CHARLIE TROTTER'S

SEAFOOD

Recipes by
Charlie Trotter

Photography by
Tim Turner

Wine Notes by
Joseph Spellman

Ten Speed Press, Berkeley, California

I would like to dedicate this book to some of the true giants of the food world, Jean Banchet, James Beard, Paul Bocuse, Julia Child, Fredy Girardet, Fernand Point, Louis Szathmary, and Roger Vergé, from whose shoulders many of us enjoy a spectacular view.

CHARLIE TROTTER

CONTENTS

9 | INTRODUCTION

15 | CHAMPAGNE & SPARKLING WINES

31 | SAUVIGNON BLANC

41 | RIESLING

69 | MUSCAT & GEWÜRZTRAMINER

85 | VIOGNIER

101 | CORTESE & ARNEIS

113 | MARSANNE & ROUSSANNE

127 | CHARDONNAY

163 | PINOT GRIS

177 | PINOT NOIR

193 | SANGIOVESE & ZINFANDEL

209 | SYRAH & BARBERA

225 | APPENDICES

234 | INDEX

INTRODUCTION

My love of seafood is fueled, first and foremost, by the sheer hedonism of eating all of the sublime things that live in water. I love the sensual pleasures involved in the handling and preparation, and then in the eating of all foods, but especially fish and shellfish. I find seafood particularly gratifying because of its beautiful textures and richness. A piece of perfectly cooked fish with a ragout of fresh seasonal vegetables and a touch of vegetable juice or delicate shellfish emulsion sauce can be an amazingly satisfying dish. By adding a wine with complementary flavors that balance with the food, you can easily take the whole combination to another level. Wine and food are a profound natural combination to me; one should not exist without the other.

Over time, I have found myself further drawn to an Eastern style of preparing seafood, eliminating cream, de-emphasizing butter, and emphasizing the utter purity of the flavors. It has been said that art is a collaboration between God and the artist, which works best when the artist contributes as little as possible; so too with the cooking of fresh fish. This is primarily accomplished by obtaining the freshest possible seafood and leaving it as unadorned as possible.

Today's many modes of overnight transportation, coupled with the dramatic growth and refinement of aquaculture and the farmed fish industry, make it easier than ever to obtain superbly fresh fish and shellfish throughout the United States. At Charlie Trotter's, I have access to many varied and high-quality prizes from the sea. One of my favorite suppliers, Rod Mitchell, of Browne Trading Company in Portland, Maine, provides us with day-boat lobster, peekytoe crab, hand-harvested sea scallops, wild striped bass, and more. I talk to Rod two or three times a week and he tells me what's running. I give him a wish list, and the next day he puts together our order from the fishing boats and the fish auction. It's airfreighted to Chicago and delivered to the back door of the restaurant. Some of the product is less than twenty-four hours out of the water when we receive it—not bad for being land-locked in the Midwest. It is nearly as easy to obtain exquisite seafood from the Gulf of Mexico, Lake Superior, or Hawaii as it is to buy fish from nearby shores. And it is definitely worth your effort to get the best.

When shopping for seafood, choose stores that are spotlessly maintained, with no fishy aroma in the air, only an indistinct sweetness. I generally prefer to work with whole fish, which are less exposed to bacteria than fish fillets. When purchasing fish, to detect if it is fresh, simply give it a couple of good, strong sniffs. Under the gills, in the belly, or along the cut flesh if it is a fillet, the product should not smell strong or fishy in any way. If there is any aroma at all, it should be faint, sweet, and of the sea. Whole fish should have eyes that are clear, not cloudy or faded, and the skin should be smooth and slick, not at all slimy.

The dishes in this book are typical of what we serve at Charlie Trotter's, where vegetable elements are frequently used to provide textural contrast to the fish or shellfish. I do not expect everyone to be able to obtain all of the variety of fish or shellfish—some eighty different items—displayed in the following pages. But, as in all cooking, many of the seafood items are interchangeable, and suggested substitutions are supplied at the end of each recipe. In most cities, salmon, shrimp, tuna, flounder, and even catfish are readily available and will work perfectly in most of the recipes in this book.

This book is designed to serve as inspiration for the myriad of possibilities in modern seafood cooking. I have included a chart describing the flavor, texture and

availability of the different types of seafood. I have also described some of the more unusual ingredients used in the recipes to aid in choosing substitutions. These tools, along with the color photographs of the finished dishes, are meant to be instructional, but more importantly, they are meant to serve as inspiration for further culinary exploration. That's what cuisine is all about: make it work for you! Let your palate be your guide as you explore and enjoy.

I have organized the recipes in this book by grape varieties in order to assist in the food and wine pairing process. By choosing a recipe based on your wine selection, you can develop a stronger understanding of the basic foods and cooking techniques that complement different wines. This will also help in putting together a multicourse meal. By starting with a sparkling wine dish, moving to a white wine dish or two and finally a red wine dish, you will have a progression of dishes from lighter appetizers to heavier entrées.

A range of wines has been suggested that celebrate their grape varieties in a unique way. These truly great wines are a convergence of perfect fruit, appropriate soil and weather, and the judicious hand of the winemaker. Some are common and some are rare, but all are the pinnacles of their variety and region or subregion. Though the chapters are organized by single variety (or pairs of varieties), many wines are blends of two or more varieties that have traditionally been grown side by side in the same vineyards.

The wine notes, like the recipes themselves, are meant to serve as a guide to the many possibilities available to you. If you can't find a particular wine, explore wines with similar characteristics. Just as there are no absolutes about wine, there are no absolutes about the pairing of food and wine. It is far from an exact science, but then, that's the beauty of it: there can be more than one right answer.

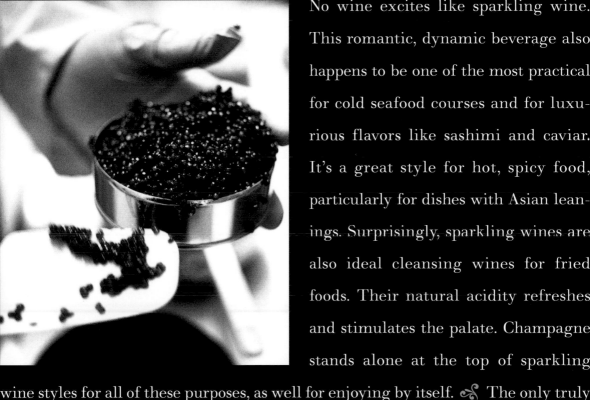

No wine excites like sparkling wine. This romantic, dynamic beverage also happens to be one of the most practical for cold seafood courses and for luxurious flavors like sashimi and caviar. It's a great style for hot, spicy food, particularly for dishes with Asian leanings. Surprisingly, sparkling wines are also ideal cleansing wines for fried foods. Their natural acidity refreshes and stimulates the palate. Champagne stands alone at the top of sparkling wine styles for all of these purposes, as well for enjoying by itself. ❧ The only truly fine sparkling wines are made with the Champagne grapes Chardonnay, Pinot Noir, and Pinot Meunier in various combinations and at various ages. Champagne has always been the first word in sparkling wine, but quality is not limited to the products of its chalky vineyards. Fine sparklings are also made in every other important growing region in France, as well as in Italy, Spain, Germany, California, Oregon, Washington, New York, Australia, and South America.

Rainbow Smelts with Caviar Rémoulade and Crispy Shallots

*This dish beautifully contrasts seafood's refinement and its simplicity:
opulent caviar, and lightly sautéed smelts. The rémoulade adds a little zing
and a creaminess and the fried shallot rings offer a sweet crispiness.
Hot smelts with cold caviar create a truly tremendous temperature contrast.
This preparation can either be consumed with a knife and fork
or as finger food, with the caviar-strewn rémoulade acting as a dipping sauce.
This combination of flavors and temperatures has enormous sensual appeal.*

Serves 4

2 tablespoons flour

Salt and pepper

4 shallots, cut into thin rings

2 tablespoons grapeseed oil
plus grapeseed oil for deep-frying

10 smelts, cleaned and filleted

1 egg yolk

1 tablespoon rice wine vinegar

½ cup olive oil

⅓ cup chopped fresh chives

1 to 2 ounces caviar

METHOD Season the flour with salt and pepper, add the shallots and toss together. Gently dust off the excess flour and fry the shallots in the grapeseed oil until golden brown. Blot on paper towels and season with salt and pepper.

Season both sides of the smelts with salt and pepper. Quickly sauté them in a very hot pan with the 2 tablespoons of grapeseed oil for about 1 minute on each side. Remove from the pan and blot on paper towels.

Place the yolk and vinegar in a small bowl and slowly whisk in the olive oil to make a thick mayonnaise. Fold in the chopped chives and season to taste with salt and pepper.

ASSEMBLY Spoon some of the chive-mayonnaise mixture and some of the caviar in the center of each plate. Arrange the smelts in a layered manner and sprinkle with the fried shallots.

Recommended Substitutions

Catfish, flounder, lobster, shrimp

Wine Notes

A crisp, lively Blanc de Blancs–style sparkler, such as the Argyle of Oregon or Guy Larmandier's Cramant Champagne, is appropriate with these fried fish. These wines use Chardonnay and a little yeastiness to remain slightly creamy, with good, refreshing acidity. This style cuts through the oil and the rich salty flavors of the caviar rémoulade, while finishing cleanly.

Arborio Rice–Crusted Belon Oysters with Baby Spinach and Sweet and Sour Beet Juice Emulsion

*I love oysters in almost every conceivable preparation, but marinated and just cooked,
they become particularly interesting. This preparation is quite simple, but the resulting combination
of flavors and textures is dazzling. The emulsion creates a very refined sweet-sour effect, and the
preserved ginger and braised spinach add sophisticated contrasting flavors. Most interesting of all is
the delicately earthy crust provided by the toasted and finely ground arborio rice.*

Serves 4

8 belon oysters, shucked

1 tablespoon chopped ginger

1 tablespoon chopped jalapeño

1 cup beet juice

2 teaspoons rice wine vinegar

3 tablespoons butter

2 cups baby spinach, cleaned

1 cup tatsoi

*8 teaspoons Preserved Ginger
(recipe follows)*

Salt and pepper

¼ cup Arborio rice

4 tablespoons chopped fresh chervil

1 egg yolk

2 tablespoons water

¼ cup flour

2 tablespoons grapeseed oil

METHOD Place the shucked oysters in a bowl with the chopped ginger and jalapeño. Refrigerate for 4 hours to infuse the flavor.

To make the beet juice emulsion, place the beet juice in a small saucepan over medium heat and simmer for 20 minutes, or until reduced to ¼ cup. Add the rice wine vinegar and whisk in 1½ tablespoons of the butter. Just prior to use, blend with a hand-held blender to create a froth.

Place the baby spinach and tatsoi in a small sauté pan with the remaining 1½ tablespoons of butter and wilt over medium heat. Fold in 6 teaspoons of the Preserved Ginger and season to taste with salt and pepper.

Place the Arborio rice on a sheet pan and toast in the oven at 375 degrees for 10 to 15 minutes, or until lightly golden brown. Once cool, purée in the blender until ground into a fine powder. Add 2 tablespoons of chopped chervil to the Arborio rice powder and mix thoroughly. Place the yolk in a small bowl and whisk in the 2 tablespoons water. Lightly toss the oysters with the flour and pat off the excess. Dip in the egg wash and dredge fully in the Arborio rice powder. Quickly cook the oysters with the grapeseed oil in a hot sauté pan for 1 to 2 minutes on each side, or until golden brown.

ASSEMBLY Place 2 separate mounds of wilted spinach in the center of each plate. Top each mound of spinach with an oyster and place a piece of Preserved Ginger on each oyster. Spoon the beet juice emulsion around the plate and sprinkle with the remaining chopped chervil.

Preserved Ginger

Yield: 3 tablespoons

4 tablespoons julienned ginger

1½ cups sugar

1½ cups water

METHOD Place the ginger, ½ cup of the sugar, and ½ cup of the water in a small saucepan. Simmer for 10 minutes, strain the liquid, and repeat the process 2 more times, reserving the final cooking liquid to store the ginger. Refrigerate until needed.

Recommended Substitutions

Lobster, any type of oysters, scallops, shrimp, tuna

Wine Notes

There are wonderful values in Loire Valley sparkling wines, generally made from Chenin Blanc, but more frequently involving Chardonnay. Brut sparkling wines from Château Moncontour, J. M. Monmousseau, and Bouvet all possess the crisp apple flavors and acidity typical of any Loire wine. Here, this wine style is a refreshing counterpoint to the spicy ginger and sweet beet flavors that embellish the creamy belons.

Marinated Onaga with Blood Orange Juice, Extra Virgin Olive Oil, and Lemon Thyme

It is hard to beat a preparation like this for simplicity and elegance. The onaga or long-tailed red snapper is fabulous when consumed raw, but it must be very fresh. The fish literally melts in your mouth, with the olive oil providing an almost decadent richness. This is a perfect way to start a light warm-weather meal.

Serves 4

1/2 cup blood orange juice

8 thin slices onaga, 4 inches long by 2 inches wide (about 1 small fish), cleaned and skin removed

Salt and pepper

1/4 cup extra virgin olive oil

1 tablespoon fresh lemon thyme leaves

METHOD Place the blood orange juice in a small saucepan and cook over medium heat for 7 to 10 minutes, or until reduced to about 5 tablespoons. Remove from heat and cool.

Season the onaga slices with salt and pepper and rub with 3 tablespoons of olive oil.

ASSEMBLY Lay 2 slices of the onaga side by side on each plate and sprinkle with some of the lemon thyme leaves. Spoon the blood orange juice reduction on and around the onaga along with the remaining olive oil. Top with freshly ground black pepper.

Recommended Substitutions

Salmon, scallops, red snapper, tuna

Wine Notes

Nearly raw fish is almost always a perfect sparkling wine food. Roederer Estate Brut Anderson Valley is among the best sparklings of California's offerings. Its balance, crisp toastiness, and unabashed fruit combine seamlessly with the citrus and thyme that refreshingly garnish the plate. True Champagne might seem a touch too biscuity or briochelike for this simple, fresh plate.

Korean Hot Pot with
Albacore Tuna and Somen Noodles

One-pot meals are complex in flavor and texture and always satisfying for the soul. This is my version of a classic Korean hot pot. I have mixed all of the elements into the broth rather than leaving them separate, with the intention of melding their flavors. Just before serving, I sear some tuna, slice it, and fan the pieces across the top. The heat or spice and the quantity of vegetables can be easily adjusted to suit your needs. In a smaller portion this preparation makes a perfect first course before a more substantial meat dish; as a larger portion, it is a perfect meal by itself.

Serves 4

½ cup thinly sliced daikon

1½ cups Pickling Juice (see Appendices)

1 jalapeño, sliced into thin rings

4 scallions, cut in half

2 tablespoons butter

¼ cup water

Salt and pepper

3 egg whites

½ cup chopped tomatoes

8 cups Beef Stock (see Appendices)

¾ cup kimchi

½ cup English cucumber, sliced thinly and slices cut into quarters

1 pound albacore tuna loin, trimmed to 1½- to 2-inch diameter, skin removed

3 tablespoons togarashi

2 tablespoons grapeseed oil

4 ounces dry somen noodles, cooked

8 medium denkos shiitake mushrooms, roasted and cut into quarters (see Appendices)

4 teaspoons fine chiffonade of cilantro leaves

METHOD Place the daikon in 1 cup of the Pickling Juice and refrigerate overnight.

Place the jalapeño in the remaining ½ cup of Pickling Juice and refrigerate overnight.

Braise the scallions in a small saucepan with the butter and water for 5 to 7 minutes, or until tender. Remove them from the liquid and season to taste with salt and pepper.

In a medium bowl, froth the egg whites with a whisk and add the tomatoes. Place the Beef Stock in a medium saucepan and add the egg white mixture. Using a wooden spoon, stir the mixture continually over medium heat until a raft begins to form (a semisolid mass of egg whites that removes the impurities from the stock). Turn the heat down and slowly simmer for 20 to 30 minutes, until the Beef Stock is crystal clear and an amber color. Strain the liquid through a fine-mesh sieve lined with cheesecloth, being careful not to break the raft. Discard the raft and season the Beef Stock with salt and pepper.

Just before serving, warm the kimchi and English cucumber in a small saucepan with a touch of the clarified Beef Stock.

Season the albacore tuna loin with salt and roll it in the togarashi. In a very hot sauté pan, sear all sides of the loin with the grapeseed oil. Cut into 24 thin slices and season with salt and pepper.

ASSEMBLY Arrange some of the somen noodles, kimchi, cucumber, shiitakes, scallions, pickled daikon, and pickled jalapeño in each bowl. Place 6 slices of the albacore tuna on top and ladle the clarified Beef Stock into each bowl. Top with cilantro.

Recommended Substitutions

Halibut, lobster, red snapper, swordfish, tuna

Wine Notes

Hot flavors require a refreshing acidity, yet perhaps not an aggressively effervescent sparkler. The lower-pressure Crémant Demi-Sec style of Scharffenberger satisfies the need for some sweetness while still providing generous fresh fruit flavors big enough for the rich tuna. Often considered more of a dessert-style sparkler, Demi-Sec can be surprisingly versatile within the meal.

Sea Urchin and Osetra Caviar with Vodka Crème Fraîche and Daikon

This decadent dish is the perfect way to kick off a special meal. The sinfully rich caviar and heady urchin are offset by the cleansing and crisp daikon. The vodka crème fraîche reintroduces richness, and the wasabi tabiko adds a little heat and a pleasant textural pop. All of the flavors and textures taken together result in an intensely sensual mouth experience.

Serves 4

2 to 3 sea urchins (yielding a total of 12 sacs of sea urchin roe)

½ cup daikon, julienned

1 tablespoon freshly squeezed lemon juice

4 teaspoons fine chiffonade of flat-leaf parsley

Salt and pepper

2 tablespoons vodka

¼ cup crème fraîche

1 teaspoon blanched lemon zest, finely chopped

1 teaspoon blanched lime zest, finely chopped

2 to 3 ounces Osetra caviar

¼ cup wasabi tabiko fish roe

Parsley Juice (recipe follows)

METHOD Remove the sea urchin roe and gently rinse them with cold water.

Toss the daikon in a small bowl with the lemon juice and parsley. Season to taste with salt and pepper.

In a separate small bowl, whisk the vodka and crème fraîche together. Fold in the lemon and lime zest and season to taste with salt and pepper.

ASSEMBLY Spread some of the daikon mixture in a circle in the center of each plate. Arrange 3 pieces of sea urchin roe on top of the daikon. Place 4 small spoonfuls of Osetra caviar at separate points around the plate. Place 4 half-teaspoons of wasabi tabiko at separate points around the plate. Spoon the vodka crème fraîche mixture and the Parsley Juice around the caviar.

Parsley Juice

Yield: about ½ cup

2 cups flat-leaf parsley

3 tablespoons grapeseed oil

3 tablespoons ice water

Salt and pepper

METHOD In a very hot pan, sauté the parsley for a few seconds in 1 tablespoon of the grapeseed oil. Immediately remove from the pan and place in the refrigerator. Coarsely chop the cooled parsley and place in a blender with the ice water and remaining 2 tablespoons of grapeseed oil.

Blend thoroughly and strain through a fine-mesh sieve. Season to taste with salt and pepper and store in the refrigerator until needed.

Recommended Substitutions

Lobster, shrimp, tuna

Wine Notes

The cleanest, most assertive style of Champagne sees no dosage, or added sweetness. Laurent-Perrier Ultra Brut may seem extremely dry and lean alone, but as a tart, cleansing Champagne for the distinctive, intense sea urchin flavor, Ultra Brut cannot be matched. This razor-sharp Champagne is also an ideal caviar accompaniment.

Sushi

*From time to time we serve sushi at the restaurant, either as canapés or
as an amuse-gueule to begin a meal. Our friends at the marvelous Sai Cafe,
located two blocks from Charlie Trotter's, prepared these pieces for us.*

**Serves 1 as an entrée
or several as an appetizer**

*1½ cups cooked sticky rice,
at room temperature*

2 tablespoons rice wine vinegar

1½ tablespoons sugar

¾-ounce piece eel (unagi)

3 tablespoons tamari

2 ½- by 3-inch pieces nori

Pinch of white sesame seeds

¾-ounce piece octopus, poached (tako)

*¾-ounce piece albacore tuna
(shiro maguro)*

¾-ounce piece halibut (hirame)

¾-ounce piece salmon (namasake)

¾-ounce piece tuna (maguro)

¾-ounce piece sea bass (suzuki)

¾-ounce piece yellowtail (hamachi)

½-ounce piece surf clam (hokigai)

½-ounce piece squid (ika)

2 to 3 tablespoons wasabi paste

2 tablespoons flying fish roe (tobiko)

⅛ teaspoon black sesame seeds

1 tablespoon thinly sliced pickled ginger

1 teaspoon shiso, cut into a fine chiffonade

METHOD Place the sticky rice in a small bowl and mix with the rice wine vinegar and sugar. Marinate the eel in 2 teaspoons of the tamari and broil for 1 minute, or until cooked. Form 2 tablespoons of rice into a firm mound and place the eel on top. Wrap with a strip of nori and moisten one end to seal. Lightly sprinkle the top with the white sesame seeds. Form 2 tablespoons of rice into a firm mound and press a piece of poached octopus on top. Wrap with a strip of nori and moisten one end to seal. To assemble the remaining sushi, form 2 tablespoons of rice into a firm mound and press a piece of fish on top of the rice. Repeat until all of the fish is used.

Whisk together the remaining 7 teaspoons of tamari and enough wasabi paste to create the amount of heat you desire. Form the remaining wasabi paste into tiny quenelles.

ASSEMBLY Arrange the various types of sushi on a serving plate. Sprinkle the tobiko and black sesame seeds around the sushi. Spoon the tamari-wasabi mixture around the plate. Place the wasabi quenelles, pickled ginger, and shiso around the sushi.

Recommended Substitutions

Any type of fish that can be eaten raw

Wine Notes

Some heat and the exceptional freshness of the fish are keys to this sparkling wine-friendly arrangement. We like the overt, yet dry, fruitiness of Iron Horse "Vrais Amis," the crisp Green Valley sparkler by this fabulous estate in Sonoma County. Though the wine has a strong Pinot Noir influence, making it almost berrylike in the nose, it works wonderfully with its continuous effervescence.

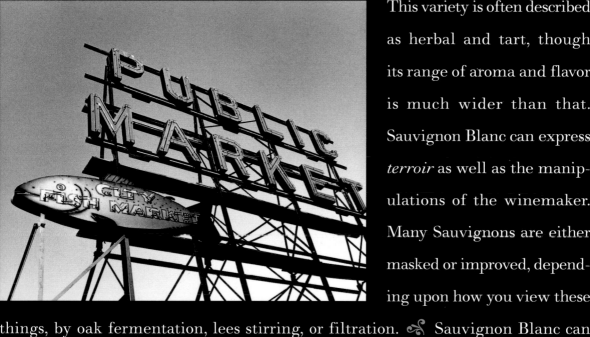

This variety is often described as herbal and tart, though its range of aroma and flavor is much wider than that. Sauvignon Blanc can express *terroir* as well as the manipulations of the winemaker. Many Sauvignons are either masked or improved, depending upon how you view these things, by oak fermentation, lees stirring, or filtration. ❧ Sauvignon Blanc can handle a wide range of flavors, from earthy vegetable to strong sea flavors. The best Sauvignons bring a lean mineral intensity to the flavor experience, an excellent foil for most seafood. The key to most good Sauvignons, with a few exceptions, is their intensely dry finish. (There is certainly a long tradition of sweet Sauvignon Blanc as well, but this style is not addressed by these recipes.) For the most part, the recipes here incorporate quite vivid, intense flavors, of the sort with which Sauvignon is comfortable. Especially notable are the spring vegetable accompaniments—always Sauvignon food—and the liberal use of leafy herbs in these dishes.

Daurade with Peruvian Potato Purée and Citrus-Tomato Vinaigrette

Daurade delicately flakes apart when cut with a fork. Its texture approximates that of sea bass and its skin turns golden and crispy when cooked, resulting in a glorious contrast with the succulent flesh. Here, a satiny mound of purple potato purée forms a superb bed for the fish. Finally, a coarsely textured vinaigrette featuring citrus, tomato, and haricots verts is spooned around the plate for a very complex palate of flavors and textures that nicely "rope in" the fish.

Serves 4

2 pounds purple potatoes

4 tablespoons butter

Salt and pepper

2 cups Fish Stock (see Appendices)

2 tablespoons chopped shallots

1 cup white wine

1/2 cup haricots verts, blanched and cut into 1/8-inch-thick pieces

1/4 cup Olive Oil–Poached Tomatoes (see Appendices)

2 teaspoons chopped fresh marjoram

4 2 1/2-ounce pieces daurade, with skin

2 teaspoons grapeseed oil

16 orange sections, peeled

METHOD Bake the purple potatoes at 400 degrees for 40 to 50 minutes, or until done. Let stand for 10 minutes and remove the skin. Pass the potato pulp through a ricer, add 2 tablespoons of the butter, and mash with a fork until smooth. Season to taste with salt and pepper.

Place the Fish Stock in a small saucepan and simmer over medium-high heat for 20 minutes, or until reduced to about 2/3 cup. In a small sauté pan, sweat the shallots in 2 teaspoons of the butter for 1 minute, or until translucent. Add the white wine and continue to simmer for 10 minutes, or until reduced to 1/2 cup. Add the reduced stock and whisk in the remaining 4 teaspoons of butter. Just before serving, stir in the haricots verts, Olive Oil–Poached Tomatoes, and chopped marjoram. Season to taste with salt and pepper.

Score the skin side of the daurade with a knife or razor blade, and season both sides with salt and pepper. Quickly sauté the daurade in the grapeseed oil in a very hot pan, skin side down, for 1 to 2 minutes. Turn over and sauté 1 to 2 minutes, or until just cooked.

ASSEMBLY Place a mound of the purple potato purée in the center of each plate and top with a piece of fish. Spoon the fish stock reduction around the plate and arrange a few orange sections around the fish.

Recommended Substitutions

Catfish, flounder, halibut, salmon, sea bass, red snapper

Wine Notes

Crisp, unoaked Sauvignon is useful here because the texture of the fish is quite delicate and the accenting flavors are not bold. We find good Sauvignons in this style from Cakebread, Havens, and Liparita: pretty, elegant wines that are not overdone with ripeness, herbal intensity, or oak. These wines also have a citrusy affinity for the orange-based vinaigrette, which is not too acidic for these wines.

Turbot Ceviche Wrapped in Smoked Salmon with Razor Clam Vinaigrette

Turbot makes a marvelous ceviche because its texture stays ever-so-slightly firm even after marinating. Here the turbot-ceviche mixture is flavored with dill and citrus and encased with slices of meltingly soft smoked salmon. A razor clam and lime juice vinaigrette is then drizzled around the plate. The textures and flavors of this combination of ingredients meld together quite nicely to make a refreshing and majestic preparation. Serve the turbot ceviche shortly after preparing so the fish will not be overcooked by the acid in the fruit juices. This would make an ideal first course for a special meal.

Serves 4

¼ cup chopped carrots

¼ cup chopped celery

¼ cup chopped Spanish onions

8 razor clams

½ cup Sauvignon Blanc or other white wine

2 cups thinly sliced bite-size pieces fresh turbot

2 tablespoons freshly squeezed pink grapefruit juice

2 tablespoons freshly squeezed orange juice

4 pink grapefruit sections, peeled

6 orange sections, peeled

½ cup diced cucumber

4 tablespoons dill sprigs

Salt and pepper

4 6½- by 2-inch thin slices smoked salmon

4 tablespoons freshly squeezed lime juice

1 tablespoon chopped shallots

½ cup olive oil

4 teaspoons finely julienned lime zest

4 teaspoons Dill Oil (recipe follows)

4 lime sections, peeled and cut into tiny pieces

METHOD Place the chopped carrot, celery, and onion on a sheet pan and lay the clams on top of the chopped vegetables. Pour the white wine over the razor clams and bake at 375 degrees for 7 minutes. Remove the clam meat from the shell, cut into thin slices on the bias, cool, and set aside.

Place the turbot slices in a medium bowl and spoon the grapefruit and orange juices over the fish. Gently toss together and refrigerate for 5 minutes. Cut the grapefruit and orange sections into small pieces and fold in ¼ cup of the diced cucumber and 2 tablespoons of the dill sprigs. Combine with the turbot ceviche and season to taste with salt and pepper. Lightly oil four 2¼-inch-diameter ring molds (any similar-size molds will work as well) and line with the smoked salmon slices. Fill each mold with some of the turbot ceviche.

Place the lime juice and chopped shallots in a small bowl. Slowly whisk in the olive oil and season to taste with salt and pepper. Fold in the razor clams and the remaining ¼ cup diced cucumber.

Quickly blanch the lime zest in boiling salted water for 30 seconds.

ASSEMBLY Place a smoked salmon—wrapped turbot ceviche in the center of each plate and carefully remove the mold. Spoon the razor clam vinaigrette around the plate. Drizzle the Dill Oil around the razor clam vinaigrette. Sprinkle the remaining 2 tablespoons dill sprigs, the tiny lime pieces, and lime zest around the plate.

Dill Oil

Yield: about ½ cup

1 cup fresh dill sprigs

½ cup grapeseed oil

½ cup olive oil

METHOD Blanch the dill in boiling salted water for 15 seconds. Immediately shock in ice water and drain. Coarsely chop the dill and squeeze out the excess water. Place in a blender with the oil and purée for 3 to 4 minutes, or until bright green. Pour into a container, cover, and refrigerate for 1 day. Strain through cheesecloth, refrigerate for 1 more day, and then decant.

Recommended Substitutions

Scallops, shrimp, red snapper, swordfish, tuna

Wine Notes

The light, extremely fresh turbot preparation needs a tart Sauvignon, and the smoked salmon needs an extra dimension of earthiness unique to Loire Sauvignon. This preparation is extremely wine-friendly. We find the exceptional Pouilly-Fumé cuvées by Didier Dagueneau compelling. The intensely ripe "Pur Sang" is an exotic merge of fruit and sassy acidity. More modest Loire approaches might include Ménétou-Salon or Quincy, with their more aggressive tartness and clean finish.

Pacific Coast Oysters with Sweet and Sour Fennel, Tarragon Oil, and Peppercorns

*Creamy, salty, and slightly briny oysters like these plump Sunset Beach morsels
from the Pacific Northwest are a tremendous way to begin any meal. I love satiny oysters
contrasted with something that has a clean, crunchy texture. Here the spicy sweet and
sour fennel is the perfect flavor and textural foil. Fennel juice and tarragon oil make a fantastic
vinaigrette, and the peppercorns add just the right amount of refined exotic heat.*

Serves 4

³/₄ cup julienned fennel

¹/₂ cup Pickling Juice (see Appendices)

¹/₂ cup chopped fennel bulb

2 teaspoons butter

¹/₂ teaspoon pink peppercorns, cracked

¹/₂ teaspoon green peppercorns, cracked

¹/₂ teaspoon black peppercorns, cracked

1 tablespoon fennel fronds

¹/₃ cup Fennel Juice (see Appendices)

Salt and pepper

12 Pacific Coast oysters, shucked

4 teaspoons Tarragon Oil (recipe follows)

2 teaspoons tarragon, julienned

METHOD Place the julienned fennel in the Pickling Juice and refrigerate for 4 hours. Place the chopped fennel in an ovenproof pan with the butter. Cover and roast in the oven at 350 degrees for 20 to 30 minutes, or until tender. Toss the peppercorns together in a small bowl. Remove the fennel from the Pickling Juice and toss in a separate bowl with the fennel fronds and half of the combined peppercorns. Purée the roasted fennel with the Fennel Juice, pass through a fine-mesh sieve, and season to taste with salt and pepper.

ASSEMBLY Place 3 mounds of the pickled fennel mixture on each plate. Top each mound with an oyster and spoon the fennel juice purée around the plate. Drizzle the Tarragon Oil on the plate and sprinkle with the tarragon and remaining peppercorns.

Tarragon Oil

Yield: about ¹/₂ cup

¹/₂ cup tarragon

¹/₄ cup grapeseed oil

¹/₄ cup olive oil

METHOD Blanch the tarragon in boiling salted water for 15 seconds. Immediately shock in ice water and drain. Squeeze out the excess water and coarsely chop the tarragon. Place in a blender with the oil and purée for 3 to 4 minutes, or until bright green. Pour into a container, cover, and refrigerate for 1 day. Strain through cheesecloth, refrigerate 1 more day, and then decant.

Recommended Substitutions

Lobster, assorted oysters, scallops, shrimp, tuna

Wine Notes

Benchmark Sauvignon Blanc from Sancerre hits the spot with these oysters—tart, even racy, Sancerre Chavignol "Les Culs de Beaujeu" by Cotat, most notably. This wine has intense herbal tones for the prominent fennel and tarragon flavors and a mineral presence that is oyster-friendly and very cleansing. Sancerre's higher acidity gives it the edge over most American Sauvignons for these oysters.

Langoustines with Braised Artichokes, Carrots, Onions, and Chervil-Infused Broth

I love all shellfish, but langoustines are a special treat. They are incredibly sweet and their texture is unbelievably delicate. The slightest pressure from your mouth, and these plump morsels explode with an almost candylike flavor. With the aromatic chervil broth and the complex flavor of the artichokes, the dish is not only simple to prepare but particularly luscious to consume.

Serves 4

1 cup chopped carrots

1 cup chopped celery

1 cup chopped yellow onions

2 tablespoons grapeseed oil

3 artichoke bottoms with stems attached

4 tablespoons plus 2 teaspoons butter

2 carrots, sliced into ¼-inch discs

1 cup julienned Spanish onion

*2 tablespoons Pickling Juice
(see Appendices)*

*1 cup yellow wax beans, blanched and
cut on the bias*

Salt and pepper

½ cup chopped fresh chervil

*8 langoustines, cooked, tail meat removed
from shells, claws reserved*

4 teaspoons Chervil Oil (recipe follows)

METHOD In a medium saucepan, caramelize the chopped carrots, celery, and onion in the grapeseed oil. Add the artichokes, cover with water, and bring to a simmer. Add 3 tablespoons of the butter and continue to cook over low heat for 30 to 40 minutes, or until the artichokes are tender. Remove the artichokes, strain the cooking liquid through a fine-mesh sieve, and reserve. Cut the artichokes into small wedges. Place the cooking liquid in a medium saucepan along with the sliced carrots and simmer for 3 minutes.

In a small pan, sweat the julienned onions in 2 teaspoons of the butter. Add the Pickling Juice and simmer for 3 minutes. Add the yellow wax beans and all of the cooking liquid and carrots from the artichokes. Slowly whisk in the remaining 1 tablespoon of butter and season to taste with salt and pepper. Add 6 tablespoons of chopped chervil to the broth just before serving.

Season the langoustines with salt and pepper and sprinkle with the remaining 2 tablespoons of chopped chervil.

ASSEMBLY Arrange some of the artichoke wedges, carrots, yellow wax beans, and onions in the center of each bowl. Place 2 of the warm langoustines and 2 of the claws on top of the vegetables. Ladle the artichoke broth in the bowl and drizzle the Chervil Oil around the bowl.

Chervil Oil

Yield: about ½ cup

1 cup fresh chervil leaves

½ cup grapeseed oil

¼ cup olive oil

METHOD Blanch the chervil in boiling salted water for 15 seconds. Immediately shock in ice water and drain. Squeeze out any excess liquid and coarsely chop. Purée in a blender with the oils for 3 to 4 minutes, or until bright green. Pour into a container, cover, and refrigerate for 1 day. Strain through cheesecloth, refrigerate for 1 more day, and then decant.

Recommended Substitutions

Lobster, salmon, scallops, shrimp, snapper

Wine Notes

The caramelized sweet flavors in this broth call for a richer style of Sauvignon Blanc, one with some oak influence and an almost melonlike ripeness. However, the delicate langoustine meat begs for a subtler style. Slightly oaky Sauvignon Blancs from Duckhorn or Araujo "Eisele" in Napa are lovely matches because their ripe fruit supports the dish while not being as aggressive as a Loire wine. A rare Bordeaux match is found in Pavillon Blanc du Château Margaux, an exceptionally clean Sauvignon-based wine that ages gracefully.

The variety with the most practicality and the least respect in the current wine fashion is Riesling. Riesling has spine. It creates bold contrast. It goes against the grain. Riesling producers in Germany, Austria, Alsace, and selected parts of North America have much to fiercely defend. This crisp, clean, rarely oaked variety gives outstanding structure to a wide range of fish preparations. ✑ Where other varieties may stifle elegant flavors, Riesling gives purity and focus to all the flavors on the plate. Riesling is a fine enhancement to arrangements that include tree fruits and citrus flavors because its inherent acidity stands up to high-acid flavors. It creates harmony with sweet shellfish and lighter-fleshed fish. Its earthy tones are a constant reminder of vineyard identity—unique confluences of soil and sun exposure. Serve great Riesling with pride and enjoy the astonished pleasure of your dining companions. They will appreciate its precision and verve.

Lemon Balm–Infused Dungeness Crab Consommé with Crab-Stuffed Squash Blossoms, White Asparagus, and Ramps

This dish definitely informs that spring is here! Everything about it is redolent of the season of rebirth. It is light and delicate, but the crab is sweet and the asparagus and ramps are feisty and assert their youthful flavors. Lemon balm seals the deal with a peppery-lemon essence that majestically emphasizes each of these special flavors.

Serves 4

2 live Dungeness crabs

2 teaspoons freshly squeezed lime juice

Salt and pepper

4 fresh squash blossoms

16 large white asparagus tips

12 ramps, cleaned

Dungeness Crab Consommé (recipe follows)

4 teaspoons Lemon Balm Oil (see Appendices)

4 tablespoons fresh tiny lemon balm leaves

METHOD Poach the live Dungeness crabs in boiling salted water for 12 minutes and immediately shock in ice water. Remove from ice water and remove all of the crabmeat from the claws, legs, and body, keeping the meat in large pieces if possible. This will take some time and strength, but the end result is well worth the effort. Reserve the crab shells for the consommé.

Carefully clean the crabmeat, removing any shell particles. Reserve 1 cup of the crabmeat for the consommé. Place the remaining crabmeat in a medium bowl, toss with the lime juice, and season to taste with salt and pepper.

Rinse the squash blossoms with cold water and remove the pistils. Carefully stuff the blossoms with some of the crabmeat. Just prior to use, place the stuffed squash blossoms in a steamer and steam for 2 minutes.

Blanch the white asparagus tips in boiling salted water, drain, and season to taste with salt and pepper.

Blanch the ramps in boiling salted water for 1 minute, drain, and season to taste with salt and pepper.

ASSEMBLY Place a crab-stuffed squash blossom in the center of each bowl. Arrange some of the ramps, white asparagus tips, and remaining crab pieces in each bowl. Ladle some consommé in each bowl, drizzle with some of the Lemon Balm Oil, and sprinkle with some of the tiny lemon balm leaves.

Dungeness Crab Consommé

Yield: about 1½ quarts

1 cup chopped Spanish onion

1 cup chopped celery

1 cup chopped carrots

2 tablespoons grapeseed oil

2 tablespoons tomato paste

½ cup dry or sweet red wine

Reserved Dungeness crab shells

2 to 2½ quarts water

4 egg whites

1 cup chopped tomatoes

1 cup reserved crabmeat

Salt and pepper

4 ounces fresh lemon balm leaves

METHOD In a large stockpot, caramelize the onion, celery, and carrot in the grapeseed oil. Add the tomato paste and continue to cook for 3 minutes. Deglaze with the red wine. Add the crab shells, cover with the water (just enough to cover the shells), and simmer over medium heat for 2 hours. Strain through a fine-mesh sieve and place in a medium saucepan.

Whisk the egg whites in a medium bowl until slightly frothy. Add the tomato and crabmeat and continue to whisk until fully incorporated. Add the egg white mixture to the shellfish stock and simmer over medium heat, stirring constantly with a wooden spoon until a raft (a semisolid mass of egg whites that removes the impurities from the stock) begins to form.

Once the raft begins to form, reduce the heat to a low simmer and stop stirring. Continue to simmer for 30 to 45 minutes, or until the consommé is crystal clear. Carefully strain through a fine-mesh sieve lined with cheesecloth. Take care not to break the raft apart or tiny particles will cloud the consommé. Season to taste with salt and pepper. Just prior to serving, steep the lemon balm in the hot consommé for 5 minutes. Discard the lemon balm and serve immediately.

Recommended Substitutions

Crab, lobster, salmon, shrimp

Wine Notes

"Pacific Rim" Riesling, the Asian cuisine–friendly style made by Bonny Doon Vineyard in California, makes a marvelous companion to the exotic lemon balm and the slightly spicy blossoms, while bearing enough richness for Dungeness crab. Though whimsically labeled, this wine is a serious one for this type of modern, globally influenced preparation.

Smoked Sturgeon Terrine with Petite Herb and Radish Salad and Yellow Bell Pepper Juice Vinaigrette

Smoked sturgeon is especially satiny and smooth. The luscious fat in the fish and the texture of the slices after the sturgeon has been cured make this preparation an incredible eating experience. The herb-radish salad adds a cleansing and refreshing bite, and the concentrated bell pepper juice provides a sweet aromatic perfume that balances superbly against the satiny terrine.

Serves 4

3 tablespoons butter, whipped

1 tablespoon chopped fresh chives

3 salted anchovy fillets, rinsed and chopped

1 pound thinly sliced smoked sturgeon

3 tablespoons fresh chervil leaves

2 tablespoons dill sprigs

2 tablespoons fresh small flat-leaf parsley leaves

2 tablespoons fresh small tarragon leaves

6 teaspoons julienned red satin radish

Lemon Oil (recipe follows)

Salt and pepper

Yellow Bell Pepper Juice (recipe follows)

METHOD Mix the whipped butter, chives, and anchovies together in a small bowl. Line a small 1½- by 4-inch dome-shaped terrine mold with plastic wrap, leaving extra to cover the terrine (other terrine molds of similar size will work as well). Cut the smoked sturgeon into 1½-inch-wide pieces (or the width of the terrine mold). Put a layer of smoked sturgeon on the bottom of the mold and spread it with a very thin layer of the anchovy butter. Continue to layer the smoked sturgeon and anchovy butter until you reach the top of the terrine mold. Cover with the plastic wrap and refrigerate for 2 hours, or until firm.

Place the chervil, dill, parsley, tarragon, and red satin radish in a small bowl and toss with 2 teaspoons of the Lemon Oil. Season to taste with salt and pepper.

Cut the terrine into ¼-inch-thick slices and carefully remove the plastic wrap.

ASSEMBLY Place some of the herb salad on each plate and arrange 2 overlapping slices of the terrine across from the salad. Spoon 1 teaspoon of the Lemon Oil and the yellow bell pepper juice around each plate and top with freshly ground black pepper.

Lemon Oil

Yield: about ¼ cup

¼ cup grated lemon zest

¼ cup grapeseed oil

METHOD Purée the lemon zest and the grapeseed oil together for 2 minutes. Refrigerate overnight and strain through a fine-mesh sieve.

Yellow Bell Pepper Juice

Yield: about ⅓ cup

3 yellow bell peppers, seeded

METHOD Juice the peppers and place in a medium saucepan. Over medium heat, reduce the liquid for 20 minutes, or until it has a light syruplike consistency. Strain through a fine-mesh sieve and refrigerate until needed.

Recommended Substitutions

Lobster, cured salmon, smoked salmon

Wine Notes

The smoked flavors of sturgeon are a perfect Riesling companion. A steely, lean style of racy Riesling comes from the Ruwer, where Maximin Grünhaus leads the way with the most prestigious vineyards. The "Abtsberg" Kabinett is an austere, crisp Riesling whose acidity punches through the anchovy butter and whose sweetness underscores the yellow bell pepper juice. Upriver a bit lie the great Brauneberg vineyards of Fritz Haag, whose somewhat fuller Brauneberger-Juffer Kabinett bears zippy acidity and an apple finish.

Steamed Lake Superior Whitefish with Fiddlehead Ferns and Potato-Apple-Celery Purée

Whitefish is rarely served in fine restaurants because it is thought to be too pedestrian. However, when it is impeccably fresh, whitefish is indeed a special treat and I love offering it at Charlie Trotter's. The fish truly melts away the moment it is in your mouth. This particular preparation is redolent of the heartland. The addition of fiddlehead ferns provides the necessary textural foil, while creamy, slightly sweet apple-potato-celery purée supplies a "comfort food" element. Strands of caramelized onions floating in the apple-celery juice broth help to push the combination over the top. This dish will surely please even the most finicky of eaters, as it is satisfying on almost every level.

Serves 4

1 cup chopped celery

2 cups chopped Granny Smith apples

1 1/2 cups chopped potatoes, boiled

Salt and pepper

2 cups celery juice

3 tablespoons plus 2 teaspoons butter

6 tablespoons chopped fresh chives

2 tablespoons chopped fresh chervil

1 cup julienned Spanish onions

1 1/2 cups fiddlehead ferns, cleaned

4 3-ounce portions Lake Superior whitefish, skin removed

4 teaspoons fresh chive blossoms

METHOD Place the celery and 1 cup of the apple in a medium saucepan, cover with water, and simmer over medium heat for 5 to 7 minutes, or until slightly soft. Drain and purée with the cooked potatoes until smooth (additional water may be needed to purée it smoothly). Place the purée in a nonstick pan and slowly dry over medium-low heat for 20 minutes, stirring constantly, until the purée has a sturdy consistency. Season to taste with salt and pepper.

Place the celery juice in a small saucepan with the remaining 1 cup of apple and simmer over medium heat for 15 minutes. Strain through a fine-mesh sieve and season to taste with salt and pepper. Whisk in the 3 tablespoons of butter, 3 tablespoons of the chives, and 1 1/2 tablespoons of the chervil. Froth with a hand-held blender just prior to use.

Caramelize the julienned onion with the 2 teaspoons butter over medium-high heat for 15 minutes, or until golden brown.

Blanch the fiddlehead ferns in boiling salted water for 2 minutes, drain, and season to taste with salt and pepper.

Season both sides of the whitefish with salt and pepper. Crust the top side with the remaining chives and chervil. Place on a rack in a steamer and steam for 3 minutes, or until just cooked.

ASSEMBLY Spoon some of the potato purée in the center of each bowl. Top with a piece of steamed fish. Arrange the fiddlehead ferns and caramelized onions in the bowl. Ladle the celery-apple broth into the bowl and sprinkle with the chive blossoms.

Recommended Substitutions

Catfish, cod, lobster, trout

Wine Notes

The Great Lakes region is not often considered fine wine country, but excellent cool-climate Riesling can come from Northern Michigan on the Leelanau and Old Mission Peninsulas. Riesling from Chateau Grand Traverse presents an opportunity for whitefish to shine in a fresh, elegant preparation. The wine's generous sweetness is fine with the apple-celery broth sweetness and is refreshing enough alongside fiddleheads, another seasonal treat from the Midwest.

Sweet Baby Maine Shrimp with Arugula, Heart of Palm, Tomato Coulis, and Spicy Herb Sauce

The tiny shrimp from Maine are as sweet as candy and their texture is so soft you barely need to chew them. Here they are paired with a Spicy Herb Sauce that gets its heat from the addition of wasabi tobiko. There is also a soothing and barely acidic tomato coulis that even further accentuates the sweet shrimp. A small salad featuring arugula and hearts of palm adds poignant textural notes. Taken as a whole, this dish is refreshing, delicately assertive, and resonant with complex flavors.

Serves 4

1 ripe plum tomato

Salt and pepper

2 tablespoons wasabi tobiko

Spicy Herb Sauce (see Appendices)

1 tablespoon chopped shallots

1 tablespoon freshly squeezed lemon juice

2 teaspoons rice wine vinegar

2 tablespoons olive oil

1 cup julienned hearts of palm

1 1/2 cups small arugula leaves

1/2 cup enoki mushrooms

28 sweet baby Maine shrimp, cleaned

2 teaspoons butter

12 yellow currant tomatoes

4 teaspoons Basil Oil (see Appendices)

METHOD Chop the plum tomato and purée in the blender until smooth. Using a spoon, push through a sieve, allowing some of the pulp to pass through. Gently warm in a small saucepan and season to taste with salt and pepper.

Fold the wasabi tobiko into the Spicy Herb Sauce.

Place the shallots, lemon juice, and vinegar in a small bowl and slowly whisk in the olive oil. Season to taste with salt and pepper. Toss in the hearts of palm, arugula, and enoki mushrooms, and season to taste with salt and pepper.

Season the shrimp with salt and pepper and quickly sauté in a hot pan with the butter for 1 to 2 minutes, or until just done.

ASSEMBLY Arrange some of the hearts of palm mixture in the center of each plate. Place 7 of the shrimp and 3 of the yellow currant tomatoes around the hearts of palm. Spoon some of the tomato purée and Spicy Herb Sauce around the plate. Drizzle the Basil Oil around the plate and top with freshly ground black pepper.

Recommended Substitutions

Crayfish, lobster, scallops, shrimp, tuna

Wine Notes

Herbs and tobiko help a traditional German Kabinett–style Riesling become a complete flavor addition. The shrimp are sweet, and the savory flavors of the arugula and tomato need only a slightly sweet lift. Hochheim, at the eastern limit of the Rheingau, produces riper, fuller Riesling than its western neighbors, from less steep vineyard sites. Franz Künstler makes remarkable full-bodied Riesling that furthers the clean flavors of this dish. The Hochheimer Hölle Kabinett is a generous, even bold, Riesling by Künstler that is atypical for the Rheingau but a great match with the spiciness of the herb sauce.

Smoked Catfish with Apple-Fennel Salad
and Pickled Pearl Onions

*Catfish is a much underrated fish, more often than not served fried with gobs of tartar sauce.
A fish this subtle in flavor deserves more civilized treatment. I like taking it directly from the smoker
while still warm and serving it with a little fruit and vegetable salad. The catfish is succulent
and melts in your mouth, while the sweet fruits and crunchy vegetables cut right into the smokiness
that lingers on your palate. A drizzle of olive oil adds a touch of satisfying richness.*

Serves 4

1 8-ounce catfish fillet, skin removed

4 cups Pickling Juice (see Appendices)

6 ounces hickory wood chips

1 cup white pearl onions, peeled

1 tablespoon grapeseed oil

1/2 cup diced Red Delicious apple

1/2 cup diced Granny Smith apple

1/2 cup diced fennel bulb

*1/2 cup satsuma mandarin sections,
cut in half*

1/2 cup golden raisins

8 teaspoons fennel fronds

4 teaspoons olive oil

METHOD Place the catfish fillet in a pan, cover with 2 cups of the cool pickling juice, and refrigerate overnight (about 12 hours). Soak half of the wood chips in 1 cup of water for 1 hour. Drain the excess water and set aside. Place the dry chips in the base of a grill or smoker. Using a propane torch, light the dry chips until you get a strong smoke. Add the wet chips. Remove the catfish from the liquid, place on a rack above the chips, and cover. (You may need to check every 15 minutes to make sure you still have a heavy smoke going.) Cold-smoke the catfish for 45 minutes, or until it has a strong, smoky flavor. Remove from the smoker, cut into 4 pieces, and serve immediately. Do not refrigerate the smoked catfish because the fat will solidify.

Cut the pearl onions in half and place in a sauté pan with 1 tablespoon of grapeseed oil. Sauté over medium-high heat until lightly caramelized. Remove from the pan and place in 2 cups of Pickling Juice. Let stand for 1 hour. Strain the onions from the Pickling Juice and place the Pickling Juice in a small saucepan. Simmer for 15 to 20 minutes, or until reduced to 1/2 cup.

In a small bowl, toss together the diced Red Delicious apple, Granny Smith apple, fennel, satsuma mandarin sections, and golden raisins. Add 4 tablespoons of the reduced Pickling Juice and 6 teaspoons of the fennel fronds and stir to combine.

ASSEMBLY Place a small mound of the diced fruit mixture on each plate. Place some of the pickled pearl onions across from the fruit and set a piece of smoked catfish on top. Spoon the remaining reduced Pickling Juice around the plate along with the remaining fennel fronds. Finish with a drizzle of olive oil around the plate.

Recommended Substitutions

Cold poached halibut, lobster, salmon, smoked salmon, shrimp

Wine Notes

Big flavors in this preparation demand a big, even somewhat sweet, Riesling. We love traditional Auslese, and the Bernkasteler Doctor Riesling Auslese 1993 by Wegeler-Deinhard is a fine, classic example. The rich sweetness has a unique flavor to complement almost any smoked food, and the fruit has a ripe apple complexity much like the salad it is paired with. This wine is astonishingly balanced, with high acidity and low alcohol.

Soft-Shell Crab with Ennis Hazelnuts, Snow Pea Shoots, and Aromatic Vegetable Broth

~~~~~~

*Nearly everyone loves soft-shell crabs. Their shellfish flavor is wonderfully sumptuous,
and their plump succulence explodes in your mouth. I have always loved soft-shells with nuts added,
and especially with hazelnuts. The sweet richness of the hazelnuts truly benefits the crab.
The crunchy nut coating almost emulates the shell of the crab. In this preparation, snow pea shoots
and slices of orange cherry tomatoes add a cleansing element that splendidly cuts into
the rich crab and nut flavors. A full-flavored but very light vegetable broth provides the
perfect backdrop for all of the ingredients, gracefully weaving them together.*

Serves 4

1 cup fresh carrot juice

1/2 cup fresh apple juice

1/2 cup fresh fennel juice

1/4 cup fresh snow pea shell juice

1 clove garlic, juiced

1 jalapeño, juiced

1 1/4 cups red bell pepper juice

1 tablespoon Spicy Vinegar (see Appendices)

1 tablespoon plus 2 teaspoons butter

Salt and pepper

1/2 cup hazelnut flour

1/2 teaspoon ground chipotle pepper

1/4 teaspoon ground cayenne pepper

1/2 teaspoon ground cumin

1 egg yolk

2 tablespoons water

4 soft-shell crabs

1/2 cup all-purpose flour

2 tablespoons grapeseed oil

2 cups fresh curry leaves

2 cups snow pea shoots

12 orange cherry tomatoes, thinly sliced

*12 Ennis hazelnuts, toasted, peeled, and
cut in half*

METHOD Combine the seven juices in a medium saucepan and gently simmer over medium heat for 2 to 3 minutes. Add the Spicy Vinegar, whisk in 1 tablespoon of the butter, and season to taste with salt and pepper. (If the juice separates, whisk just prior to serving.)

Place the hazelnut flour, chipotle pepper, cayenne, and cumin in a small bowl and stir together. Place the yolk in a separate small bowl and whisk in the water. Lightly dust the soft-shell crabs with the all-purpose flour. Dip the crabs in the egg yolk mixture and sprinkle both sides with the hazelnut flour mixture. Place the soft-shell crabs with the grapeseed oil in a very hot sauté pan and cook for 2 minutes on each side, or just until crispy. Remove from the pan and blot on paper towels.

In a medium sauté pan, quickly wilt the curry leaves and snow pea shoots with 2 teaspoons of the butter and a splash of water for 1 minute. Season to taste with salt and pepper.

ASSEMBLY Place some of the wilted greens in the center of each bowl. Lay a soft-shell crab on top of the greens and arrange some of the tomato slices and hazelnut halves around the bowl. Ladle some of the vegetable broth into each bowl.

Recommended Substitutions

Crayfish, lobster, scallop, shrimp, tuna

Wine Notes

Though not technically a Riesling, Morgadio Albariño is thought to be a Riesling ancestor from Galicia, on the western coast of Spain. Albariño is not as sweet as many Rieslings, and this variety is sensational with the nut-coated crab. It has refreshing acidity when young (use the most recent vintage) and aromatic complexity for the vegetable broth with its spicy ingredients.

Pickled Mackerel with Caraway Vinaigrette and Warm Fingerling Potato Salad

I love pickled fish of any kind, but there's something truly special about pickled mackerel.
It has just the right fat content to balance the acid in the Pickling Juice.
The tremendous flavor of the mackerel seems to call out for potato, caraway, and onion.
It is a combination of flavors that works perfectly together. A little
hard-boiled egg rounds out this incredible mixture of ingredients and flavors.

Serves 4

1 cup julienned Spanish onion

2 teaspoons grapeseed oil

3 cups Pickling Juice (see Appendices)

2 teaspoons caraway seeds, toasted

*3 tablespoons chopped fresh herbs
(such as fresh parsley and chives)*

1/3 cup olive oil

Salt and pepper

8 1 1/2-ounce pieces mackerel, with skin

1/4 cup finely julienned celery

1 cup roasted fingerling potatoes

*4 hard-boiled quail eggs,
sliced into thin discs*

2 lady apples, cut into small wedges

1/2 cup toasted rye bread batons

METHOD To make the caraway vinaigrette, in a small pan, sauté the Spanish onion in the grapeseed oil until translucent. Add 1 cup of the Pickling Juice and continue to cook for 3 minutes. Remove the pan from the heat and let stand in the Pickling Juice for 1 hour. Strain and reserve both the onions and 1/2 cup of the Pickling Juice. Place the reserved 1/2 cup of Pickling Juice in a small bowl. Add the caraway seeds and chopped herbs and slowly whisk in the olive oil. Season to taste with salt and pepper.

Place the mackerel in a small, deep pan with straight sides. Pour the remaining Pickling Juice into a saucepan, bring to a boil, and pour over the mackerel. Let stand for 2 minutes, turn the fish over, and let stand until fully cooked, about 3 more minutes. (It may be necessary to remove the mackerel, bring the Pickling Juice back to a boil, and pour over the mackerel in order to fully cook the fish.)

Place the julienned celery in a small bowl and cover with ice water. Let stand for 10 to 15 minutes, until the celery begins to curl.

Slice the warm roasted fingerling potatoes into small wedges, toss with 2 tablespoons of the caraway vinaigrette, and season to taste with salt and pepper.

ASSEMBLY Arrange some of the fingerling potatoes, quail eggs, lady apples, celery, and rye bread batons on each plate. Place a small mound of the pickled Spanish onions at the front end of the plate and top with 2 pieces of the pickled mackerel. Spoon the caraway vinaigrette around the plate and over the mackerel and the potato salad.

Recommended Substitutions

Cold poached cod, halibut, pickled herring, lobster, salmon

Wine Notes

Dry Alsatian Riesling can take on diverse and even extreme flavors and make them work. Pickling juices can be unsettling to just about any other style of dry wine, but Alsatian Riesling carries through without a blink. Charles Schleret "Herrenweg" Riesling 1993 is a perfect example of varietally intense wine with clean, rich, yet dry flavors.

Flounder with Pink Oyster Mushroom—Stuffed Mini Evergreen Tomato, Wilted Baby Beet Greens, and Beef Juices

Flounder is among the most common fish found in supermarkets around North America. Like whitefish, when it is fresh, flounder is very flaky and delicate and it has an appealingly refined mild flavor. Here, on a mound of beet greens, and with a roasted Evergreen tomato stuffed with delicate pink oyster mushrooms, the flavor comes alive. Beef Stock Reduction lends the final significant element, profoundly tying all of the ingredients together.

Serves 4

4 mini Evergreen tomatoes

2 tablespoons chopped shallots

2 tablespoons butter

1 1/2 cups tiny pink oyster mushrooms

Salt and pepper

3 cups baby beet greens

1/2 cup Beef Stock Reduction (see Appendices)

8 1 1/2-ounce pieces flounder

1 tablespoon grapeseed oil

4 teaspoons Basil Oil (see Appendices)

METHOD Blanch the green tomatoes in boiling salted water for 30 to 60 seconds, just to loosen the skin. Immediately shock in ice water. Using a paring knife, carefully pull the skin away from the base of the tomato, drawing it toward the top. Do not remove the skin completely; leave a small amount attached to the top of the tomato. Cut off the top portion of the tomato and twist the skin to form a point.

Hollow out the bottom half of the tomato and discard flesh.

Sweat 1 tablespoon of the shallots in 1 tablespoon of the butter until translucent. Add the pink oyster mushrooms and continue cooking for 2 to 3 minutes, or until tender. Season to taste with salt and pepper. Fill each of the green tomatoes with some of the pink oyster mushroom mixture. Place in the oven at 350 degrees for 5 minutes, or until the tomato is hot in the center.

In a small sauté pan, wilt the beet greens and the remaining shallots in the remaining butter over medium heat for 3 to 5 minutes, or until the raw flavor of the beet greens has been cooked out. Season to taste with salt and pepper.

Warm the Beef Stock Reduction in a small saucepan over medium heat.

Season both sides of the flounder with salt and pepper. Sauté in a hot pan with

the grapeseed oil for 30 to 45 seconds on each side.

ASSEMBLY Place 1 of the stuffed green tomatoes on each plate with the tomato top positioned behind it. Spoon 1 teaspoon of the Basil Oil over each tomato. Arrange some of the wilted beet greens in front of the tomato and place 2 pieces of the flounder on the greens. Spoon the Beef Stock Reduction around the plate.

Recommended Substitutions

Salmon, red snapper, trout, whitefish

Wine Notes

Among the great dry Riesling districts, Austria's Wachau produces uniquely full and intense dry wines. The exciting Riesling Federspiel by Franz Prager in the Ried "Steinriegl" is a dry Riesling that does not overwhelm the flounder (as the richer Smaragd might) or come up short for the tart tomato element here. The fresh greens are a fine balance for both fish and wine.

Steamed Gindai and Mussels with Lemongrass Broth, Braised Swiss Chard, and Soba Noodles

This seafood stew has wonderfully complex flavors and textures, yet it is an easy dish to savor. The Hawaiian reef fish gindai is ethereal in its lightness, especially when steamed. The mussels and Swiss chard add a complementary heartiness. The radishes and jalapeño provide an elegant bite, and the shiso and lemongrass, a haunting perfume. Water chestnuts and cucumber offer a refreshing crunch, and a few drops of sesame oil bring forth a dignified richness. Additional soba noodles can be used for a more substantial dish, and wild mushrooms could easily be added if an even heartier dish is desired.

Serves 4

4 cups Fish Stock (see Appendices)

2 12-inch stalks lemongrass, coarsely chopped

Salt and pepper

4 3-ounce pieces gindai, with skin

1 cup blanched Swiss chard, coarsely chopped

4 ounces soba noodles, cooked

1/2 cup julienned red satin radish

1/2 cup julienned cucumber

1 jalapeño, seeded and finely julienned

16 thin slices of water chestnuts

16 mussels, steamed and shucked

4 tablespoons julienned nori

4 tablespoons julienned shiso

1/2 cup onion sprouts

4 teaspoons sesame oil

METHOD Place the Fish Stock in a medium saucepan with the lemongrass. Simmer over medium heat for 20 minutes to infuse the lemongrass. Strain through a fine-mesh sieve and season to taste with salt and pepper.

Season the gindai with salt and pepper and score the skin. Place in a steamer for 3 to 5 minutes, or until just done.

Warm the blanched Swiss chard in the Fish Stock over low heat for 2 minutes. Serve immediately.

ASSEMBLY In the center of each bowl, place some of the soba noodles, radish, cucumber, and jalapeño. Place a piece of the steamed gindai on top of the noodles. Place a slice of water chestnut at the four corners of the gindai, and set a mussel on top of each water chestnut. Ladle 1 cup of the Fish Stock and Swiss chard into each bowl. Sprinkle the nori, shiso, and onion sprouts around the bowl. Drizzle the sesame oil around the bowl and top with freshly ground black pepper.

Recommended Substitutions

Halibut, lobster, any type of oysters, salmon, red snapper, whitefish

Wine Notes

A crisp Middle Mosel Riesling, such as a spicy Ürziger or an earthy Graacher, is a classic style for the Asian flair of this dish. Gindai is a delicate fish, and with grain and green flavors all around, perfect for Graacher Domprobst Kabinett by Willi Schaefer, whose mineral aromas add to the already complex array of spices and vegetables.

Nairagi with Squid Ink Fettucine and Red Bell Pepper—Cardamom Emulsion

Nairagi is the Hawaiian name for striped marlin. This fish is firm, similar to tuna, and it has a very mild, elegant flavor. I like to leave it underdone in the middle to fully enjoy the succulence of the meat. Here, an exotic froth imbued with the flavors of cardamom is spooned around the fish. Chewy Squid Ink Fettucine adds a pleasant textural balance and a divine muskiness, while the onion sprouts add a playful bite.

Serves 4

4 red bell peppers, juiced (about 2¹/₂ cups juice)

¹/₄ cup cardamom seeds, toasted

4 tablespoons butter

Salt and pepper

4 3-ounce pieces nairagi

4 teaspoons chopped fresh parsley

4 teaspoons chopped fresh chives

2 teaspoons grapeseed oil

1 tablespoon freshly squeezed lime juice

2 teaspoons chopped shallots

2 tablespoons fresh thyme leaves

3 tablespoons olive oil

Squid Ink Fettucine (recipe follows)

2 tablespoons onion sprouts

8 small sprigs thyme

1 tablespoon butter

METHOD Heat the red bell pepper juice in a medium saucepan with the cardamom seeds. Simmer over medium heat for 45 minutes, or until reduced to 1¹/₂ cups, and strain through a fine-mesh sieve. Whisk in 3 tablespoons of the butter and season to taste with salt and pepper. Froth with a hand-held blender just prior to use.

Season both sides of the nairagi with salt and pepper and sprinkle one side with 2 teaspoons of the parsley and 2 teaspoons of the chives. Quickly sauté in a very hot pan with the grapeseed oil for 2 minutes on each side, or until just golden brown (the fish should be undercooked). Remove from the pan and slice in half on the diagonal.

To make the lime-thyme vinaigrette, place the lime juice, shallots, and thyme leaves in a small bowl. Whisk in the olive oil and season to taste with salt and pepper. Toss the Squid Ink Fettucine with the remaining butter, the remaining chopped parsley and chives, and half of the vinaigrette. Season to taste with salt and pepper.

ASSEMBLY Twist some of the fettucine around a long fork and place it in the center of each plate. Place 2 halves of the nairagi next to the fettucine. Spoon some of the red bell pepper juice around the plate. Sprinkle the onion sprouts and fresh thyme sprigs around the plate and over the fettucine. Drizzle the remaining vinaigrette on top of the fish.

Squid Ink Fettucine

Yield: about 4 cups

1 egg
1 tablespoon squid ink
³/₄ cup extra-fine semolina flour

METHOD Blend the egg and squid ink in a blender on high for 20 to 30 seconds. Place the semolina flour in a medium bowl and form a well in the center. Pour the squid ink—egg mixture into the well and combine with a wooden spoon or your hands until fully incorporated. Form into a ball and knead for 2 minutes. Wrap in plastic and refrigerate for 1 hour. Roll into thin sheets using a pasta machine and cut into fettucine strips. Cook in boiling salted water, for 1 to 2 minutes, or until al dente.

Recommended Substitutions

Lobster, marlin, salmon, scallops, swordfish, tuna

Wine Notes

The intense fresh thyme presence makes a dry, though not totally dry, Riesling an exciting match. Some sweetness in the red bell pepper juice makes a Halbtrocken from the Rheinhessen fit beautifully; the lovely J. & H. A. Strub Niersteiner Paterberg Riesling Kabinett Halbtrocken 1994 is crisp and parallels the citrus influence in the frothed sauce. The liveliness of this or another good Nierstein producer, such as Gunderloch, is a sensational flavor for this exotic fish.

Seafood Sausage with Baby Greens, Pineapple Sage, and Peppered Pineapple Vinaigrette

Over the years, I have served seafood sausage in a number of preparations.
This version features a dice of salmon, scallop, and lobster piped into a lamb casing.
The lamb casing is very delicate and allows you to cook the seafood to a slightly
underdone degree without resulting in a chewy wrapping the way a hog casing would.
This version features playful tropical flavors working off the succulent fish and shellfish.
Pineapple sage and garden sprout salad provide perfect foils to the rich elements on the plate.
Serve this as an appetizer before a big, robust tuna dish, or as a prelude
to a glorious whole roasted fish, possibly carved at tableside.

Serves 4

12 fresh pineapple sage leaves

Grapeseed oil for frying

1 cup chopped fresh pineapple

2/3 cup diced pineapple

Salt and pepper

2 cups tiny lettuces and sprouts
(such as pea sprouts, sunflower sprouts, fresh
young basil leaves, and mixed baby greens)

3 tablespoons olive oil

1 cup small-diced sea scallops

1 cup small-diced salmon,
skin and bones removed

1 cup small-diced cooked lobster

2 tablespoons chopped fresh chervil

20 inches lamb casing

Ginger Oil (recipe follows)

Red Chile Oil (recipe follows)

12 fresh pineapple sage blossoms, halved

METHOD Fry 8 of the pineapple sage leaves in grapeseed oil for 5 to 7 seconds and blot on paper towels. Cut the remaining pineapple sage leaves into a fine chiffonade.

Purée the chopped pineapple until smooth and pass through a fine-mesh sieve with a spoon.

In a small bowl, toss the diced pineapple with freshly ground black pepper.

Place the tiny lettuces and sprouts in a small bowl and toss with 1 tablespoon of the olive oil. Season to taste with salt and pepper.

Place the scallops, salmon, and lobster in a small bowl. Fold in the remaining olive oil and the chopped chervil, and season to taste with salt and pepper.

Rinse the lamb casing thoroughly under running water. Place the seafood mixture in a pastry bag fitted with a ¼-inch round tip. Tie a knot at one end of the lamb casing and place the other end over the round pastry tip. Hold the casing on the pastry tip while piping the seafood mixture into the casing. Slowly fill the casing with the seafood mixture, packing it tightly. Once the casing is full of the seafood mixture, twist it into 2½-inch-long sausages and tie a knot at the open end. Poach the sausage in boiling salted water for 40 seconds. Slice each sausage in half on the bias.

ASSEMBLY Arrange 4 of the seafood sausage pieces in the center of each plate. Place a small mound of the lettuce mixture on top of the seafood sausage along with 2 fried pineapple sage leaves. Spoon some of the pineapple purée, Ginger Oil, and Red Chile Oil around the plate. Place some of the diced pineapple, sage blossoms, and sage chiffonade around the seafood sausage.

Ginger Oil

Yield: about ⅓ cup

½ cup chopped ginger
½ cup grapeseed oil

METHOD Purée the ginger and grapeseed oil in a blender for 3 to 4 minutes, or until smooth. Refrigerate overnight. Strain through a fine-mesh sieve and refrigerate until needed.

Red Chile Oil

Yield: about ⅓ cup

½ cup chopped red chiles
½ cup grapeseed oil

METHOD Purée the red chiles and grapeseed oil in a blender for 3 to 4 minutes, or until smooth. Refrigerate overnight. Strain through a fine-mesh sieve and refrigerate until needed.

Recommended Substitutions

Halibut, shrimp, snapper, swordfish, whitefish

Wine Notes

The slight earthiness and sweetness of a classic Mosel are perfect for sausage, whether it be meat or seafood. Selbach-Oster's Zeltinger Himmelreich Riesling Spätlese, at only 8 percent alcohol, is refreshing, with a touch of appley sweetness. Peppered pineapple is a fascinating food element that mirrors the effect of this wine.

These two varieties are really not similar except for the wonderful floral intensity of their wines. Their best examples also happen to grow side by side in Alsace. These aromatic wines can sometimes have some sweetness, which helps in numerous tropical preparations, and plenty of flamboyance, which suits a colorful or whimsical plate. ❧ We have found fine Muscat Blanc a Petits Grains (the full name of the best Muscat variety) in many areas, and the Muscat Ottonel and Gelber Muskateller equally useful for their flashy, sometimes spicy character. Gewürztraminer can be a more brooding, powerful wine, whose most intense examples can have a knockout perfume followed by a down-for-the-count finish. The styles of wines that we recommend from these varieties are very much on the dry end of the spectrum. In their dry manifestations, Muscat and Gewürztraminer are excellent early-course wines of attention-grabbing flash. Either variety is sure to provide stimulation of both palate and cerebellum.

African Pompano with Macadamia Nut Crust, Bok Choy, and Spicy Lemongrass-Coconut Emulsion

The combination of foodstuffs in this dish makes for a fascinating array of flavors and textures.
The overall effect is of eating something quite light and refreshing.
African pompano is just firm enough to stand up to the other flavors, yet its delicate flavor,
while not mild enough to get lost, melds magnificently into the fragrant cloudlike broth.
This preparation is especially refreshing on an intensely hot day.

Serves 4

4 3-ounce pieces African pompano

Salt and pepper

³/₄ cup chopped macadamia nuts

2 tablespoons grapeseed oil

2 tablespoons chopped ginger

1 cup finely julienned leeks

3 teaspoons butter

1 cup julienned cucumber

2 cups coarsely chopped bok choy

*¹/₂ cup julienned roasted yellow bell pepper
(see Appendices)*

*¹/₂ cup julienned roasted red bell pepper
(see Appendices)*

Coconut Broth (recipe follows)

*4 tablespoons shaved toasted
macadamia nuts*

4 teaspoons fresh cilantro leaves

4 teaspoons julienned flat-leaf parsley

METHOD Season both sides of the African pompano with salt and pepper and crust the top side with the chopped macadamia nuts. Place in a hot sauté pan with the grapeseed oil and sauté for 2 minutes on each side, or until done.

Sauté the ginger and leeks with the butter for 2 to 3 minutes, or until translucent. Add the cucumber, bok choy, and roasted red and yellow peppers and continue to cook for 2 minutes or until the ingredients are hot. Season to taste with salt and pepper.

ASSEMBLY Arrange some of the leek—bok choy mixture in the center of each bowl and top with a piece of the African pompano. Ladle the warm Coconut Broth into the bowl. Sprinkle the shaved macadamia nuts, cilantro leaves, and julienned parsley around the bowl.

Coconut Broth

Yield: about 1 quart

3 fresh coconuts

1¹/₂ cups chopped lemongrass

2 cups water

2 cups milk

Salt

METHOD Strain the milk from the coconuts and place in a medium saucepan with the lemongrass. Finely grate the coconut meat. Add the coconut meat, water, and milk to the coconut milk and simmer over medium heat for 30 minutes. Purée in a blender and strain through a fine-mesh sieve. Season to taste with salt.

Recommended Substitutions

Halibut, lobster, salmon, red snapper, swordfish

Wine Notes

Spicy Gewürztraminer is often considered an ideal mate for Thai-influenced cuisine. Coconut, lemongrass, and cilantro are classic ingredients that prove this to be true. Ostertag "Fronholz" Gewürztraminer is a very ripe Alsace Gewürztraminer with a touch of sweetness that parallels the broth, and with enough richness for the texture of the fish.

Hawaiian Blue Prawn with Tropical Fruit Salsa and Spicy Persimmon Sauce

*My wife, Lynn, loves Hawaii, and we travel there once a year. Not only is it a restful getaway,
but the sophisticated cuisine that has developed there is truly splendid. Over the years, I have gained
much inspiration from my dining experiences in Hawaii. This preparation is a prime example
of a Pacific Rim–inspired idea, a dish that is light and healthful and full of great flavors and textures.
The succulent prawns burst with a richness that is tamed by the myriad flavors supplied
by the fruits. Finally, an important heat is provided by the spicy persimmon sauce and the
jalapeño-sesame vinaigrette. This dish practically demands to be eaten in the sunshine.*

Serves 4

6 whole kumquats

3 tablespoons sugar

1/2 cup Pickling Juice (see Appendices)

1/4 cup thinly sliced red onion

*4 Hawaiian blue prawns, deveined, peeled,
and tail attached*

Salt and pepper

2 teaspoons grapeseed oil

12 thin slices sapote

12 thin slices mango

12 thin slices avocado

12 thin slices persimmon

12 thin slices pineapple guava

12 thin slices star fruit

Cilantro-Chile Vinaigrette (recipe follows)

Spicy Persimmon Sauce (recipe follows)

METHOD Place the kumquats in a small saucepan, cover with water, and bring to a simmer. Strain and repeat once more. Cut open the kumquats and discard the seeds and pulp. Place the skin back in the saucepan, cover with water and add the sugar. Simmer over medium heat for 30 minutes, remove from heat, and cool in the syrup.

Place the Pickling Juice in a small saucepan with the sliced red onion. Simmer over medium heat for 5 minutes, remove from the heat, and cool in the Pickling Juice. Strain the onions just prior to use.

Season both sides of each prawn with salt and pepper. Tie with twine so the tail is standing upright. Quickly cook in a very hot sauté pan with the grapeseed oil for 1 to 2 minutes on each side, or until done. Remove the twine before serving.

ASSEMBLY Arrange 3 slices of each of the different types of fruit in the center of each plate with some of the pickled red onion. Place a prawn on top of the fruit and spoon the Cilantro-Chile Vinaigrette on top of the prawn. Spoon the Spicy Persimmon Sauce around the fruit.

Cilantro-Chile Vinaigrette

Yield: about 1/4 cup

1/4 cup Pickling Juice (see Appendices)

1 red jalapeño, minced

1 tablespoon chopped fresh cilantro

1 1/2 teaspoons sesame oil

Salt and pepper

METHOD Combine the Pickling Juice, jalapeño, and cilantro in a small bowl. Slowly whisk in the sesame oil and season to taste with salt and pepper.

Spicy Persimmon Sauce

Yield: about 3/4 cup

1 small ripe persimmon, peeled and chopped

*3 tablespoons Spicy Vinegar
(see Appendices)*

3 tablespoons water

Salt and pepper

METHOD Purée the persimmon with the Spicy Vinegar and water until smooth. Season to taste with salt and pepper. Warm in a small saucepan just prior to use.

Recommended Substitutions

Lobster, salmon, scallops, any type of shrimp, tuna

Wine Notes

Muscat's intense perfume takes on a strong mineral character in the unique Pfalz wines of Müller-Catoir. The opulent Gelber Muskateller grown at Haardt (Haardter Burgergarten) offers apricot and wet stone aromas and richness on the palate. The traditional Spätlese is a powerful, slightly sweet wine, a great fusion with the tropical fruit in this recipe. The flavors are extraordinarily clean, and the finish lingers because of the sweetness and acidity in tandem.

Mahimahi with Wilted Greens, Chinese Longbeans, Fried Hawaiian Ginger, and Star Anise Vinaigrette

Mahimahi is among the most succulent of the seafoods featured in this book,
and it is also one of the most versatile. In spite of its delicate flesh it holds up very well to
assertive flavors, and its flavor even seems to be highlighted by contrasting textures.
Here, the crunchy Chinese longbeans pair with barely wilted greens for an exquisite textural foil
to the fish. A fragrant star anise vinaigrette harmonizes with the meltaway fish
and the crispy vegetables. Flakes of fried Hawaiian ginger add a final perfumy crispness.

Serves 4

1 medium white squash, unpeeled

Salt and pepper

1/4 cup Hawaiian ginger juice or young ginger juice

1/4 cup orange juice

1/4 cup banana juice

1/4 cup pineapple juice

1/4 cup blood orange juice

4 pieces star anise

1/3 cup plus 1 tablespoon grapeseed oil, plus extra for frying

4 teaspoons chopped fresh chervil

1/4 cup sliced Hawaiian ginger or young ginger

4 Chinese longbeans

2 teaspoons butter

2 cups baby bok choy

2 cups frisee

2 cups baby red romaine

1/4 cup julienned water chestnuts

1/4 cup water

12 1 1/2-ounce pieces mahimahi, skin removed

METHOD Place the whole white squash on a sheet pan with 1/4 inch of water. Bake at 375 degrees for 45 to 60 minutes, or until cooked through. Remove from oven, let cool for 10 minutes, and thinly slice. Season the slices with salt and pepper and reheat if necessary just before serving.

Place the ginger, orange, banana, pineapple, and blood orange juices in a small pot with 2 pieces of the star anise. Simmer over medium heat for 15 to 20 minutes, or until reduced to about 1/3 cup. Strain the juices through a fine-mesh sieve. Grind the remaining star anise and add to the reduced juices. Slowly whisk in 1/3 cup of the grapeseed oil and season to taste with salt and pepper. Stir in the chopped chervil.

Heat some grapeseed oil (about 1 inch) in a small saucepan. Fry the ginger pieces just until slightly golden, about 30 to 45 seconds. Remove the ginger from the oil and blot on paper towels.

Blanch the longbeans in boiling salted water for 2 to 3 minutes, or until tender. Toss with 1 teaspoon of the butter and season to taste with salt and pepper.

Place the baby bok choy, frisee, and baby red romaine in a hot pan with the julienned water chestnuts, the remaining teaspoon of butter, and the water, and gently wilt over medium heat for 1 to 1 1/2 minutes.

Season to taste with salt and pepper.

Season both sides of the mahimahi with salt and pepper and sauté in a hot pan with 1 tablespoon of the grapeseed oil for 2 minutes on each side, or until just cooked.

ASSEMBLY Place some of the white squash slices on the plate and top with some of the wilted greens. Layer 3 pieces of mahimahi with some of the remaining wilted green mixture. Wrap a longbean around the mahimahi. Sprinkle some of the fried ginger around the plate. Spoon the star anise vinaigrette around the mahimahi.

Recommended Substitutions

Swordfish, trout, tuna, whitefish

Wine Notes

Spicy Muscat from Tement (Gelber Muskateller) in Styria or Eyrie (Muscat Ottonel) in Oregon are the recommended wines as they possess less sweetness than German or Alsatian versions. Ginger and star anise, the exotic, aromatic elements of this dish, are well highlighted by either of these Muscats. Both wines are more delicate styles of Muscat, yet they have the finesse needed for the meaty mahimahi.

Hamachi Three Ways

*Hamachi, or yellow tail, is a very versatile fish. It is tremendous both raw and barely seared.
It can be marinated and then roasted, grilled, or braised. It can be flavored with Asian seasonings,
paired with mushrooms and a meat stock reduction, or simply poached in a court
bouillon made from this incredible fish's bones. Here, it is offered up as a light appetizer featuring
three distinct preparations that showcase hamachi's very unique characteristics.
The spicy papaya sauce and the pulped avocado nicely emphasize the hamachi's richness.
And finally, serving three warm pieces of fish with chilled accompanying ingredients
and cold Gewürztraminer lends a very exotic and sensuous mouthfeel to this dish.*

Serves 4

1 hamachi jaw bone

1 cup chopped Spanish onion

1 cup chopped celery

1 cup chopped leeks

4 tablespoons fine chiffonade of opal basil

1 cup thinly sliced fresh papaya

1 cup Pickling Juice (see Appendices)

1 ripe avocado, peeled and pit removed

1 tablespoon chopped shallots

2 tablespoons chopped fresh cilantro

1 tablespoon freshly squeezed lime juice

Salt and pepper

½ cup fresh ogo seaweed

½ cup water

½ cup julienned daikon

2 teaspoons freshly squeezed lemon juice

12 1-ounce pieces hamachi

6 teaspoons sesame oil

¼ cup Thai barbecue sauce

2 tablespoons grapeseed oil

2 teaspoons black sesame seeds

2 teaspoons white sesame seeds

METHOD To make the hamachi broth, place the hamachi jaw bone in a medium saucepan with the chopped onion, celery, and leeks. Cover with about 2 quarts water and simmer over medium-high heat for 1 hour. Strain and continue to reduce over medium-high heat for 30 minutes, or until reduced to about 1 cup. Add the opal basil just prior to serving.

Steep the papaya in the Pickling Juice for 2 hours. Set aside ⅓ cup of the preserved papaya. Purée the remaining papaya with just enough of the Pickling Juice to purée smoothly.

Place the avocado in a small bowl and mash with a fork until it has a semismooth consistency. Add the chopped shallots, cilantro, and lime juice and season to taste with salt and pepper. Cover and store in the refrigerator until needed.

Place the ogo seaweed in a small saucepan with the water, simmer over medium heat for 3 minutes, drain, and use while warm.

Toss the daikon and lemon juice together in a small bowl and season to taste with salt and pepper.

Season the hamachi with salt and pepper. Place 4 pieces in a small container, toss with the sesame oil, and let marinate in the refrigerator for 1 hour before cooking. Place 4 pieces in a separate container with the Thai barbecue sauce and let marinate in the refrigerator for 1 hour before cooking. Gently grill the sesame oil–marinated hamachi over a low flame for 2 minutes on each side, or until just underdone. Sauté the Thai barbecue–marinated hamachi in a hot pan with 1 tablespoon of the grapeseed oil for 1 to 2 minutes on each side, or until just underdone. Sprinkle one side of the remaining hamachi with the black and white sesame seeds and cook in a very hot

sauté pan with the remaining 1 tablespoon grapeseed oil, seed side down first, for 1 to 2 minutes on each side.

ASSEMBLY Place 3 quenelles of the pulped avocado mixture in the center of each plate. Place some of the preserved papaya slices at the outer edge of one of the quenelles and top with a piece of the sesame seed–crusted hamachi. Place some of the daikon at the end of another quenelle and top with a piece of the Thai barbecue–marinated hamachi. Place some of the ogo seaweed at the end of the remaining quenelle and top with a piece of grilled hamachi. Spoon some hamachi broth on top of the grilled hamachi and around the plate. Spoon some of the preserved papaya purée around the plate.

Recommended Substitutions

Salmon, scallops, red snapper, swordfish, tuna

Wine Notes

The wine must embellish the three very different treatments of this succulent fish without creating flavor conflicts. One of the richest dry Gewürztraminers we know is by Navarro Vineyards in Anderson Valley, California, a fragrant yet balanced wine that seems closest to the Alsace model by F. E. Trimbach. Either wine works because of its less dense aroma and dry finish.

Fluke Sashimi with Baby Lettuces and Pickled Vegetable Maki Rolls with Spicy Peanut-Miso Sauce

Fluke is ideal for marinating and serving raw because its flesh is delicate but at the same time firm enough to stand up to the flavors of a marinade. In a larger serving, this preparation is almost a complete meal. The spicy peanut-miso sauce adds an exotic flavor and a welcome richness. It's hard to imagine a more perfect lunch on a hot day.

Serves 4

¹/₃ cup baby red romaine
¹/₃ cup frisee
¹/₃ cup baby arugula
¹/₃ cup tatsoi
¹/₃ cup green oak
¹/₃ cup lolla rossa
3 tablespoons olive oil
6 teaspoons Key lime juice
Salt and pepper
8 thin slices fresh fluke
12 thin slices avocado
Maki Rolls (recipe follows)
¹/₄ cup red clover sprouts
4 teaspoons julienned shiso
4 teaspoons julienned primroses
Spicy Peanut-Miso Sauce (see Appendices)
1 teaspoon black sesame seeds

METHOD Place all of the greens in a small bowl and toss together with 2 tablespoons of the olive oil and 2 teaspoons of the Key lime juice. Season to taste with salt and pepper.

Rub the fluke pieces with the remaining olive oil and Key lime juice and season with salt and pepper.

ASSEMBLY Arrange a mixture of the lettuce greens on each plate, incorporating some of the sliced avocado and a small piece of the fluke. Place 2 slices of the Maki Rolls on one side of the lettuce greens. Sprinkle a few of the red clover sprouts, some of the shiso, and some of the primroses on top of the lettuce greens. Lay a piece of the fluke in front of the lettuce greens and spoon some of the Spicy Peanut-Miso Sauce around the plate and on the fluke. Sprinkle a few black sesame seeds around the plate and top with freshly ground black pepper.

Maki Rolls

Yield: 2 Maki Rolls

4 4-inch-long carrot batons
4 4-inch-long mango batons
1 cup Pickling Juice (see Appendices)
¹/₂ teaspoon wasabi
1¹/₂ teaspoons water
1 cup cooked sticky rice
1¹/₂ tablespoons sugar
2 tablespoons rice wine vinegar
2 sheets nori
6 4-inch-long chives
4 4-inch-long red bell pepper batons
4 4-inch-long avocado batons

METHOD Place the carrots and mango in a small bowl, cover with the Pickling Juice, and refrigerate for 2 hours.

Place the wasabi and the water in a small cup and stir until smooth to make a paste.

Place the rice, sugar, and rice wine vinegar in a small bowl. Stir gently until incorporated.

Lay a sheet of nori on a bamboo maki roller. Place ¹/₂ cup of the rice on top of the nori. (Moisten your hands with water before touching the rice to prevent it from sticking to your hands.) Using your hands, spread the rice flat and leave a 2-inch border at the top of the nori. Spoon 1 teaspoon of the wasabi paste on top of the rice. Lay 3 of the chives across the rice. Drain the Pickling Juice and place 2 mango pieces end to end on top of the chives. Repeat the process with the carrot, red bell pepper, and avocado. Using the maki roller, carefully roll up the nori sheet, creating a firm, smooth maki roll. Moisten the 2-inch border of the nori with water and pinch the sheet to create a seal. Set aside. Repeat this process with the remaining ingredients.

Let the rolls stand for 30 minutes at room temperature, then slice them on the bias into 1¹/₂-inch pieces.

Recommended Substitutions

Scallops, shrimp, red snapper, swordfish, tuna

Wine Notes

Alsace produces exciting Muscat as one of the four permitted varieties for Grand Cru vineyard designation. Though the variety seems to be overshadowed by Riesling and Gewürztraminer in reputation, its unique floral intensity can be more satisfying than earthy Riesling or opulent Gewürztraminer. Zind-Humbrecht makes great Muscat from the "Goldert" Grand Cru, a clean, full wine with peach and orange blossom tones. This wine has an affinity for the miso and peanut flavors in this elegant raw fish preparation and vibrant acidity that parallels the pickled maki roll.

Farmed Baby Abalone with Bok Choy, Jicama, and Asian Vinaigrette

*I have always considered abalone a special treat, especially in a preparation that
really shows off its delicate, regal flavor. I don't like to bread this majestic mollusk or deep-fry it.
I prefer a simple, quick sauté, and then dress it lightly with an aromatic vinaigrette.
I find that the smaller, farmed abalone don't need pounding to tenderize them. I like their delicate,
natural chewiness, but if you prefer, you can pound them a little to avoid that textural
aspect altogether, or simply slice them thinly after cooking. Here, braised bok choy and zesty Asian
vinaigrette are all that are needed to create a sublime first course for a special dinner.*

Serves 4

⅓ cup freshly squeezed orange juice

½ teaspoon hoisin sauce

¾ teaspoon chile paste with garlic

2 tablespoons chopped fresh cilantro

1 tablespoon plus 2 teaspoons sesame oil

Salt and pepper

1 tablespoon julienned ginger

1 tablespoon chopped shallots

16 baby bok choy leaves

2 tablespoons water

8 fresh baby abalone, shelled

2 tablespoons grapeseed oil

2 tablespoons butter

¾ cup jicama batons

2 teaspoons fine chiffonade of cilantro

METHOD Whisk together the orange juice, hoisin sauce, chile paste, chopped cilantro, and 1 tablespoon of the sesame oil in a small bowl. Season to taste with salt and pepper.

In a medium sauté pan, sweat the ginger and chopped shallots in the 2 teaspoons of sesame oil. Add the baby bok choy leaves and 2 tablespoons water and continue cooking over medium heat for 2 minutes. Remove the baby bok choy leaves and reserve the cooking juices that remain in the pan. Season the leaves with salt and pepper.

Season both sides of the baby abalone with salt and pepper. In a hot pan, quickly sauté the abalone with the grapeseed oil and butter for 2 minutes on each side, or until it is slightly firm and golden brown. (The abalone may be sliced thinly after cooking.)

ASSEMBLY Arrange some of the baby bok choy leaves and jicama in the center of each plate. Place 2 of the abalone on top of the bok choy. Spoon the reserved cooking juices on top of the abalone and around the plate. Spoon the orange juice–chile paste mixture around the plate. Sprinkle the julienned cilantro on top of the abalone.

Recommended Substitutions

Lobster, shrimp, red snapper, swordfish, tuna

Wine Notes

Crisp Gewürztraminer from Washington or Oregon is well-balanced and lighter-bodied than many from California or Alsace. This recipe requires a lighter wine because of the heat in the bok choy and the vinaigrette. We recommend Gewürztraminer from Yakima Valley by Hogue Cellars; this crisp, lean version keeps the heat in check and offers typical floral spiciness for the aromas in the dish.

Once the little-known local wine of great Lyon restaurants, this grape of Condrieu was drifting to near extinction just a few short years ago. Today, the fine wine world seems to scramble for this exotic, heady variety. It grows well in numerous areas of California, in the mid-Atlantic states, and in the south of France; however, it is only in greater quantity, not in greater quality, in these regions than in Condrieu. Yield is the key to maintaining Viognier's intensity. Higher yielding vineyards produce a wine of less tension. ❧ Viognier's peachy, nectarlike perfume and strong finish make it a great variety for bold seafood flavors. Many Viogniers give a deceptively sweet impression and can be equally expressive when made in oak or in stainless steel. We find that Viognier is best drunk young, even in its grandest renditions from single vineyards in Condrieu or in the singular appellation of Château Grillet. The same can be said of the best California Viogniers, which often lack the requisite acidity for cellaring.

Cumin-Crusted Turbot with Yuca Purée, Wild Watercress, and Red Wine Vinaigrette

Turbot has great texture. It's like eating a piece of meat, yet the flavor is quite delicate.
Here, the sturdy flesh is met with the peppery, fresh flavor of the watercress and the satiny yuca.
A luscious red wine vinaigrette is made right in the pan in which the turbot was cooked.
This preparation shows why turbot is among the royals from the sea.

Serves 4

3 cups peeled and chopped fresh yuca

3 cups milk

Salt and pepper

8 2-ounce pieces turbot, skin removed

3 tablespoons cumin seeds,
toasted and crushed

2 tablespoons grapeseed oil

2 tablespoons chopped shallots

1 cup red Zinfandel

1 tablespoon olive oil

2 tablespoons chopped fresh chervil

2 tablespoons chopped fresh chives

2 cups wild watercress

1 tablespoon butter

METHOD Place the yuca in a small sauce-pan with the milk. Simmer over medium heat for 40 to 50 minutes, or until tender. Drain the liquid and purée the yuca until smooth. Season to taste with salt and pepper.

Season both sides of the turbot with salt and pepper and sprinkle the top side with the crushed cumin. Sauté the turbot in a hot pan with the grapeseed oil for 1 to 2 minutes on each side. Remove the turbot from the pan and set aside. Place the shallots in the sauté pan and lightly caramelize. Deglaze with the Zinfandel and simmer for 5 minutes, or until reduced to 1/2 cup. Quickly whisk in the olive oil. Stir in the chervil and chives, and season to taste with salt and pepper.

In a separate sauté pan, quickly wilt the wild watercress in the butter and season to taste with salt and pepper.

ASSEMBLY Spoon some of the yuca purée in the center of each plate and top with the watercress. Place 2 pieces of turbot on top of the watercress and spoon the pan sauce on and around the fish.

Recommended Substitutions

Halibut, lobster, salmon, swordfish, tuna

Wine Notes

Condrieu's dryer styles suit this dish, so look for René Rostaing's or Georges Vernay's fresh versions to give the turbot-yuca combination some floral spiciness and good structure in the background. These more firm Condrieus also play a good foil to the red wine vinaigrette's acidity.

Gulf Shrimp with Potato Purée and Turmeric-Fennel Emulsion

*These sweet Gulf shrimp absolutely melt into the satiny yellow Finn potato purée.
A fennel-turmeric emulsion adds a complex but soothing exotic quality, and the crispy potato tuile
provides a playful crunch. Once the prep work is done, this dish just takes moments to put together.
The amount of heat in the emulsion can be altered by adding more or less togarashi.*

Serves 4

2 cups Fennel Juice (see Appendices)

1 small Granny Smith apple, chopped

*3 tablespoons Turmeric Butter
(recipe follows)*

1 teaspoon togarashi

2 tablespoons freshly squeezed lemon juice

Salt and pepper

*12 ounces yellow Finn potatoes
(about 3 potatoes)*

3 tablespoons butter

3 tablespoons half-and-half

*12 jumbo shrimp, deveined,
with tail attached*

2 teaspoons grapeseed oil

12 Potato Tuiles (recipe follows)

4 teaspoons Fennel Oil (see Appendices)

4 teaspoons fennel fronds

METHOD Place the Fennel Juice in a small saucepan and simmer 10 to 15 minutes, or until reduced to 1 cup. Add the chopped apples, simmer for 5 minutes, and strain through a fine-mesh sieve. Just prior to serving, whisk in the Turmeric Butter, togarashi, and lemon juice. Season to taste with salt and pepper and keep warm.

Peel the yellow Finn potatoes and cut into a large dice. Place in a medium saucepan and cover with salted water. Simmer for 15 to 20 minutes, or until tender. Drain and pass through a ricer or sieve. Place in a small mixer with the butter and the half-and-half and whip until smooth. Season to taste with salt and pepper.

Season both sides of the shrimp with salt and pepper and quickly sauté in a hot pan with the grapeseed oil for 1 to 2 minutes on each side.

ASSEMBLY Place a mound of the potatoes in the center of each bowl and arrange 3 shrimp upright around the potatoes. Place a Potato Tuile standing on an angle between each shrimp. Ladle some of the turmeric broth in each bowl and drizzle the Fennel Oil in the broth. Place a few fennel fronds in each bowl.

Turmeric Butter

Yield: ¼ cup

¼ cup diced Spanish onions

2 teaspoons grapeseed oil

¼ cup diced Granny Smith apples

1 tablespoon turmeric

¼ cup water

¼ cup butter, softened

METHOD In a small saucepan, sauté the onion with the grapeseed oil. Add the apple, turmeric, and water and continue to cook for 10 minutes. Cool, purée, and pass through a fine-mesh sieve. Fold into the softened butter and refrigerate until needed.

Potato Tuiles

Yield: about 1 cup batter

*1 Idaho potato (about 10 ounces),
baked and peeled*

3 tablespoons butter

4 egg whites

*2 tablespoons fine chiffonade
of flat-leaf parsley*

Salt and pepper

METHOD Place the warm potato in a mixing bowl with the butter and the egg whites. Using an electric mixer fitted with the paddle attachment, mix on medium for 3 to 4 minutes, or until smooth. Pass the potato mixture through a fine-mesh sieve, fold in the parsley, and season to taste with salt and pepper.

Cut a template out of a thin piece of cardboard with a 2-inch-square center removed. Place the template on a nonstick sheet pan, spread a thin layer of the potato batter in the center, and remove the template. Repeat until you have 12 squares of batter. (Extra tuile batter can keep for 2 days in the refrigerator.) Place the sheet pan in the oven at 300 degrees for 12 to 15 minutes, or until the batter is golden brown. Remove the squares from the sheet pan and cool.

Recommended Substitutions

Crayfish, lobster, salmon, scallops, shrimp, tuna

Wine Notes

These big flavors require bold wines. The heady, spicy intensity is matched by a few varieties, but Viognier is the most exciting. Young Condrieu by Guigal, especially the rare "La Doriane" cuvée, is a powerful, spicy match for the turmeric emulsion and does not overwhelm the meaty shrimp. Good, full American Viogniers are produced by Calera, Arrowood, and La Jota, though none have the earthiness of the Condrieu.

Whole Roasted Red Mullet with French Green Lentils, Roasted Yellow Beets, Baby Turnips, and Veal Stock Reduction

*Roasting a fish whole yields a more succulent meat as the fish juices do not evaporate as quickly.
It is also fun to present it this way. The red mullet, with its delicious skin,
simply melts in your mouth. Here, with the buttery lentils, sweet roasted beets,
and playfully sharp turnips, the result is elegantly robust.*

Serves 4

2 large yellow beets, unpeeled
¼ cup small-diced carrots
¼ cup small-diced celery
2 tablespoons plus 2 teaspoons butter
2 cups cooked French green lentils
Salt and pepper
24 whole baby turnips, peeled
4 whole small red mullet, cleaned and gutted
4 teaspoons olive oil
½ cup Veal Stock Reduction (recipe follows)

METHOD Place the whole beets in the oven at 400 degrees for 1 hour, or until tender. (The beets will have shrunken and the skin may appear bubbly.) Cut away the outer skin and slice each beet into 12 thin discs.

Sweat the carrots and celery in a small saucepan with 2 tablespoons of the butter for 3 minutes. Add the cooked lentils and season to taste with salt and pepper.

Cook the turnips in boiling salted water until tender. Toss with the remaining 2 teaspoons of butter and season to taste with salt and pepper.

Season both sides of the red mullet with salt and pepper and rub with the olive oil.

Place on a small sheet pan with the gutted side down. Roast in the oven at 450 degrees for 5 to 7 minutes, or until golden brown and crispy.

Place the Veal Stock Reduction in a small saucepan and warm over medium heat.

ASSEMBLY Arrange 6 beet slices in 2 rows side by side in the center of each plate. Spoon some of the hot lentils on top of the beets and top with the whole roasted red mullets. Arrange 6 of the turnips around the mullet and spoon the Veal Stock Reduction around the plate.

Veal Stock Reduction

Yield: 1¼ cups

10 pounds veal bones
2 carrots, coarsely chopped
2 stalks celery, coarsely chopped
1 yellow onion, coarsely chopped
1 leek, cleaned and coarsely chopped
1 bulb garlic, cut in half
2 tablespoons grapeseed oil
½ cup tomato concassée
4 cups dry red wine (such as Burgundy)

METHOD Place the bones in a roasting pan and roast in the oven at 450 degrees for 2 hours, or until golden brown. When bones are browned, caramelize the carrots, celery, onion, leek, and garlic in the grapeseed oil in a large stockpot. Add the tomato concassée and cook for 5 minutes. Deglaze with the red wine and reduce until most of the wine has been cooked out. Add the browned bones and cover with cold water. Bring to a boil, then reduce heat and let simmer over medium heat for 8 hours. Strain through a fine-mesh sieve and simmer over medium heat for 45 minutes, or until it coats the back of a spoon. Extra reduction can be stored in the freezer for several months.

Recommended Substitutions

Lobster, salmon, snapper, trout, whitefish

Wine Notes

Some of the best Condrieus come from small landholders who make minuscule quantities of exquisite Viognier. The grower we are most fond of is Yves Cuilleron. The exceptional Condrieu "Les Chaillets *Vieilles Vignes*" is a concentrated, yet not too opulent, wine for the earthy, rooty elements that surround the red mullet. Cuilleron's Condrieu is perfumed yet dry and firm enough for the stock-based sauce.

There now is your insular city of the Manhattoes, belted round by wharves as

Indian isles by coral reefs – commerce surrounds it with her surf. – HERMAN MELVILLE

Scallop "Ravioli" with Hokkaido Squash, Broccoli Raab, and Red Wine–Beet Sauce

To the eye, these little morsels actually appear to be ravioli, but there is no pasta present on the plate.
Roasted hokkaido squash is placed between two razor-thin slices of diver scallop
to create a raviolilike effect. The sweet squash melts perfectly into the luscious scallop.
The red wine–beet sauce provides an acidic sweetness that helps to further enhance the richness of
the scallops, and broccoli raab is earthy and cleansing and supplies just the right crunchy texture.

Serves 4

1 cup cooked hokkaido squash

6 teaspoons butter

Salt and pepper

12 pieces blanched broccoli raab

3 tablespoons Red Wine Reduction
(see Appendices)

3 tablespoons Beet Juice Reduction
(recipe follows)

24 thin slices raw sea scallops

2 teaspoons chopped fresh chervil

METHOD Place the hokkaido squash in a small saucepan with 2 teaspoons of the butter. Warm over medium heat and mash with a fork. Season to taste with salt and pepper.

Warm the broccoli raab in a sauté pan with 2 teaspoons of butter and season to taste with salt and pepper.

Place the Red Wine Reduction and Beet Juice Reduction in a small saucepan and warm over medium heat.

Season the scallop slices with salt and pepper. Lay 12 slices of the scallops on an oiled sheet pan. Place 1 tablespoon of the hot hokkaido squash in the center of each scallop. Top with another slice of scallop and press the edges together. Melt the remaining 2 teaspoons of butter and brush over the scallops. Place in the oven at 350 degrees for 2 to 3 minutes, or just long enough to barely cook the scallops. Sprinkle with the chopped chervil.

ASSEMBLY Place 3 of the scallop "ravioli" in the center of each plate. Arrange 3 pieces of broccoli raab around the scallops and spoon the red wine–beet sauce around the plate.

Beet Juice Reduction

Yield: about ¼ cup

1 cup red beet juice

METHOD Place the beet juice in a small saucepan over medium heat and simmer for 20 to 30 minutes, or until reduced to about ¼ cup. Strain through a fine-mesh sieve and store in the refrigerator until needed.

Recommended Substitutions

Halibut, salmon, swordfish, tuna

Wine Notes

Sweet vegetable flavors surround the sweet, tender scallop slices here, so an overly sweet, alcoholic Viognier might be too intense. We like Qupe Viognier for its dry palate and lower than typical alcohol level (12.5 percent). This style of Viognier quietly pushes forward the squash and beet flavors while allowing the scallop to maintain some sea sweetness.

Frog Legs with Roasted Eggplant Purée and Saffron–Yellow Squash Coulis

Frog legs are not usually considered seafood, but since most frogs spend so much of their existence in or near water, it seems fitting to include a recipe for their preparation in this book. Frog leg meat is lean and delicate but full-flavored enough to stand up to such sturdy flavors as saffron, chile vinegar, and garlic. A smooth mound of rich eggplant purée is a profound backdrop.

Serves 4

1 small eggplant, peeled

Salt and pepper

2 tablespoons plus 4 teaspoons olive oil

3 tablespoons Roasted Garlic Purée (recipe follows)

20 frog legs

4 teaspoons chopped garlic

4 tablespoons grapeseed oil

1 small yellow squash, peeled and chopped

¼ cup water

1 teaspoon saffron threads

1 tablespoon Spicy Vinegar (see Appendices)

2 tablespoons chopped flat-leaf parsley

METHOD Cut the eggplant into a large dice and toss with 1 teaspoon of salt. Let stand at room temperature for 30 minutes. Drain the liquid and rinse the salt off the eggplant. Toss the eggplant with 2 tablespoons of the olive oil, place on a nonstick sheet pan with ½ inch of water, and roast at 400 degrees for 40 to 50 minutes, or until cooked. Remove the eggplant from the oven, coarsely purée with the Roasted Garlic Purée, and season to taste with salt and pepper.

Season the frog legs with salt and pepper and coat with the chopped garlic. Quickly sauté in a hot pan with the grapeseed oil for 2 minutes on each side. Remove from the pan and blot on paper towels.

Place the squash in a small saucepan with the water, saffron, and Spicy Vinegar. Cook over medium heat for 5 to 7 minutes, or until the squash is cooked. Purée with the remaining liquid in the pan until smooth, and pass through a fine-mesh sieve. Season to taste with salt and pepper.

ASSEMBLY Place a large spoonful of the roasted eggplant purée in the center of each plate and arrange the frog legs upright around the purée. Spoon some of the yellow squash sauce around the frog legs and sprinkle with the chopped parsley. Top with freshly ground black pepper and spoon the remaining olive oil around the plate.

Roasted Garlic Purée

Yield: about ¼ cup

2 bulbs garlic, tops removed

3 cups milk

½ cup olive oil

Salt and pepper

METHOD Place the garlic in a small saucepan, cover with the milk, and simmer for 10 minutes. Drain the milk, place the garlic bulbs bottom side down in an oven-proof pan, add the olive oil, and cover. Bake at 350 degrees for 1 to 1½ hours, or until the bulbs are soft. Once cool, squeeze the soft garlic out of the skins and place in a blender with the olive oil it baked in. Purée until smooth and season to taste with salt and pepper. If you prefer a thinner purée, you may adjust the consistency with Chicken Stock (see page 228) or water.

Recommended Substitutions

Lobster, scallops, shrimp, red snapper, tuna

Wine Notes

These garlicky treats need full, floral Condrieu to embellish them, and a wine with a couple of years' cellaring might give the combination more depth as well. Try the late-released Condrieu "Côteau de Vernon" by Georges Vernay, which has a Burgundian roundness while still exhibiting floral Viognier aromatics. This fuller, more developed Condrieu matches the sealike flavors of the frog legs and the richness of the eggplant purée while still preserving the delicacy of the saffron flavoring the squash.

Baby Eels with Seaweed Salad and Spicy Herb Sauce

These little eels, known as pibales, are an unusual and special treat.
They are tossed live into a hot sauté pan and crisped up almost like tiny fried vegetables.
Here, they sit on a small mound of seaweed salad, which provides a wonderful
crunchy texture and a beautiful sesame perfume. The spicy herb sauce adds a touch of acid
and a delicate heat. Fried onions in lieu of the tiny eels would also make a splendid treat.

Serves 4

8 ounces live baby eels
¼ cup grapeseed oil
Salt and pepper
2 cups seaweed salad
Spicy Herb Sauce (see Appendices)

METHOD In a very hot pan, quickly sauté the baby eels in the grapeseed oil for 2 minutes, stirring constantly. Season to taste with salt and pepper.

ASSEMBLY Place some of the seaweed salad in the center of each plate and top with a mound of the baby eels. Spoon the Spicy Herb Sauce around the plate and top with freshly ground black pepper.

Recommended Substitutions

Lobster, fried onions, smoked salmon, shrimp, tuna

Wine Notes

John Alban's Estate Viognier is the best in California for its balance, ripeness, and flavor purity. With the very delicate baby eel flavor and the distinctly spicy seaweed and sauce, the wine carves a perfect delineation of flavor. Like this dish, it is clean, has personality, and finishes boldly.

Pink Porgy and Conch Fritter with Bacon Fat Vinaigrette

Pink porgy has soft, delicate flesh that is mild tasting and works well with a variety of flavor accents. Here, it is paired with fruits and vegetables that provide complex texture and flavor contrasts as well as different levels of acid and sweetness. Crispy bacon and a drizzle of bacon fat provide a satisfying richness that perfectly mellows the acids of tomato, persimmon, and papaya. A conch fritter is added for a whimsical touch. In all, this is a full-flavored and satisfying preparation that is deceptively refined.

Serves 4

1 cup cooked bacon batons, fat reserved
2 teaspoons freshly squeezed lemon juice
1/4 cup freshly squeezed orange juice
2 tablespoons tamari
Salt and pepper
1/4 cup lemon sections, skin removed
1/2 cup diced strawberry papaya
1/2 cup diced tomato
1/2 cup diced peeled persimmon
1/4 cup diced sunchoke
8 1 1/2-ounce pieces pink porgy, with skin
2 tablespoons grapeseed oil
Conch Fritters (recipe follows)
4 teaspoons flat-leaf parsley chiffonade

METHOD To make the vinaigrette, place the reserved warm bacon fat in a small bowl. Whisk in the lemon juice, orange juice, and tamari, and season to taste with salt and pepper. Break the lemon sections into small wedges.

Place the lemon, papaya, tomato, persimmon, and sunchoke in a medium bowl and toss together with 3 tablespoons of the vinaigrette.

Season both sides of the pink porgy with salt and pepper and score the skin side with a razor blade. Quickly sauté in a very hot pan with the grapeseed oil, skin side down first, for 1 to 2 minutes on each side.

ASSEMBLY Spoon some of the fruit mixture in the center of each plate. Place 2 pieces of the pink porgy overlapping each other on top of the fruit. Place a conch fritter on the side of the plate and sprinkle the flat-leaf parsley around the plate. Spoon the remaining vinaigrette and the bacon batons around the plate.

Conch Fritters

Yield: 6 to 8 fritters

1/2 pound conch meat
2 tablespoons chopped fresh chives
1 egg
1/3 cup milk
3/4 cup flour
1 1/4 tablespoons baking powder
2 teaspoons shallots, chopped
1/2 teaspoon chopped jalapeño
3 tablespoons beer
3 dashes Tabasco or hot sauce
Salt and pepper
Grapeseed oil for deep-frying

METHOD Lay the conch flat and cover with plastic wrap. Pound with a mallet to an even thickness. Chop into a small dice and fold in the chopped chives.

Whisk the egg and milk together in a separate bowl. Stir in the flour, baking powder, shallots, jalapeño, beer, and Tabasco. Stir until smooth. Fold in the conch and season with salt and pepper.

Heat the grapeseed oil to 350 degrees in a large, deep skillet. Using a small ice cream scoop or two soup spoons, drop some of the conch fritter batter into the grapeseed oil. Cook for about 1 minute on each side, or until golden brown. Remove to a paper towel.

Recommended Substitutions

Catfish, cod, flounder, lobster, trout

Wine Notes

The panoply of fresh fruit demands an aromatically intense wine, and the bacon presence suggests a wine of greater smokiness as well as richness. Porgy itself has a clean, almost sweet flavor, requiring a perfumed but light Piedmont white. We find the nuttiness of Arneis quite useful. This aromatic grape is unique to Piedmont and a lovely match here. Good Arneis is made by Ceretto in a light style and by Bruno Giacosa in a more hefty, full-throttle style.

Wreck Bass with Lobster-Strewn Amaranth, Braised Scallions, Poached Quail Egg, and Red Wine–Shellfish Sauce

Succulent wreck bass melts in your mouth. Here, it is used with a complex shellfish theme.
Braised scallions add a little bite and just the right textural contrast.
The amaranth provides a complex earthiness, and the herb crust, a light, springlike fragrance.

Serves 4

12 3-inch pieces scallion, root attached

2 tablespoons butter

1 cup water

Salt and pepper

¼ cup Veal Stock Reduction (recipe follows)

2 tablespoons Red Wine Reduction (see Appendices)

6 tablespoons Shellfish Stock (see Appendices)

1 cup cooked amaranth

4 teaspoons finely chopped scallion greens

8 small lobster medallions, cooked

1 cup blanched diced turnips

6 teaspoons chopped fresh herbs (such as chives and parsley)

4 3-ounce pieces wreck bass

2 teaspoons grapeseed oil

4 poached quail eggs

METHOD Place the scallions in a medium sauté pan with the butter and the water. Bring to a simmer and continue to cook for 5 to 7 minutes, or until tender. Remove from the liquid and season to taste with salt and pepper.

Place the Veal Stock Reduction, Red Wine Reduction, and Shellfish Stock in a small saucepan and simmer for 3 minutes, or until hot.

Warm the amaranth in a small saucepan and fold in the chopped scallion greens and lobster medallions. Season to taste with salt and pepper.

Place the diced turnips in a small pan and warm over medium heat. Season to taste with salt and pepper and toss with 2 teaspoons of the chopped herbs.

Season both sides of the bass with salt and pepper and crust the top side with the remaining 4 teaspoons of chopped herbs. Quickly sauté in a very hot pan with the grapeseed oil for 2 minutes on each side.

ASSEMBLY Place 3 scallions side by side on the front of each plate and top with a piece of fish. Place some of the amaranth-lobster mixture in a small timbale mold behind the fish, remove the mold, and top with one of the cooked quail eggs and freshly ground black pepper. Spoon some of the red wine–shellfish sauce around the plate and arrange the diced turnips around the sauce.

Veal Stock Reduction

Yield: 1¼ cups

10 pounds veal bones

2 carrots, coarsely chopped

2 stalks celery, coarsely chopped

1 yellow onion, coarsely chopped

1 leek, cleaned and coarsely chopped

1 bulb garlic, cut in half

2 tablespoons grapeseed oil

½ cup tomato concassée

4 cups dry red wine (such as Burgundy)

METHOD Place the bones in a roasting pan and roast in the oven at 450 degrees for 2 hours, or until golden brown. When bones are browned, caramelize the carrots, celery, onion, leek, and garlic in the grapeseed oil in a large stockpot. Add the tomato concassée and cook for 5 minutes. Deglaze with the red wine and reduce until most of the wine has been cooked out. Add the browned bones and cover with cold water. Bring to a boil, then reduce heat and let simmer over medium heat for 8 hours. Strain through a fine-mesh sieve and simmer over medium heat for 45 minutes, or until it coats the back of a spoon. Extra reduction can be stored in the freezer for several months.

Recommended Substitutions

Flounder, halibut, salmon, shrimp, snapper, whitefish

Wine Notes

The unique perfume of Cortese makes the aromatic range of this dish harmonize. Shellfish, root vegetable, and earthy grain all bond with the flavors of Gavi Neirano. The deft wood influence does not mask the grape in this underrated wine. And the central wreck bass element makes a great Gavi-friendly nucleus of flavor.

Silence is golden, they say – and yet, cuisine, one must speak of that! – FERNAND POINT

Wild Striped Bass with Stinging Nettles, Wild Mushroom–Balsamic Emulsion, and Hot and Sour Golden Beet Sauce

Wild striped bass is a great treat. It has a wonderful clean flavor that is light and delicate, but that remains unique against more assertive elements. Here, the fish sits on a pedestal of braised stinging nettles, which, because of their complex flavor, come across as thinking man's collard greens. For some playful texture a little mound of diced chayote is added to the nettles. Spicy Vinegar helps to offset the natural sweetness of the golden beets to create a very simple golden beet sauce. This, in turn, is exquisitely balanced with the regal wild mushroom–balsamic emulsion. In total, this preparation sings with harmonizing earthiness.

Serves 4

2 cups Mushroom Stock (see Appendices)

2 tablespoons aged balsamic vinegar

6 tablespoons butter

Salt and pepper

1/2 cup chopped yellow beet

1/4 cup Spicy Vinegar (see Appendices)

1/4 cup water

2 tablespoons chopped uncooked bacon

4 cups stinging nettles

1 tablespoon brown sugar

3 tablespoons rice wine vinegar

1 1/2 cups diced chayote

4 3-ounce pieces wild striped bass, skin removed

2 teaspoons grapeseed oil

METHOD Place the Mushroom Stock in a small saucepan and simmer for 20 to 30 minutes, or until reduced to 3/4 cup. Add the balsamic vinegar, whisk in 3 tablespoons of the butter, and season to taste with salt and pepper. Froth with a hand-held blender just prior to use.

Cook the chopped beets in boiling salted water for 15 to 20 minutes, or until tender. Drain and purée the beets with the Spicy Vinegar and water. Pass through a fine-mesh sieve, whisk in 1 tablespoon of the butter, and season to taste with salt and pepper.

Render the bacon in a medium sauté pan. Add the stinging nettles; use gloves when handling the raw stinging nettles, or they will cause a stinging sensation in your hands. Cook for 5 minutes, then add the brown sugar and rice wine vinegar. Continue to cook over low heat for 30 to 40 minutes, or until the stinging nettles are tender. Remove pan from heat and carefully discard the woody stems of the nettles. Place the nettles in a large bowl and season the stinging nettles with salt and pepper.

Place the diced chayote in a medium pan with 2 tablespoons of the butter and sauté for 2 to 3 minutes, or until tender. Season to taste with salt and pepper.

Season both sides of the fish with salt and pepper and sauté in the grapeseed oil in a very hot pan for 1 to 2 minutes on each side, or until just cooked.

ASSEMBLY Use a 3-inch triangle-shaped mold or any other mold of a similar size. Fill the bottom of the mold with some of the chayote mixture and top with some of the stinging nettles. Remove the mold and place a piece of wild striped bass on top of the stinging nettles. Spoon some of the golden beet sauce and mushroom–balsamic emulsion around the plate.

Recommended Substitutions

Catfish, cod, halibut, red snapper, trout

Wine Notes

This dish contains many sweet flavors—sweet greens, sweet chayote, and sweet beets—and a dry wine seems to intensify the sweetness. A round Gavi, youthful and fresh, supports the rich fish and allows the vegetable and fruit flavors to remain pure. The Massone "Vigneto Masera" 1995 is perfect. Clean and more steely than most Gavi, the Massone offers a lightly nutty richness and crisp citrusy acidity.

Spiny Lobster with Potato Gnocchi, Wilted Spinach, and Saffron-Infused Mussel Emulsion

Spiny lobster seems to have a slightly firmer texture and sweeter meat than Maine lobster and is ideally suited for this preparation. The gnocchi are elegant pillows of flavor that help showcase the exotic flavor and texture of the saffron-mussel emulsion. The wilted spinach and a rich Gavi act as cleansing agents to these luscious flavors and complex textures. A little drizzle of spicy bell pepper juice serves to further highlight these distinctive flavors and textures, helping to weave together the disparate but compatible elements.

Serves 4

¼ cup chopped shallots

½ teaspoon saffron threads

1½ cups dry white wine

1 pound mussels, cleaned and debearded

1½ cups chopped yellow squash

½ cup water

1 tablespoon plus 1 teaspoon Spicy Vinegar (see Appendices)

2 teaspoons freshly squeezed orange juice

Salt and pepper

2 tablespoons half-and-half

2 cups fresh spinach leaves

2 tablespoons butter

1 to 2 spiny lobster tails, shell removed (about 8 ounces)

2 tablespoons Red Bell Pepper Juice (recipe follows)

1 teaspoon freshly squeezed lemon juice

¼ cup mayonnaise

Potato Gnocchi (recipe follows)

METHOD Place the shallots, saffron, and white wine in a large sauté pan and bring to a simmer over medium-high heat. Add the mussels, cover, and steam for 3 to 4 minutes. Discard the mussel shells and meat.

Place the yellow squash in the sauté pan with the mussel juice and water. Cook the squash for 3 to 5 minutes, or until tender. Purée with all of the cooking liquid, 1 teaspoon of the Spicy Vinegar, and the orange juice until smooth. Pass through a fine-mesh sieve and season to taste with salt and pepper. Just prior to use, warm in a saucepan with the half-and-half and froth using a hand-held blender.

Wilt the spinach in a medium sauté pan with 1 tablespoon of the butter. Season to taste with salt and pepper.

Season the lobster with salt and pepper and sauté in a hot pan with the remaining 1 tablespoon of butter for about 2 minutes, or until just done. Slice into 4 medallions.

Whisk the red bell pepper juice, lemon juice, and the remaining 1 tablespoon Spicy Vinegar into the mayonnaise and season to taste with salt and pepper.

ASSEMBLY Place some of the wilted spinach in the center of each bowl. Place a lobster medallion on top of the spinach and arrange some of the Potato Gnocchi around the bowl. Ladle the saffron-infused mussel emulsion in the bowl and spoon some of the red bell pepper mayonnaise over the lobster and around the bowl.

Red Bell Pepper Juice

Yield: about ⅓ cup

3 red bell peppers, seeded

METHOD Juice the peppers and place in a medium saucepan. Over medium heat, reduce the liquid for 20 minutes, or until it has a light syruplike consistency. Strain through a fine-mesh sieve and refrigerate until needed.

Potato Gnocchi

1 egg yolk

1 large Idaho potato (about 8 ounces), peeled, cooked, and riced

½ to ¾ cup flour

Salt and pepper

2 teaspoons butter

METHOD Mix the egg yolk into the potato with a wooden spoon and knead in enough flour so that the dough is not sticky. Season to taste with salt and pepper.

Divide the mixture into 4 sections. Roll each section into a long cigar shape about ½ inch in diameter. Cut the rolls into ¾-inch pieces and delicately pinch the pieces in the middle along their lengths. Refrigerate on a lightly floured sheet pan until ready to cook. Shortly before serving, poach the gnocchi in boiling salted water for 2 to 3 minutes, or until they float. Remove with a slotted spoon. Place in a small bowl, toss with the butter, and season to taste with salt and pepper.

Recommended Substitutions

Lobster, salmon, scallops, shrimp, tuna

Wine Notes

Here is a full range of gutsy flavors for Piedmontese white. The heady saffron and chewy lobster need a full and assertive wine like Gavi di Gavi La Scolca, a powerful rendition of the Cortese, with substantial barrel influences. Almost a Burgundian-style wine, though perhaps not as smoky and earthy, this great Gavi is a world class dry white.

These dry wine grapes from the Rhône Valley provide its most ageworthy white wines. They give wines that balance rich, earthy flavors, and are fine textural foils for firmer-fleshed fish. Young, lighter wines based on these varieties are also surprising successes with leafy herbs and greens, while heartier wines are fabulous legume matches. They are often blended together to yield an aromatic, full wine that deserves serious cuisine. Wines

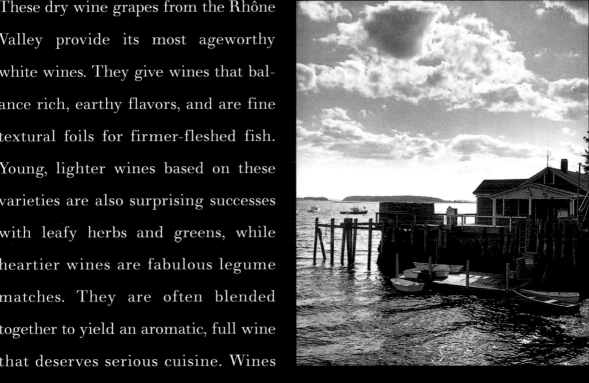

that include both varieties, like Domaine de Trevallon Blanc, can be grander than single-variety versions. ❧ Hermitage Blanc can be a huge, gangly Marsanne when young, but at ten years has the refinement of great white Burgundy with more aromatic nuance. Châteauneuf-du-Pape Blanc is more variable, but Roussanne-intense blends are also ageable, rich wines. In North America, California viticulturists have found numerous good sites for Marsanne and a few for Roussanne, and in Australia's Victoria there are many fine good-value Marsannes.

Farmed Sturgeon with Banana Fingerling Potatoes, Veal Stock Reduction, and Truffle Oil

Like monkfish, sturgeon has firm-textured flesh and is well-suited for pairing with bolder flavors and textures. The slightly astringent braised chard and the buttery fingerling potatoes make a perfect bed for the sturgeon. The Veal Stock Reduction drizzled with a little truffle oil adds an extraordinary complexity. To finish, tomato confit flavored with chile vinegar sits on top of the fish, a combination of sweet and heat to calmly marry these wonderful elements.

Serves 4

1 ½ cups banana fingerling potatoes, peeled and cut into a small dice

4 teaspoons butter

Salt and pepper

¾ cup Olive Oil–Poached Tomatoes (see Appendices)

4 teaspoons fresh tiny oregano leaves

2 teaspoons Spicy Vinegar (see Appendices)

½ cup Veal Stock Reduction (recipe follows)

3 cups chopped red Swiss chard

4 3-ounce pieces farmed sturgeon, cut into round discs, skin removed

1 tablespoon grapeseed oil

4 teaspoons white truffle oil

METHOD Place the diced potatoes in a small pot and cover with salted water. Simmer for 5 to 7 minutes, or until the potatoes are tender. Drain, toss with 2 teaspoons of the butter, and season to taste with salt and pepper.

Coarsely chop the warm Olive Oil–Poached Tomatoes and toss with 2 teaspoons of the oregano leaves and the Spicy Vinegar in a small bowl. Season to taste with salt and pepper.

Warm the Veal Stock Reduction in a small saucepan over medium heat.

Just prior to use, wilt the red Swiss chard with the remaining 2 teaspoons of butter over medium-high heat for 1 to 2 minutes, and season to taste with salt and pepper.

Season both sides of the sturgeon with salt and pepper. Quickly sauté in a very hot pan with the grapeseed oil for 1 to 2 minutes on each side, or until just cooked.

ASSEMBLY Arrange some of the diced potatoes and wilted red Swiss chard in the center of each plate. Place a piece of sturgeon on the red Swiss chard and top the sturgeon with a quenelle of the tomato confit. Spoon the warmed Veal Stock Reduction and white truffle oil around the plate. Top with freshly ground black pepper. Sprinkle with the remaining tiny oregano leaves.

Veal Stock Reduction

Yield: 1¼ cups

10 pounds veal bones

2 carrots, coarsely chopped

2 stalks celery, coarsely chopped

1 yellow onion, coarsely chopped

1 leek, cleaned and coarsely chopped

1 bulb garlic, cut in half

2 tablespoons grapeseed oil

½ cup tomato concassée

4 cups dry red wine (such as Burgundy)

METHOD Place the bones in a roasting pan and roast in the oven at 450 degrees for 2 hours, or until golden brown. When bones are browned, caramelize the carrots, celery, onion, leek, and garlic in the grapeseed oil in a large stockpot. Add the tomato concassée and cook for 5 minutes. Deglaze with the red wine and reduce until most of the wine has been cooked out. Add the browned bones and cover with cold water. Bring to a boil, then reduce heat and let simmer over medium heat for 8 hours. Strain through a fine-mesh sieve and simmer over medium heat for 45 minutes, or until it coats the back of a spoon. Extra reduction can be stored in the freezer for several months.

Recommended Substitutions

Catfish, halibut, salmon, swordfish, whitefish

Wine Notes

Bonny Doon "Le Sophiste" is a Roussanne-Marsanne blend that captures the honeyed essence of Marsanne in the powerful framework established by Roussanne. The oregano-steeped rich sturgeon meat needs a slightly fuller yet not so stern Rhône style, and among the growing number of American practitioners of these varieties, Randall Grahm is the best.

Israeli Couscous and Cold Poached Halibut with Teardrop Tomato, Mint, and Red Jalapeño Vinaigrette

This light and refreshing preparation is ideally suited for a warm summer day.
The Israeli couscous, which is larger and chewier than the more common North African couscous,
is the perfect foil for the soft-textured fish and barely crunchy vegetables.
A zingy jalapeño vinaigrette spooned on and around the halibut provides an exciting finish.

Serves 4

1/2 cup finely julienned Spanish onion

1/2 cup Pickling Juice (see Appendices)

1 red jalapeño, seeded and minced

4 teaspoons fresh mint chiffonade

1/2 cup olive oil

Salt and pepper

1 1/2 cups cooked Israeli couscous

1/2 cup thinly sliced yellow teardrop tomatoes

8 yellow patty pan squash, blanched and thinly sliced

8 green patty pan squash, blanched and thinly sliced

Poaching Liquid (recipe follows)

4 3 1/2-ounce pieces halibut, skin removed

METHOD Place the Spanish onion and Pickling Juice in a small saucepan and simmer over medium heat for 2 minutes. Let cool in the juice.

To make the vinaigrette, place the red jalapeño, 1/4 cup of the Pickling Juice, and 2 teaspoons of the mint in a medium bowl. Slowly whisk in the olive oil and season to taste with salt and pepper.

Toss the Israeli couscous with half of the vinaigrette. In a separate bowl, toss the sliced tomatoes and the squash with 2 tablespoons of the vinaigrette and season to taste with salt and pepper.

Place the Poaching Liquid in a saucepan and bring to a boil.

Season both sides of the fish with salt and pepper and place in a small, deep dish with straight sides. Pour the boiling Poaching Liquid over the halibut to cover. Let stand for 2 minutes, then turn the halibut over and let stand for 2 more minutes, or until the fish is just done. (If the halibut is not thoroughly cooked, return the Poaching Liquid to the saucepan, bring it back to a boil, and pour it over the fish again.) Remove the cooked halibut from the Poaching Liquid, season with salt and pepper, and serve immediately.

ASSEMBLY Arrange some of the Israeli couscous, tomatoes, pickled Spanish onion, and patty pan squash in the center of each plate. Place a piece of the halibut on top of the Israeli couscous and spoon the remaining vinaigrette over the halibut. Sprinkle the remaining mint around the plate.

Poaching Liquid

Yield: about 1 quart

3 cups Fish Stock (see Appendices)

1 cup white wine

1/2 cup chopped Spanish onion

1/2 cup chopped leeks

1 tablespoon pink peppercorns

1 cup fresh lemon thyme

Salt and pepper

METHOD Place the Fish Stock, wine, onion, leeks, and peppercorns in a medium saucepan and simmer over medium heat for 10 minutes. Add the lemon thyme and simmer for 5 minutes. Strain, season to taste with salt and pepper, and bring to a boil just prior to use.

Recommended Substitutions

Flounder, lobster, salmon, swordfish, whitefish

Wine Notes

Rhône whites are often multivariety blends, and Châteauneuf-du-Pape Blanc is a prime example. The Domaine du Vieux Télégraphe produces an exceptional white from its stony vineyards that features Clairette and Grenache Blanc prominently along with Roussanne and Bourboulenc. This wine's lively perfume is exciting when fresh and young and has a natural leaning toward the mint and cucumber featured here. Oak is not a factor in this wine, and with its freshness and mineral tones, the clean flavors of the cold halibut shine through.

Rainbow Trout with Shellfish Eggdrop Soup

Crispy skin against the soft flesh allows rainbow trout to be among the most sumptuous seafood treats. In this eggdrop soup, made richer with a base of Shellfish Stock, the trout's delicate traits are splendidly exploited. Adzuki beans add substance, and slices of chiles, steeped in the stock, bring on a complex, lingering heat that threads all of the components together. This would be a perfect main course after a plate of marinated tuna.

Serves 4

6 cups Shellfish Stock (see Appendices)

2 jalapeño peppers, diced

2 eggs

Salt and pepper

12 1-ounce pieces rainbow trout, with skin

2 tablespoons grapeseed oil

12 baby corn, cooked

1/2 cup cooked adzuki beans

12 yellow pattypan squash, cooked and cut in half

3/4 cup julienned sunchoke

4 teaspoons chopped fresh chervil

METHOD Place 5 1/2 cups of the Shellfish Stock and the jalapeño peppers in a medium saucepan and bring to a simmer.

Place the eggs in a small bowl and whisk together, incorporating some air. Slowly pour the whisked eggs into the simmering stock, remove from heat, and gently stir. Season to taste with salt and pepper.

Season both sides of the rainbow trout with salt and pepper and score the skin with a knife or razor blade. Place the trout, skin side down, in a very hot pan with the grapeseed oil. Sauté 1 to 2 minutes on each side.

Gently warm the corn, beans, squash, and sunchoke in separate small saucepans with a touch of the remaining Shellfish Stock, and season to taste with salt and pepper.

ASSEMBLY Arrange some of the hot vegetables and 3 pieces of the rainbow trout in the center of each bowl. Ladle in some of the hot eggdrop soup and sprinkle with the chopped chervil.

Recommended Substitutions

Flounder, halibut, lobster, trout, whitefish

Wine Notes

Hermitage Blanc by J. L. Chave is a fabulous Marsanne with a fennel-like flavor that adds to the elegant broth in this preparation. The nutlike bean presence is white Rhône–friendly. Chave's Hermitage Blanc is best from five to eight years old, as it can be extremely hard in its youth. It is an almost meaty wine, a good, rich, dry style for the trout.

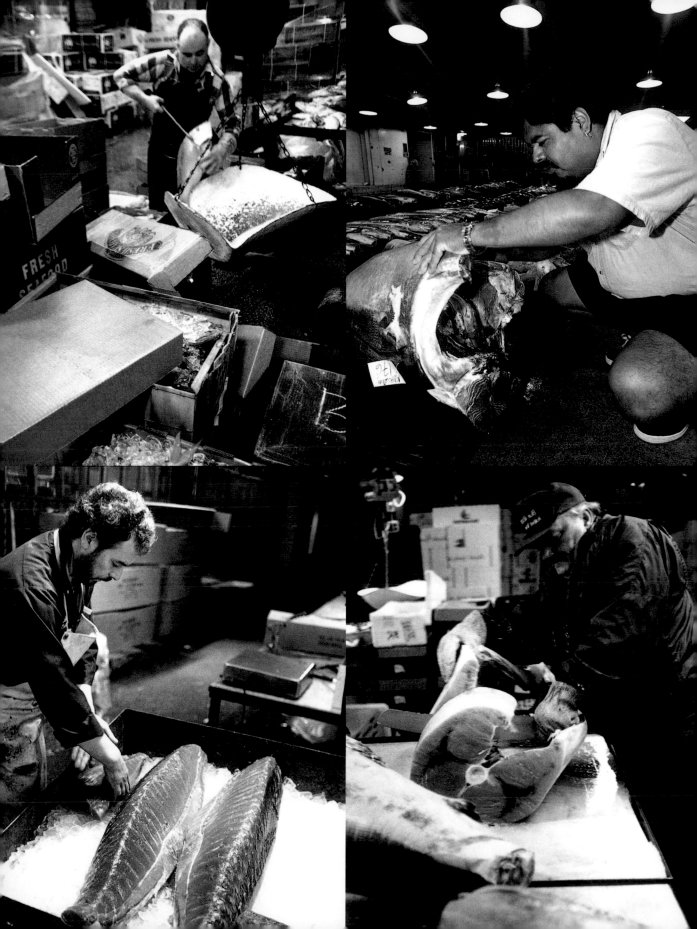

Olive Oil–Poached Swordfish with Oven-Dried Tomatoes, Roasted White Eggplant, and Black Olives

*The technique of very slowly poaching swordfish in olive oil was first demonstrated to me
by the brilliant chef David Bouley when we prepared a special seafood meal together in 1990 to benefit
the Chicago Fund on Aging and Disability. This has become my favorite way to prepare swordfish.
The results are truly spectacular. Here, it is in a warm-cool preparation. The swordfish and eggplant
are warm, and everything else is at room temperature. The combination is refreshing and
light, yet the flavors jump off the plate. This is a great warm-weather dish for eating on the patio.*

Serves 4

2 cups peeled and diced white eggplant

Salt and pepper

*7 tablespoons olive oil plus extra olive oil
for poaching (about 2 cups)*

3 artichoke bottoms, cooked, choke removed

*4 tablespoons chopped fresh herbs
(such as fresh chives and parsley)*

*1 1/2 cups chopped Oven-Dried Tomatoes
(recipe follows)*

4 3-ounce pieces swordfish, skin removed

*1/2 cup pitted oil-cured French black olives,
cut into thin wedges*

*1/4 cup Red Wine Reduction
(see Appendices)*

METHOD Sprinkle the eggplant with salt and let stand for 1 hour. Rinse off the salt and drain. Place the eggplant in a medium sauté pan with 2 tablespoons of the olive oil and cook over medium heat for 20 minutes, or until done. Add water if necessary to keep the eggplant from sticking. Season to taste with salt and pepper.

Slice the artichokes into paper-thin slices. Brush with 4 tablespoons of the olive oil, sprinkle with chopped herbs, and season to taste with salt and pepper.

Place the Oven-Dried Tomatoes in a small saucepan and warm over medium heat. Season to taste with salt and pepper.

Place 2 cups of the olive oil in a medium saucepan. Warm over a very low flame; the oil should feel warm to the touch but not too hot. Season both sides of the swordfish with salt and pepper and place in the warm oil. The oil should cover the fish. Cook the fish for 3 minutes, turn over and cook for an additional 3 minutes, or until just done. Remove from the oil and cover the top with some of the Oven-Dried Tomatoes.

ASSEMBLY Lay some of the artichoke slices overlapping, in the center of each plate. Place a small mound of the eggplant in the center of the slices and top with a piece of the fish. Arrange the olives and the remaining Oven-Dried Tomatoes around the artichokes. Spoon the Red Wine Reduction and the remaining 1 tablespoon olive oil around the plate.

Oven-Dried Tomatoes

Yield: about 1 1/2 cups

6 plum tomatoes, cut in 1/4-inch-thick slices

3 tablespoons olive oil

Salt and pepper

4 sprigs thyme

METHOD Lay the sliced tomatoes on a wire rack and drizzle with the olive oil. Season the tomatoes with salt and pepper and place the thyme on top. Place in the oven on a sheet pan at 250 degrees for 2 1/2 to 3 hours, or until slightly firm and dry to the touch. Remove from the rack and refrigerate until needed. The tomatoes may be stored in the refrigerator for up to 3 days.

Recommended Substitutions

Catfish, halibut, salmon, trout, whitefish

Wine Notes

The Roussanne-based Châteauneuf-du-Pape Blanc by Château de Beaucastel is a unique wonder of concentration and floral tones in its youth, and it becomes earthier and heartier with several years' aging. It's a big wine, without the caramellike oakiness of Burgundy, but with similar structure. The hearty flavors of eggplant, olive, and artichoke in this dish call for this dry, full wine, whose slight herbal flair in the finish adds a nuanced seasoning.

Escolar with Braised Endive, Fava Beans, and Veal Stock Reduction

~~~~~~

Escolar is wonderfully succulent; a spoon is all you really need to break through the flesh.
Its flavor is mild, yet it still holds up well to stronger flavors. Here, braised endive and fava beans
complement the fish with contrasting astringency and buttery starchiness.
Fava bean purée is drizzled on to bring on a creamy richness, and Veal Stock Reduction is
added to lend even further complexity and to help weave all of the elements together.

Serves 4

½ cup blanched fresh spinach

2 cooked artichoke bottoms, stems attached

Salt and pepper

¼ cup chopped carrots

¼ cup chopped celery

¼ cup chopped Spanish onions

2 teaspoons grapeseed oil

2 medium heads red Belgian endive

1 tablespoon sugar

1½ cups blanched fava beans

¼ cup water

2 tablespoons olive oil

1 tablespoon butter

½ cup Veal Stock Reduction (recipe follows)

1 cup Pickling Juice (see Appendices)

4 3-ounce pieces escolar, skin removed

2 teaspoons crushed pink peppercorns

METHOD Purée the spinach and artichokes until smooth and season to taste with salt and pepper. In a medium saucepan, caramelize the chopped carrots, celery, and onion in the grapeseed oil. Add the red Belgian endive and the sugar and cover two-thirds of the way with water. Cover and simmer for 20 to 30 minutes, or until tender and cooked through. Remove from the cooking liquid, cut off the endive base, and carefully separate the leaves.

Purée ½ cup of the fava beans with the water and olive oil until smooth. Warm in a small saucepan and season to taste with salt and pepper. Place the remaining fava beans in a small saucepan with the butter and warm over medium-low heat. Season to taste with salt and pepper.

Just prior to use, heat the Veal Stock Reduction in a small saucepan.

Place the Pickling Juice in a small saucepan and reduce over medium heat to a glaze (about 3 tablespoons). Season both sides of the escolar with salt and pepper. Pour the Pickling Juice glaze over the escolar and place in the broiler for 1 to 2 minutes, or until cooked. Sprinkle with the pink peppercorns.

ASSEMBLY Arrange 5 leaves of the braised red Belgian endive in a fan in the center of each plate. Place a spoonful of the artichoke-spinach purée at the top of the endive and place a piece of the escolar on top of the purée. Spoon the warm fava beans and fava bean purée around the endive. Spoon the Veal Stock Reduction around the plate.

Veal Stock Reduction

Yield: 1¼ cups

10 pounds veal bones

2 carrots, coarsely chopped

2 stalks celery, coarsely chopped

1 yellow onion, coarsely chopped

1 leek, cleaned and coarsely chopped

1 bulb garlic, cut in half

2 tablespoons grapeseed oil

½ cup tomato concassée

4 cups dry red wine (such as Burgundy)

METHOD Place the bones in a roasting pan and roast in the oven at 450 degrees for 2 hours, or until golden brown. When bones are browned, caramelize the carrots, celery, onion, leek, and garlic in the grapeseed oil in a large stockpot. Add the tomato concassée and cook for 5 minutes. Deglaze with the red wine and reduce until most of the wine has been cooked out. Add the browned bones and cover with cold water. Bring to a boil, then reduce heat and let simmer over medium heat for 8 hours. Strain through a fine-mesh sieve and simmer over medium heat for 45 minutes, or until it coats the back of a spoon. Extra reduction can be stored in the freezer for several months.

Recommended Substitutions

Halibut, lobster, red snapper, whitefish

Wine Notes

For this preparation we like young Marsanne in the form of Saint-Joseph Blanc. Grippat is a producer known for fine Hermitage and Saint-Joseph, which is a touch less dense and more forward. Saint-Joseph is a lively match for the fava beans and the artichokes, and the mild veal stock is appropriate for white wine.

Chardonnay is a practical, hedonically satisfying, food-friendly variety, if chosen carefully. Some foodstuffs, like mushrooms and truffles, seem made for Chardonnay's richness when made in oak; other foods, like fennel or sprouts, are attractive when the wine is a bland but high-acid quaffer. These dishes seek to add richer, earthier flavors to simply flavored fish. ❧ Chardonnay is the white wine darling of our generation, but this is a recent phenomenon. Even white Bur-

gundy was a marginal style well into this century. The fashion of sweet white wine persisted throughout the nineteenth century, while dry whites were the odd exception—they are very difficult to make and preserve without perfect growing conditions and cooled fermentation, among other issues. Now that Chardonnay is ubiquitous, we can really appreciate how great Burgundy is. ❧ Good wines are made elsewhere from Chardonnay. Unfortunately, so are sweetened and overoaked commercial versions of the variety that magnify its worst traits. The wines we recommend are extraordinary, unique Chardonnays and Burgundies.

Tuna-Crab Roll and Tuna "Tartare" with Avocado, Crushed Black Sesame Seed Vinaigrette, and Coriander Juice

The tuna-crab roll in this playful dish is meant to emulate a maki roll. The "tartare" is simply a large dice of tuna strewn about the plate. Avocado is used to add richness, and pea sprouts add an important textural contrast to the soft crab and fleshy tuna. The vinaigrette has a little spiciness, which is refreshing against the rich seafood, and the Coriander Juice perfectly cuts into all of the flavors, weaving the varied components together.

Serves 4

1/2 cup thinly sliced papaya

1/2 cup Pickling Juice (see Appendices)

3 ounces peekytoe crabmeat

2 teaspoons chopped fresh chives

1 tablespoon plus 1 teaspoon freshly squeezed lime juice

Salt and pepper

2 thin slices raw tuna (7 by 3 1/2 inches)

1 tablespoon chopped black sesame seeds

1 tablespoon sesame oil

1 1/2 tablespoons freshly squeezed orange juice

1 teaspoon tamari

1 1/2 tablespoons rice wine vinegar

2 teaspoons Spicy Vinegar (see Appendices)

1/3 cup diced raw tuna

1/3 cup diced avocado

1/4 cup snow pea sprouts

Coriander Juice (recipe follows)

METHOD Place the sliced papaya and Pickling Juice in a small container and refrigerate for at least 4 hours. Strain and coarsely chop the papaya. Place the papaya, crabmeat, chives, and 1 tablespoon of the lime juice in a small bowl. Season to taste with salt and pepper.

Lay the tuna slices on top of separate pieces of plastic wrap and season with salt and pepper. Place some of the crab salad along the 7-inch side of the tuna and carefully roll up the tuna, peeling back the plastic wrap as you go. Tighten the tuna-crab roll

by carefully wrapping it in the plastic wrap and gently pulling the plastic tight. Refrigerate until ready to use. Repeat this process with the remaining tuna and crab salad.

Cut one tuna-crab roll into four 1 1/2-inch-long pieces, and cut the remaining roll into four 1 1/2-inch-long pieces on the bias. Remove the plastic wrap.

Whisk together the sesame seeds, sesame oil, orange juice, tamari, rice wine vinegar, and Spicy Vinegar in a small bowl and season to taste with salt and pepper. Toss the diced raw tuna with 2 tablespoons of the black sesame seed vinaigrette and season to taste with salt and pepper.

Toss the diced avocado with 1 teaspoon of the lime juice and season to taste with salt and pepper.

Snip 4 teaspoons of the snow pea sprouts into small pieces, keeping the remainder whole.

ASSEMBLY Place 1 straight-cut tuna-crab roll and 1 roll cut on the bias in the center of each plate. Place a small amount of the whole snow pea sprouts standing upright between the 2 rolls. Arrange some of the diced tuna and avocado around the plate. Spoon some of the Coriander Juice and black sesame seed vinaigrette around the tuna and avocado and sprinkle with the snipped snow pea sprouts.

Coriander Juice

Yield: about 1/2 cup

2 cups tightly packed fresh coriander, blanched

3 tablespoons water

2 tablespoons grapeseed oil

2 tablespoons olive oil

Salt and pepper

METHOD Squeeze any excess water from the coriander and place in a blender with the water and oils. Purée for 3 to 4 minutes, or until smooth. Strain through a fine-mesh sieve and season to taste with salt and pepper. Refrigerate until ready to use.

Recommended Substitutions

For stuffing: crab, lobster

For wrapping: red snapper, smoked salmon

Wine Notes

This fresh preparation adds rich flavors (avocado and sesame) to fresh seafood. We find a tropical fruit–style Chardonnay from California or Australia most useful. Mer et Soleil is a somewhat pineapple- and mango-flavored Chardonnay from Monterey that lets full, ripe fruit stand in front of oak. Its fullness is appropriate for the sweet fresh tuna and crab, and its creaminess adds to the complex flavors without being cloying. Scotchmans Hill is a striking Australian Chardonnay; it is butterscotchy, yet without the flabbiness so common in commercial, or even "show"-style, Australian Chardonnay.

Mako Shark with French Navy Beans, Bleeding Heart Radish, Crispy Pig's Feet, and Wild Mushroom—Foie Gras Sauce

Mako shark has a meaty flesh and full flavor that stands up beautifully to many big flavored, sturdy elements. In this preparation, a hearty but refined wild mushroom—foie gras sauce and some pieces of braised and crisped pig's feet combine for a perfect contrast of sea and earth. The sharpness of the bleeding heart radish playfully cuts into the rich flavors, and the braised navy beans lend a comforting butteriness. This preparation is wonderful for a chilly winter evening, along with a cool but not cold Puligny-Montrachet.

Serves 4

¼ cup chopped carrots

¼ cup chopped celery

¼ cup chopped Spanish onions

3 tablespoons grapeseed oil

1 bleeding heart radish

Salt and pepper

¼ cup carrot, cut into a brunoise

2 teaspoons butter

12 1-ounce pieces mako shark, skin removed

½ cup Mushroom Stock (see Appendices)

⅓ cup Red Wine Reduction (see Appendices)

⅓ cup Foie Gras Butter (recipe follows)

1 cup cooked French navy beans

½ cup Crispy Pig's Feet (recipe follows)

¼ cup chopped fresh chives

METHOD In a small saucepan, caramelize the chopped carrots, celery, and onion in 2 tablespoons of the grapeseed oil. Add the whole bleeding heart radish, cover with water, and simmer over medium heat for 1 to 1½ hours, or until tender. Remove the radish from the liquid and carefully peel. Slice into thin discs and season to taste with salt and pepper.

In a small pan, sauté the brunoise of carrot with the butter for 2 to 3 minutes, or until tender. Season to taste with salt and pepper.

Season both sides of the mako shark with salt and pepper and quickly sauté in a very hot pan with the remaining 1 tablespoon of grapeseed oil for 1 to 2 minutes on each side, or until golden brown.

Warm the Mushroom Stock and Red Wine Reduction in a medium saucepan and slowly whisk in the Foie Gras Butter. Season to taste with salt and pepper.

ASSEMBLY Arrange some of the French navy beans, Crispy Pig's Feet, and bleeding heart radish in the center of each plate. Place the mako shark on top of the radish slices and spoon the brunoise of carrot on top. Spoon the wild mushroom—foie gras sauce around the plate and sprinkle with the chopped chives.

Foie Gras Butter

Yield: ⅓ cup

3 tablespoons foie gras

3 tablespoons butter

METHOD Purée the foie gras and butter in a food processor or blender until smooth. Pass through a fine-mesh sieve and chill until ready to use.

Crispy Pig's Feet

1 whole pig foot

4 teaspoons grapeseed oil

½ cup chopped Spanish onions

½ cup chopped carrots

½ cup chopped celery

3 to 4 cups Chicken Stock (see Appendices)

Salt and pepper

METHOD In a medium roasting pan, sear the pig foot on all sides in 2 teaspoons of the grapeseed oil. Add the vegetables and continue cooking until they begin to caramelize. Add enough Chicken Stock to cover the pig foot, cover, and braise at 350 degrees for 2½ hours. Remove the pig foot from the liquid, debone the meat, and chop into small pieces.

Heat the remaining 2 teaspoons of grapeseed oil in a small sauté pan over very high heat. Add the meat, cover, and cook for 1½ minutes or until golden brown and crispy. Turn the meat over (the pieces will be stuck together) and cook for 1½ minutes. Remove and chop into small pieces again. Season to taste with salt and pepper.

Recommended Substitutions

Catfish, lobster, salmon, red snapper, swordfish, tuna

Wine Notes

The pig's feet and foie gras make this an unusual fish preparation. Shark is up to the challenge because it is firm-fleshed, with a touch of wild flavor. Good Puligny-Montrachet will have a slight meaty streak, along with a smoky, earthy pungency. The better premier crus of Domaine Leflaive such as Clavoillon, Les Pucelles, and Les Combettes are subtle but ageable versions of this style. All will work magically here.

Steamed Cod in Bok Choy with Preserved Ginger, Mung Bean Sprouts, and Flageolet Emulsion

Cod already has a flesh that is so tender it almost melts away. When it is steamed rather than sautéed, it is even more delicate. In this preparation, the cod is served with an ethereal dairyless flageolet emulsion that elevates the elegance of the cod. Daikon and mung bean sprouts are clean, poignant accents to the fish and the buttery legumes. Preserved ginger wisps add a delicate bite, and the mushroom crust provides a wonderful earthiness.

Serves 4

1 large roasted portobello mushroom, finely chopped (see Appendices)

2 teaspoons chopped shallots

1 tablespoon plus 2 teaspoons butter

Salt and pepper

3 teaspoons chopped fresh chives

1 1/2 cups cooked flageolet beans

1/2 cup Chicken Stock (see Appendices)

1 1/2 cups fresh mung bean sprouts

1/2 cup Vegetable Stock (recipe follows)

4 teaspoons Preserved Ginger (recipe follows)

4 2 1/2-ounce pieces cod, skin removed

8 large baby bok choy leaves, blanched and thick stem removed

1/4 cup daikon sprouts

METHOD In a medium pan, sauté the portobello mushroom and the shallots in 2 teaspoons of the butter. Season to taste with salt and pepper and fold in the chopped chives.

Purée 1/2 cup of the cooked flageolet beans with the Chicken Stock and season to taste with salt and pepper. Just prior to use, warm in a small saucepan and froth using a hand-held blender.

In a small sauté pan, gently wilt the mung bean sprouts with the remaining 1 tablespoon of butter and the Vegetable Stock. Season to taste with salt and pepper and fold in the Preserved Ginger.

Place the remaining 1 cup of flageolet beans in a small saucepan and warm over medium heat. Season to taste with salt and pepper.

Season the cod pieces with salt and pepper and place in a steamer for 2 minutes. Remove fish from the steamer and spread a crust of the portobello mixture on the top. Place 2 bok choy leaves end to end and wrap them around the cod, slightly exposing the ends of the fish. Return to the steamer for about 3 minutes, or until fully cooked.

ASSEMBLY Place some of the warm flageolet beans and the mung bean sprout—Preserved Ginger mixture in the center of each plate. Set a steamed cod package on top of the sprouts. Spoon the flageolet emulsion around the plate and top with a few of the daikon sprouts.

Vegetable Stock

Yield: about 6 cups

2 leeks, cleaned and coarsely chopped

4 Spanish onions, coarsely chopped

6 stalks celery, coarsely chopped

1 celery root, peeled and coarsely chopped

2 carrots, peeled and coarsely chopped

1 bulb fennel, cleaned and coarsely chopped

2 red bell peppers, seeded and coarsely chopped

1 bulb garlic, cut in half

2 parsnips, peeled and coarsely chopped

1 tablespoon whole black peppercorns

METHOD Place all of the vegetables and the peppercorns in a large stockpot. Cover with cold water and bring to a boil. Reduce heat and simmer for 1 hour. Strain and simmer for about 45 minutes, or until reduced to about 6 cups. Extra stock can be stored in the freezer for several months.

Preserved Ginger

Yield: 4 teaspoons

1 1/2 tablespoons julienned ginger

3/4 cup sugar

3/4 cup water

METHOD Place the ginger, 1/4 cup of the sugar, and 1/4 cup of the water in a small saucepan. Simmer for 10 minutes, strain the liquid, and repeat the process 2 more times, reserving the final cooking liquid to store the ginger. Refrigerate until needed. Extra stock can be stored in the freezer for several months.

Recommended Substitutions

Lobster, red snapper, tuna, whitefish

Wine Notes

The delicate cod needs a delicate Chardonnay, and the legumes and Asian greens demand a wine that combines earth and good acidity. Burgundy works best here. A Saint-Aubin by Marc Colin is an apt wine, less dense than most Meursault or Puligny-Montrachet, refreshing, and still wonderfully earthy.

Eel with Olive Oil–Poached Tomato, Cucumber Sauce, Petite Salad, and Horseradish Vinaigrette

Because of its rich, slightly chewy meat, eel is frequently served slowly braised in a red wine preparation. In this version I have adapted it for lighter tastes. The full-flavored sautéed eel melts perfectly into the olive oil–poached tomato, while the tomato retains just the right amount of acidity to cut into the rich meat. The salad of mizuna and watercress provides a necessary textural foil, and the horseradish vinaigrette supplies an important degree of heat and sharpness. The fragrant cucumber sauce keeps everything in balance and maintains an overall lightness.

Serves 4

3 tablespoons grated horseradish

1 1/2 tablespoons rice wine vinegar

4 tablespoons olive oil

Salt and pepper

4 purple pearl onions

1/4 cup Pickling Juice (see Appendices)

1 cup mizuna

1 cup watercress

2 tablespoons fresh chervil

4 1-ounce pieces eel, skin removed

2 teaspoons grapeseed oil

Cucumber Sauce (recipe follows)

12 slices peeled cucumber

2 olive oil–poached yellow tomatoes, chopped (see Appendices)

1 cup miners' lettuce

1 1/2 tablespoons chopped fresh herbs (such as fresh parsley and chives)

METHOD In a small bowl, place the horseradish and the vinegar and slowly whisk in the olive oil. Season to taste with salt and pepper.

Thinly slice the pearl onions and pour the hot Pickling Juice over them. Let stand for 30 minutes and strain.

Place the mizuna, watercress, chervil, and pearl onions in a small bowl. Toss with 1 tablespoon of the horseradish vinaigrette and season to taste with salt and pepper.

Season both sides of the eel with salt and pepper and quickly sauté in a very hot pan with the grapeseed oil for 1 to 2 minutes on each side, or just until cooked.

ASSEMBLY Spoon a full circle of the Cucumber Sauce on each plate. Place a pinwheel of 3 cucumber slices on one side of the plate and top with some of the mizuna mixture. Place some of the tomatoes on the other side of the plate and top with a piece of the eel. Spoon some of the horseradish vinaigrette on top of the fish and around the plate. Sprinkle a few pieces of miners' lettuce and the chopped herbs around the plate.

Cucumber Sauce

Yield: about 1/3 cup

1 cucumber

2 tablespoons cold water

1/4 cup grapeseed oil

Salt and pepper

METHOD Peel the skin from the cucumber in thick strips. Blanch the strips in boiling salted water, shock in ice water, and drain. Coarsely chop the cucumber and place in a blender with the water and oil. Purée until smooth and strain through a fine-mesh sieve. Season to taste with salt and pepper.

Recommended Substitutions

Catfish, halibut, snapper, trout, whitefish

Wine Notes

The dense, flavorful eel meat and the lighter cucumber and greens need a rich wine. A pair of quite full-bodied Chardonnays stand out: Villa Mount Eden "Signature Series" Bien Nacido, and Lewis Cellars "Reserve," Napa Valley. These wines use ripe fruit and oak to their best full-bodied advantage, yielding higher-alcohol wine and more flavor to enhance the rich eel and horseradish combination.

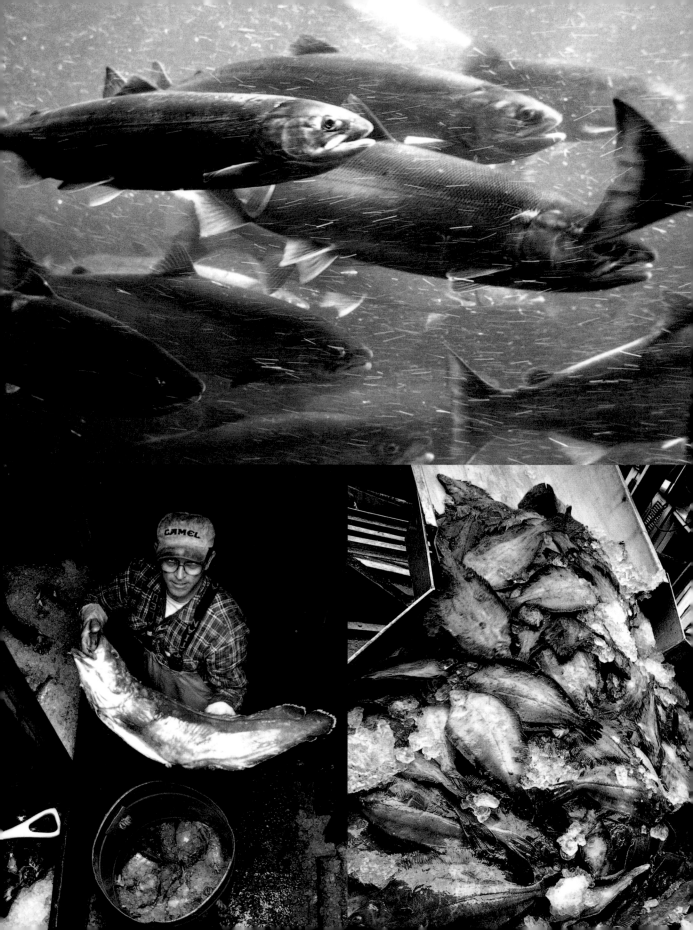

Baby Monkfish Tail Roasted on the Bone, with Hedgehog Mushrooms, Artichokes, Black Truffles, and Chicken Stock Reduction

Fish cooked or roasted on the bone is more succulent and tends to stay more moist.
Tiny monkfish are perfect for this preparation as they are quite easy to carve off the bone once
cooked. I love to mix the monkfish with artichokes, hedgehog mushrooms, haricots verts,
and, for a special treat, black truffles. This dish is earthy and satisfying, and the truffle aspect
hints at just the right amount of opulence. The preparation only needs some herbs and
a little chicken stock reduction to make a beautifully satisfying and simultaneously elegant
seafood ragout. This dish also works fantastically with a heavier meat stock reduction.

Serves 4

1 cup Chicken Stock (see Appendices)

5 tablespoons butter

Salt and pepper

2 artichoke bottoms, cooked, chokes removed, and cut into thin wedges

2 tablespoons chopped fresh herbs, such as chives or parsley

1 1/2 cups haricots verts

1 1/2 cups roasted hedgehog mushrooms (see Appendices)

4 baby monkfish tails (about 1 pound), with bone

1 tablespoon grapeseed oil

2 teaspoons freshly squeezed lemon juice

1 black truffle, thinly sliced

8 teaspoons white truffle oil

METHOD Place the Chicken Stock in a saucepan and reduce to 1/2 cup. Whisk in 3 tablespoons of the butter and season to taste with salt and pepper. Sauté the artichoke wedges in a very hot pan with 1 tablespoon of the butter, season to taste with salt and pepper, and toss with 1 teaspoon of the chopped herbs.

In a separate pan, sauté the haricots verts and hedgehog mushrooms with 1 tablespoon of the butter. Season to taste with salt and pepper.

Season both sides of the monkfish with salt and pepper. In a very hot ovenproof pan, quickly brown both sides of the monkfish in the grapeseed oil. Place the whole pan in the oven at 400 degrees for 3 minutes, or until done. Drizzle the lemon juice on top of the monkfish, cut it away from the bone, and slice it into 12 pieces on the bias.

ASSEMBLY Arrange some of the artichokes, mushrooms, haricots verts, monkfish pieces, and black truffle slices in the center of each plate. Sprinkle with the remaining chopped herbs and top with freshly ground black pepper. Spoon some of the Chicken Stock reduction around the plate. Drizzle the white truffle oil over the ragout.

Recommended Substitutions

Salmon, scallops, shrimp, red snapper, tuna

Wine Notes

Monkfish is a sweet, rich meat, requiring a rich wine. The artichoke, truffle, and hedgehog mushroom add more flavors that beg for a rich Chardonnay. A smoky, toasty style like Au Bon Climat's "Reserve Talley" Chardonnay uses great fruit, with a trademark Burgundian oak touch. The artichoke, which often presents wine-matching problems, seems tamed here, and truffle and mushroom earthiness merge well with this sophisticated Chardonnay.

Amberjack with Periwinkle Vinaigrette, Wild Watercress, and Shallot Blossoms

Amberjack's medium-firm texture and medium-full flavor perfectly suit it for pairing with elements of fairly robust character. Here, the slightly chewy periwinkles successfully show off the amberjack's delightful texture. Shallot blossoms, watercress, and elegant hints of garlic provide a necessary but refined foil to the succulent fish. This preparation is refreshing and light, yet full-flavored and ideal for a luncheon meal.

Serves 4

1 quart periwinkles, in shells

1 cup white wine (such as Chardonnay)

1 cup water

2 tablespoons chopped shallots

1/2 cup olive oil

1 clove elephant garlic, chopped

2 tablespoons freshly squeezed lemon juice

Salt and pepper

2 cups wild watercress

4 3 1/2-ounce pieces amberjack, skin removed

1 tablespoon grapeseed oil

8 shallot blossoms

METHOD Rinse the periwinkles thoroughly in cold water. Simmer the white wine, water, and shallots in a large sauté pan. Add the periwinkles and cover for 2 to 3 minutes, or until the periwinkles begin to come out of their shell. Immediately remove periwinkles from the pan and reduce the cooking liquid to 1/2 cup.

Remove the periwinkles from their shells by discarding the black scaly matter on top of the periwinkle. Use the tip of a paring knife to gently pull out the periwinkle.

In a small bowl, whisk together the reduced cooking liquid, olive oil, garlic, and lemon juice. Season to taste with salt and pepper. In a medium sauté pan, gently wilt the watercress over low heat for 1 to 2 minutes. Add the cleaned periwinkles to the vinaigrette.

Season both sides of the amberjack with salt and pepper. Quickly sauté in a hot pan with the grapeseed oil for 2 minutes on each side, or until just undercooked. Remove from the pan and cut in half.

ASSEMBLY Spoon some of the periwinkle mixture onto each plate. Place 2 halves of the amberjack on top of the periwinkles. Arrange the wilted watercress around the plate and place 2 shallot blossoms on top of the amberjack.

Recommended Substitutions

Catfish, flounder, halibut, swordfish, trout

Wine Notes

The delicious periwinkles are earthy, garlicky morsels that need a rich and earthy Chardonnay, and the amberjack seems to support and absorb all the surrounding Chardonnay flavors. The wine should pierce through the rich flavors yet maintain its fruit identity. This is a hallmark of the winemaking of Jean-Marie Guffens of Verget. Meursault "Rougeots" and Puligny-Montrachet "Sous le Puits" are fresh, modern Chardonnays with just a touch of Burgundian tang. Both of these Verget 1994s are appropriate balancing wines for this dish.

Percebes, Jasmine Rice, and
Red Wine–Mushroom Juice–Saffron Oil Vinaigrette

*Percebes, or gooseneck barnacles, are a little unusual in the United States, but they are quite common
in Spain and Portugal, and they are certainly worth the trouble it may take to locate them.
They have a mild mussel-like shellfish flavor with a very elegant soft-textured flesh once you have
peeled away a sheath of tougher skin. An unadorned mound of jasmine rice helps to offset
the texture and superb flavor of the barnacles. Wild mushroom juice and Saffron Oil add heady
and exotic notes, and help to transform the overall effect into something celestial.*

Serves 4

24 percebes

1/4 cup water

2 tablespoons butter

Salt and pepper

2 cups flat-leaf parsley leaves

1 cup Mushroom Stock (see Appendices)

1 tablespoon Red Wine Reduction
(see Appendices)

1 tablespoon chopped shallots

1 tablespoon rice wine vinegar

1/2 cup white truffle oil

1/2 cup Olive Oil–Poached Tomatoes
(see Appendices)

2 cups cooked jasmine rice

4 teaspoons Saffron Oil (recipe follows)

METHOD Place the percebes in boiling
salted water, cook for 3 minutes, drain, and
shock in ice water. Cut the percebes away
from each other, leaving as long of a stem
as possible. Carefully insert the blades of
small scissors between the rough skin and
the meat of the percebes. Cut down and
through the skin and carefully peel it away
from the meat, leaving the toe intact. Just
prior to use, warm the percebes over
medium heat with the water and butter for

1 to 2 minutes, or until warm. Remove the
percebes from the pan and season to taste
with salt and pepper.

Wilt the parsley leaves in the remaining
cooking liquid for 1 minute over medium
heat.

Place the Mushroom Stock in a small
saucepan over medium heat for 10 minutes,
or until reduced to 1/3 cup. Add the Red
Wine Reduction, shallots, and vinegar.
Slowly whisk in the white truffle oil and
season to taste with salt and pepper. Dice
the Olive Oil–Poached Tomatoes and add
the vinaigrette.

ASSEMBLY Place a mound of the cooked
jasmine rice in the center of each plate.
Arrange six of the percebes and some of the
wilted parsley around the jasmine rice.
Spoon the Saffron Oil and vinaigrette
around the plate.

Saffron Oil

Yield: 1/2 cup

1 teaspoon saffron threads

2 tablespoons water

2 tablespoons olive oil

6 tablespoons grapeseed oil

METHOD Pan-roast the saffron over low
heat for 20 seconds to help release the oils
present in the saffron. Add the water and
quickly remove from the heat. Most of the
water will immediately steam away. With a
rubber spatula, scrape the saffron and any
remaining liquid into a blender. Add the
oils, blend on high speed for 45 seconds,
and refrigerate for 1 day. Extra oil can be
stored in the refrigerator for several weeks.

Recommended Substitutions

Lobster, salmon, shrimp

Wine Notes

These exotic morsels are delectable shell-
fishlike treats that benefit from pairing
with a firm white Burgundy. Saffron and
truffle flavors somehow do not clash when
a great Chevalier-Montrachet is on the
table—Sauzet, Domaine Leflaive, and
Niellon make prime examples of this luxury wine. A more modest but nearly as successful approach may be taken with
Madame Ferret's Pouilly-Fuissé "Le Clos,"
or even a bold Chablis Grand Cru by
Raveneau. These wines are all firm coun-
terbalances to the heady, sweet aromas on
this plate.

Fennel-Stuffed Dover Sole Wrapped in Black Radish with Fennel Broth

Dover sole is certainly among the most regal of fish, with its very delicate texture and mild flavor. Here, it has a fennel theme, which doesn't assert itself so much as to overtake the profoundly simple flavor of the fish. The slices of black radish encasing the fish help to keep it moist and provide a sophisticated bite and slightly crunchy texture. This preparation is light and simple, but the resulting flavors are quite complex.

Serves 4

1 ½ cups finely julienned fennel

½ cup plus 2 teaspoons butter, softened

4 cups Fennel Juice (see Appendices)

¼ cup chopped fennel fronds

Salt and pepper

1 clove elephant garlic, finely chopped

1 large unpeeled black radish, thinly sliced across its width

8 small Dover sole fillets

2 tablespoons grapeseed oil

4 teaspoons white truffle oil

METHOD Sauté the julienned fennel in 2 teaspoons of the butter over medium heat for 8 to 10 minutes, or until golden brown. Remove from the heat and set aside. Reheat just prior to use if necessary.

Place the Fennel Juice in a medium saucepan and warm over medium heat. Whisk in ¼ cup butter and 2 tablespoons of the fennel fronds, and season to taste with salt and pepper. Froth using a hand-held blender just prior to use.

Place 3 tablespoons softened butter in a small bowl with 2 tablespoons of the fennel fronds and the chopped garlic. Stir together until fully incorporated.

Place the black radish slices and 1 tablespoon of the butter in a small saucepan and cover with water. Simmer over medium heat for 4 to 6 minutes, or until tender (the slices should be in one piece yet soft enough to wrap around the sole). Remove from the liquid and blot on a paper towel.

Score the skin side of the sole fillets with a knife to prevent curling during cooking. Season both sides with salt and pepper. Spread the fennel-butter mixture on one side of 4 of the fillets, cover with a similar size piece of sole and refrigerate until needed.

Arrange ¼ of the black radish slices in an overlapping manner on a piece of plastic the length of the fillet and three times its width. Repeat 3 more times on separate pieces of plastic wrap. Season the black radish with salt and pepper. Place one of the pairs of Dover sole in the center of each radish wrap. Carefully wrap the sole tightly in the radish and wrap with the plastic wrap. Refrigerate for at least 30 minutes.

Remove the plastic wrap and place the sole, seam side down, in a hot nonstick pan with the grapeseed oil. Quickly place a smaller sauté pan, bottom side down, directly on top of the sole. (This will help keep the black radish from curling away from the fish.) Cook over medium-high heat for 3 minutes, turn over carefully, and continue cooking for 2 to 3 more minutes, or until the black radish is golden brown and the Dover sole is cooked through. Remove from the pan and cut each piece in half.

ASSEMBLY Arrange 2 halves of the Dover sole in the center of each bowl. Spoon some of the caramelized fennel around the sole. Ladle the fennel broth in the bowl and drizzle with the white truffle oil.

Recommended Substitutions

Catfish, flounder, halibut, trout, whitefish

Wine Notes

Radish and fennel both add snap to this sole dish, with elephant garlic giving the Burgundian direction for the wine. The Meursault "Les Tessons," by Pierre Morey, gives the acid support as well as the generosity of fruit needed. Though not overly creamy or buttery in the classic Meursault sense, this style of Meursault is a better food companion than many fuller, rounder Meursaults such as Lafon.

Diver Scallop and Black Truffle Wrapped in Caul Fat with Saffron Fettucine Noodles, Portobello Mushrooms, and Rosemary

~~~~~~

This decadent dish would be perfect for a special celebration served with Grand Cru Burgundy. The truffles provide a luxury element and the caul fat a near-sinful richness. The flavors of saffron and rosemary lend refined accents and the strips of roasted portobello add an earthiness and a delicate heartiness. The preparation is finished with a delicate pan sauce featuring rosemary-scented fish stock, portobello mushroom juice, and chopped shallots. The combination of rich caul fat, luscious scallop, and heady black truffle melting in your mouth creates a great sensual feel. Wild mushroom duxelle could easily be substituted for the black truffle if economy is of concern.

Serves 4

4 large diver scallops

2 black truffles, thinly sliced

1 cup blanched fresh spinach leaves

4 ounces caul fat, soaked in water

1 cup Fish Stock (see Appendices)

1 sprig rosemary

¼ cup Mushroom Stock (see Appendices)

1 tablespoon chopped shallots

¼ cup butter

2 tablespoons Burgundy

Salt and pepper

2 roasted portobello mushrooms, cut into long strips (see Appendices)

Saffron Pasta (recipe follows)

3 tablespoons plus 1 teaspoon Rosemary Oil (see Appendices)

2 tablespoons chopped herbs (such as parsley or chives)

METHOD Slice each of the scallops into 5 thin slices. Place a few of the black truffle pieces on top of one of the scallop slices and lay a piece of blanched spinach on top of the truffles. Continue the layering until you have used all 5 scallop slices. Repeat this procedure with the remaining scallops. Carefully wrap each truffle-layered scallop in caul fat and place in the refrigerator.

Place the Fish Stock in a small saucepan with the rosemary sprig. Simmer for 5 to 10 minutes, or until reduced by half. Remove the rosemary sprig and add the Mushroom Stock.

In a separate saucepan, sweat the shallot with 1 teaspoon of the butter, and deglaze with the Burgundy and the infused Fish Stock. Simmer for 7 minutes. Slowly whisk in the remaining butter and season to taste with salt and pepper.

Reheat the portobello mushroom strips in their own juices if necessary and season to taste with salt and pepper.

Season the caul fat–wrapped scallops with salt and pepper and place in a very hot sauté pan with the seam side down. Carefully caramelize all sides of the caul fat, about 3 to 4 minutes. Remove from the pan and slice in half lengthwise.

Cook the Saffron Pasta in boiling salted water. Season to taste with salt and pepper and toss with 2 tablespoons of the Rosemary Oil and the chopped herbs.

ASSEMBLY Place a mound of the Saffron Pasta in the center of each plate along with some of the portobello mushroom strips. Place 2 halves of the layered scallops on top of the pasta. Spoon some of the Fish Stock sauce and drizzle the remaining Rosemary Oil around the plate.

Saffron Pasta

Yield: about 1 pound

2 eggs, beaten

2 tablespoons saffron threads

2 tablespoons water

1½ cups extra-fine semolina flour

METHOD In a medium bowl, thoroughly blend the eggs with the saffron and water. Work in the flour with a wooden spoon or in a mixer until a loose ball is formed. Cover with plastic wrap and refrigerate for at least 1 hour.

Roll dough out by hand or with a pasta machine. Cut into fettucine noodles and spread noodles out on a lightly floured sheet pan. Cover and refrigerate until needed.

Cook the fettucine in boiling salted water for 2 to 3 minutes, or until al dente.

Recommended Substitutions

Lobster, swordfish, tuna

Wine Notes

The sweet scallop makes Chardonnay the best variety for this heady recipe, and the caul fat element, along with truffles and portobellos, makes Burgundy the best choice. A great Corton-Charlemagne would not be out of order for the luxury level of the dish; Bonneau du Martray, Tollot-Beaut, and Olivier Leflaive are prime examples. These wines have a richness that is not oily, and possess the requisite acidity to stand up to rosemary and shallot.

Dairyless Three-Clam Chowder with Sweet Corn, Celery, and Bacon

~~~~~~

Who doesn't love clam chowder? It is the ultimate comfort food, with chewy sweet clams,
smoky bacon, crunchy celery, and a satiny broth redolent of the sea. In this version
I have eliminated all dairy products in the interest of showcasing the explosive clam flavor.
Beautiful cherrystones and countnecks are left whole rather than ground, and they
are barely cooked so that their aesthetic nature can be enjoyed. Potatoes blended into the
clam juice make the soup smooth and potent. Sweet corn and celery add
sweetness and crunch, while a drizzle of tomato purée provides the perfect bite,
cutting into these luscious flavors alongside a lean Napa Chardonnay.

Serves 4

1 cup chopped celery

1 cup chopped carrots

1 cup chopped Spanish onions

8 sprigs thyme

2 cups white wine

1 small geoduck clam

12 cherrystone clams

4 countneck clams

2 cups cooked white potatoes

2 tablespoons Spicy Vinegar
(see Appendices)

½ cup water

Salt and pepper

¼ cup uncooked bacon, cut into batons

½ cup chopped tomatoes

1 cup cooked diced potatoes

⅓ cup blanched diced celery

1 cup cooked yellow corn

2 tablespoons fine chiffonade of celery leaves

METHOD Place ½ cup of the celery, ½ cup of the carrot, ½ cup of the onion, 3 sprigs of the thyme, and 1 cup of the white wine in a large pan. Remove and discard the shell from the geoduck clam and add the meat to the pan. Add enough water to cover halfway up the clam. Cover and simmer for 20 minutes, or until tender.

Remove the geoduck from the pan, reserving the liquid. Cool the clam slightly and peel away the thick skin. Slice the meat into thin slices and set aside.

Place the remaining ½ cup celery, ½ cup carrots, ½ cup onion, 5 sprigs of thyme, and 1 cup of the white wine in a large sauté pan. Bring to a simmer and add the cherrystone and countneck clams. Cover and continue to simmer for 3 to 4 minutes, removing each clam as soon as it opens. Remove the meat from the shells and set aside. Reserve 1¼ cups of the cooking liquid (if there is not enough, make up the difference with the remaining geoduck cooking liquid).

Purée the cooked potatoes with the reserved cooking liquid, Spicy Vinegar, and water. Season to taste with salt and pepper. Heat the chowder in a medium saucepan just prior to use.

In a small pan, sauté the bacon until it is golden brown and slightly crispy. Remove from the pan and blot on paper towels. Purée the bacon fat and the chopped tomato and pass through a fine-mesh sieve. Warm in a small saucepan and season to taste with salt and pepper.

Place the diced potatoes in a small saucepan with a touch of water and warm over medium heat.

ASSEMBLY Ladle some of the chowder into each bowl. Place a countneck clam in the center and arrange the cherrystones and sliced geoduck around the bowl. Sprinkle the bacon, diced celery, corn kernels, diced potato, and celery leaves around the clams. Drizzle some of the tomato purée on top of the soup and finish with cracked black pepper.

Recommended Substitutions

Other clams, mussels, oysters

Wine Notes

This recipe emphasizes the clam flavors while using no dairy in the base. A lower level of oak is therefore a better choice. California's typically lower acidity is preferable to Burgundy because acid elements in the chowder are minimal. Napa Valley Chardonnays stood out in our tastings: Vine Cliff "Proprietress' Reserve" for its steely version (made from Liparita Vineyards—grown fruit, itself a good, lean style), and the always understated but beautifully made Forman, a classic Chardonnay whose reputation seems to lurk in the shadows of Ric Forman's great Cabernets.

Black Pomfret with Garnet Yam, Yellow Wax Beans, Duck Gizzards, Veal Stock Reduction, and Olive Oil

Black pomfret has a medium-firm body and is rich enough in flavor to stand up to meat stock or other meat products. I love it against the sweet, starchy garnet yam and the sumptuous and meltingly soft duck gizzards. The barely crunchy wax beans add just the right textural refinement, and the veal stock pushes this entire preparation into the realm of hearty sensuality.

Serves 4

5 duck gizzards

Grapeseed oil or duck fat to cover gizzards

2 cloves garlic

2 tablespoons chopped Spanish onions

3 sprigs thyme

1 large garnet yam, baked

4 teaspoons butter

Salt and pepper

24 yellow wax beans, blanched

2 tablespoons chopped fresh herbs (such as fresh parsley and chives)

Veal Stock Reduction (recipe follows)

4 3-ounce pieces black pomfret, skin removed

2 teaspoons grapeseed oil

8 teaspoons olive oil

METHOD Place the duck gizzards in a small saucepan and cover with the grapeseed oil or duck fat. Add the garlic, onion, and thyme and simmer slowly over low heat for 3 hours, or until the gizzards are tender. Cool in the cooking fat and refrigerate until needed. Just prior to serving, cut the gizzards into 16 slices and warm in some of the cooking fat.

Peel the baked yam and place in a small saucepan. Coarsely mash with a fork. Add 2 teaspoons of the butter and season to taste with salt and pepper. Warm over medium heat just prior to use.

Cut the yellow wax beans on the bias and sauté in a small pan with 2 teaspoons of the butter for 2 minutes. Toss with the chopped herbs and season to taste with salt and pepper.

Warm the Veal Stock Reduction in a small saucepan.

Season both sides of the black pomfret with salt and pepper and quickly sauté in a very hot pan in the grapeseed oil for 1 to 2 minutes on each side. Remove from pan and cut each piece in half.

ASSEMBLY Place some of the yams in the center of each plate and top with 2 halves of the fish. Arrange 4 of the gizzard slices on top of the fish and place some of the yellow wax beans around the plate. Spoon some of the Veal Stock Reduction and olive oil around the beans.

Veal Stock Reduction

Yield: 1¼ cups

10 pounds veal bones

2 carrots, coarsely chopped

2 stalks celery, coarsely chopped

1 yellow onion, coarsely chopped

1 leek, cleaned and coarsely chopped

1 bulb garlic, cut in half

2 tablespoons grapeseed oil

½ cup tomato concassée

4 cups dry red wine (such as Burgundy)

METHOD Place the bones in a roasting pan and roast in the oven at 450 degrees for 2 hours, or until golden brown. When bones are browned, caramelize the carrots, celery, onion, leek, and garlic in the grapeseed oil in a large stockpot. Add the tomato concassée and cook for 5 minutes. Deglaze with the red wine and reduce until most of the wine has been cooked out. Add the browned bones and cover with cold water. Bring to a boil, then reduce heat and let simmer over medium heat for 8 hours. Strain through a fine-mesh sieve and simmer over medium heat for 45 minutes, or until it coats the back of a spoon. Extra reduction can be stored in the freezer for several months.

Recommended Substitutions

Lobster, scallops, swordfish, tuna

Wine Notes

The combination of the medium-rich textured black pomfret garnished with sweet vegetable flavors and the gizzard and veal stock demands a rich, complex Chardonnay. Our favorite specialists make rich, oaky, dramatic Chardonnay: Matanzas Creek "Journey" Sonoma Valley and Talbott "Diamond T" Monterey are rarities with immense concentration and a major Burgundian-style oak presence. Also amazingly dense and ripe are the rare Marcassin Chardonnays from Helen Turley. All are best enjoyed about a year after release.

Skate Wing with Zucchini, Black Trumpet Mushrooms, Brussels Sprouts, Mushroom Sauce, and Curry

Skate wing is delicately fleshed yet sturdy enough to stand up to hearty flavors. The zucchini in this preparation provides a natural backdrop to the earthiness of the black trumpet mushrooms and the brussels sprouts. A touch of curry is added to this combination of well-balanced flavors to lend an exotic element. Orange juice is drizzled on and around the fish, adding just the right amount of acid to enhance the skate's natural flavors.

Serves 4

1 ¹/₂ cups julienned roasted black trumpet mushrooms, roasting juices reserved (see Appendices)

Salt and pepper

8 brussels sprouts, blanched

1 cup julienned zucchini

4 tablespoons Curry Butter (recipe follows)

4 1 ¹/₂-ounce pieces skate wing

2 tablespoons grapeseed oil

2 tablespoons freshly squeezed orange juice

2 teaspoons chopped fresh chervil

2 teaspoons chopped fresh chives

Zucchini Sauce (recipe follows)

METHOD Purée ¹/₂ cup of the black trumpet mushrooms with the roasting juices and just enough water to purée smoothly. Season to taste with salt and pepper. Warm in a small saucepan just prior to use.

Carefully remove 12 of the larger leaves from the brussels sprouts, keeping the shape intact. Julienne the remaining brussels sprouts. Place the julienned brussels sprouts and julienned zucchini in a medium sauté pan with 2 tablespoons of the Curry Butter. In a separate sauté pan, heat the remaining black trumpet mushrooms and season to taste with salt and pepper. Gently warm the brussels sprout leaves and fill with some of the warm black trumpet mushrooms. Add the remaining 1 cup black trumpet mushroom pieces to the brussels sprout and zucchini mixture (reserve any mushroom liquid).

Whisk the remaining 2 tablespoons Curry Butter into the mushroom juice to make a pan sauce. Season to taste with salt and pepper.

In a very hot pan, sauté the skate in the grapeseed oil. Spoon the orange juice over the cooked skate and sprinkle with the chopped chervil and chives.

ASSEMBLY Place some of the zucchini and mushroom mixture in the center of each plate. Top with a piece of the skate and arrange the brussels sprout cups at 3 points. Spoon the Zucchini Sauce and black trumpet mushroom sauce around the plate. Spoon the Curry Butter pan sauce on top of the fish and around the plate.

Curry Butter

Yield: about ¹/₄ cup

¹/₄ cup chopped Granny Smith apples

1 clove garlic, chopped

1 shallot, chopped

1 teaspoon grapeseed oil

2 teaspoons curry powder

¹/₂ teaspoon hot paprika

2 tablespoons water

¹/₄ cup butter, softened

METHOD In a small saucepan, sauté the apple, garlic, and shallot in the grapeseed oil. Cook for 5 to 7 minutes over medium heat, then add the curry powder, paprika, and water. Continue to cook for 3 more minutes, cool, and fold in the soft butter. Purée for 1 to 2 minutes, or until smooth.

Pass through a fine-mesh sieve, cover, and refrigerate until needed.

Zucchini Sauce

Yield: about ³/₄ cup

¹/₂ cup zucchini skins

¹/₄ cup water

2 tablespoons olive oil

Salt and pepper

METHOD Blanch the zucchini skins in boiling salted water and shock in ice water. Purée the skins with the ¹/₄ cup water and the olive oil until smooth. Strain through a fine-mesh sieve and season to taste with salt and pepper. Warm in a small saucepan just prior to serving.

Recommended Substitutions

Catfish, salmon, shrimp, swordfish, tuna,

Wine Notes

This delicately curried preparation needs an elegant wine, a supple Chardonnay with a touch of earthiness. Many American Chardonnays are thick with sweet oak flavors, but Italian or French Chardonnays present a higher acidity advantage. A fresh and citrusy Collio Chardonnay from Puiatti is clean and lively. Its freshness is a fine enhancement to the mild curry and is round enough for the skate wing texture.

Poached Octopus with Braised Leeks, Parsley Root, Tiny Zucchini, Barley, Marjoram, and Wild Mushroom Broth

This stew of octopus, barley, and assorted vegetables is hearty and yet it is quite light. The Wild Mushroom Broth provides a beautiful woodsy flavor that shows off the texture and flavor of the octopus superbly, while serving as an excellent Burgundy foil. The octopus, with its slightly chewy eloquence, accentuates the barley, tomato, and clam mushrooms quite nicely. Tiny leaves of marjoram provide a refreshing pepperiness that helps to send this preparation over the top.

Serves 4

1 fresh baby octopus (about 1 pound), cleaned

½ cup rice wine vinegar

1 tablespoon plus 4 teaspoons butter

Salt and pepper

1½ cups cooked pearl barley

½ cup Chicken Stock (see Appendices)

1 cup chopped leeks

8 baby zucchini, blanched

Wild Mushroom Broth (recipe follows)

2 cups roasted clam mushrooms (see Appendices)

40 tiny Parisian balls of carrot, blanched

40 tiny Parisian balls of parsley root, blanched

1½ cups diced Olive Oil–Poached Tomatoes (see Appendices)

½ cup julienned daikon

8 Roasted Garlic Cloves (recipe follows)

4 teaspoons reserved cooking oil from Roasted Garlic Cloves

4 teaspoons chopped fresh marjoram

METHOD Poach the octopus in boiling salted water with the vinegar for 10 to 15 minutes, or until tender. Shock in ice water, cut the tentacles into 1½-inch pieces on the bias, and discard remaining octopus. Just before serving, quickly sauté the tentacles in a very hot pan with 1 tablespoon of the butter. Season to taste with salt and pepper.

In a small saucepan, heat the barley with the Chicken Stock. Season to taste with salt and pepper.

Place the chopped leeks in a small sauté pan with 2 teaspoons of the butter. Cook over medium heat for 5 to 7 minutes, or until tender. Season to taste with salt and pepper.

Cut the zucchini into 1-inch pieces on the bias and warm in a small saucepan with the remaining 2 teaspoons of butter. Season to taste with salt and pepper.

Warm the Wild Mushroom Broth in a medium saucepan and season to taste with salt and pepper.

ASSEMBLY Arrange the barley, leeks, zucchini, mushrooms, carrots, parsley root, Olive Oil–Poached Tomatoes, daikon, Roasted Garlic Cloves, and sautéed octopus in the bowl. Ladle in the Wild Mushroom Broth and spoon some of the reserved olive oil from cooking the the roasted garlic around the bowl. Top with the fresh marjoram.

Roasted Garlic Cloves

Yield: 8 cloves

8 cloves garlic, peeled

1 cup milk

⅓ cup olive oil

METHOD Place the garlic cloves in a small saucepan, cover with the milk, and simmer for 10 minutes. Drain the milk, place the garlic cloves in an ovenproof pan, add the olive oil, and cover. Bake at 350 degrees for 30 to 50 minutes, or until the cloves are soft. Remove the cloves from the oil and use as needed.

Wild Mushroom Broth

Yield: 1 quart

2 cups (8 ounces) chopped cremini mushrooms

1 cup (4 ounces) chopped portobello mushrooms

2 cups (8 ounces) chopped button mushrooms

2 tablespoons olive oil

Salt and pepper

6 cups water

METHOD Sauté the mushrooms in the olive oil in a medium saucepan over medium-high heat for 5 to 7 minutes. Season with salt and pepper. Add the water and simmer for 45 minutes, or until reduced by one-third. Strain through a fine-mesh sieve and season to taste with salt and pepper.

Recommended Substitutions

Lobster, salmon, shrimp, squid

Wine Notes

Here, the central element, octopus, is densely meaty, while the vegetables are aromatic and texturally satisfying in a less challenging way for wine. A Burgundy producer whose wines have wonderfully earthy aromas and ripe, creamy texture is Michel Niellon. Chassagne-Montrachet "Les Champs Gains" is ripe and earthy, not overly oaky, and ages well; an older version (at six to ten years) would harmonize all the elements of this dish, while echoing the grain flavors of the barley.

White Alaskan Salmon with Summer Truffles, White Trumpet Mushrooms, and Alaskan Peanut Potatoes

White Alaskan salmon melts in your mouth with its unctuous, sweet, fatty flesh. Here, with white asparagus tips, early summer truffles, Alaskan peanut potatoes, and small boiler onions, we have the ultimate springtime dish. A simple pan sauce made from the cooking juices of the salmon, a little white wine, and some chopped chervil is all that is needed to create this ultrasensual plate of great food. There is no question that this preparation will impress anyone who tries it.

Serves 4

3 cups Alaskan peanut potatoes

2 tablespoons olive oil

Salt and pepper

25 white asparagus tips

1 1/2 cups roasted white trumpet mushrooms (see Appendices)

8 boiler onions

4 tablespoons plus 2 teaspoons butter

4 3 1/2-ounce pieces white salmon, skin removed

1 tablespoon grapeseed oil

2 tablespoons chopped shallots

3/4 cup white Burgundy

3 tablespoons chopped fresh chervil

1 small summer truffle, thinly sliced

METHOD Toss the potatoes with the olive oil and season to taste with salt and pepper. Place on a sheet pan and bake at 400 degrees for 20 to 25 minutes, or until done. Slice into thick discs.

Blanch the asparagus tips in boiling salted water for 2 minutes, or until tender. Drain and season to taste with salt and pepper.

Reheat the roasted white trumpet mushrooms in the cooking juices and season to taste with salt and pepper. Blanch the boiler onions in boiling salted water. Shock in ice water and peel. Cut the onions into quarters and quickly sauté in 2 teaspoons of the butter over medium-high heat for 3 to 4 minutes, or until slightly caramelized. Season to taste with salt and pepper.

Season both sides of the white salmon with salt and pepper. Sauté in a very hot pan with the grapeseed oil. Sauté for 1 to 2 minutes on each side; the fish should be just underdone. Remove the fish from the pan, sweat the shallot in the cooking juices, and deglaze with the white Burgundy. Simmer for 3 minutes, whisk in the remaining 4 tablespoons of butter and the chopped chervil.

ASSEMBLY Arrange some of the onions, white asparagus tips, roasted white trumpet mushrooms, potato slices, and summer truffle slices in the center of each plate. Place a piece of white salmon on top. Spoon the pan sauce over the white salmon and around the plate.

Recommended Substitutions

Catfish, halibut, lobster, salmon, swordfish, whitefish

Wine Notes

Some lighter flavors of the early summer season point to a lighter appellation for the Burgundy choice here. Whereas pink salmon might require a heavier wine, the white salmon needs more delicacy. Elegant truffle and mushroom flavors are enhanced by a less heralded commune like Auxey-Duresses. The Duc de Magenta holding, made now by Maison Louis Jadot, is a beautiful, slightly earthy match, as is the extraordinary Auxey-Duresses of Maison Leroy. Whites from Auxey-Duresses are excellent values for Burgundy and offer deftly employed oak and firm acidity for the truffles and potatoes.

Brandade and Mushroom Tart
with Lobster Sauce and Braised Celery

Brandade has to be among the most sensually satisfying foods. It's somewhat mousselike, but the olive oil and garlic give it an opulent pungency. Texturally, the mixture of dried fish, potato, and olive oil literally dissolves in your mouth. Here, in a tart layered with mushroom and more potato, it comes across especially earthy in its flavor, yet it holds up to the intense lobster sauce, and to an oaky Chardonnay. The delicate lobster dresses up the dish, and a small mound of braised celery is the necessary balance for all of the textures.

Serves 4

2 Idaho potatoes, peeled

¼ cup olive oil

Salt and pepper

4 whole roasted portobello mushroom caps (see Appendices)

Tart Dough (recipe follows)

Brandade (see Appendices)

1 egg yolk

½ cup water

3 cups Shellfish Stock (see Appendices)

1 cup cooked sticky rice

¾ cup lobster meat, cooked and chopped

1 stalk celery, peeled and sliced thinly on the bias

1 teaspoon butter

4 celery leaves

¼ cup grapeseed oil

METHOD Slice the Idaho potatoes into ¼-inch-thick discs, brush with olive oil, and season with salt and pepper. Lay flat on a nonstick sheet pan and bake at 400 degrees for 15 to 20 minutes, or until tender.

Cut the portobello mushroom caps in half horizontally and into 8 discs the diameter of the tart mold you will be using.

Roll out the Tart Dough ⅛ inch thick on a lightly floured surface. Cut into 8 circles large enough to line and cover four 3- by ½-inch ring molds. (Other molds of a similar size will also work.) Place the ring molds on a parchment-lined sheet pan and fill with the Tart Dough, allowing for some overhang. Place some of the Brandade in the bottom of each tart. Arrange some of the potato discs on top of the Brandade and top with a portobello mushroom disc. Place another layer of Brandade on top of the potato, arrange some of the potato discs on top of the Brandade and top with a portobello mushroom disc. Lay another circle of tart dough on top of the mushroom and seal the edges. Repeat for the other 3 molds. Refrigerate for 30 minutes.

In a small bowl, whisk together the yolk and 2 tablespoons of the water. Using a pastry brush, lightly coat the top of the tarts with the egg wash.

Bake at 375 degrees for 35 to 40 minutes, or until golden brown. Let stand for 5 minutes, remove from the molds, and cut into thirds (or serve whole).

Place the Shellfish Stock in a small saucepan, simmer, and reduce by half. Add the cooked rice and continue to simmer for 5 minutes, or until it has a thick consistency. Strain and season to taste with salt and pepper. Add the chopped lobster meat just prior to use.

Place celery in a small sauté pan with the butter and remaining 6 tablespoons of water and braise over medium heat until tender. Season to taste with salt and pepper.

Fry the celery leaves in the grapeseed oil for 5 to 10 seconds, or until they begin to crisp. Blot on paper towels.

ASSEMBLY Place the 3 wedges (or whole tart) on each plate. Arrange some of the braised celery next to the tart with a fried celery leaf standing upright. Spoon the lobster and shellfish sauce around the plate.

Tart Dough

Yield: 12 ounces dough

1½ cups flour

1 teaspoon kosher salt

1 cup cold butter, chopped

⅓ cup ice water

METHOD Place the flour, salt, and butter in a bowl. Using a fork or pastry cutter, cut the butter into the flour until it is in pea-sized chunks. Add the ice water and mix until just combined (the dough should have visible pieces of butter). Form dough into a ball, wrap in plastic, and refrigerate for 1 hour before rolling out.

Recommended Substitutions

Lobster, salmon rillette, shrimp, whitefish

Wine Notes

Brandade is a formidable flavor for wine, needing richness and even a hint of spice. Many California Chardonnay makers use charred oak to "spice" a wine with nutmeg, cinnamon, or clove aromas—ideal counterflavors for this dish. Mushroom, celery, and lobster are all Chardonnay-friendly flavors as well. Try Newton "Unfiltered," Pahlmeyer "Not Filtered," or Shafer "Red Shoulder Ranch," all benchmark Napa Valley producers extracting big flavor and spice from both grapes and oak.

Pinot Gris has the most remarkably different character in its three most prominent growing areas: power and length in Alsace; effortless lightness and purity in Northern Italy; and appley, spicy charm in Oregon. As a genetic mutation from Pinot Noir, this should come as no surprise, as unpredictability seems to be the hallmark of both varieties. The surge of Pinot Gris's popularity has been astounding; it is Oregon's best calling card in white wine. ❧ The wines are so different one could develop separate sets of recipes for each of these areas, yet they have a family resemblance that bonds them. Pinot Gris is comfortable with foie gras and salmon, with lobster, and even with meat flavors. Pinot Gris's versatility is evident in light, elegant recipes like the John Dory, and rich, meaty preparations like the shad roe. The great sweet Tokay Pinot Gris of Alsace are especially attractive in foie gras dishes as an alternative to Sauternes. This exciting variety deserves a prestigious place on the world's table.

Peekytoe Crab Cake, Haddock, and Olympia Oysters with Rice Noodles, Kelp, Wasabi Root, and Kaffir Lime–Celery Broth

There are a lot of flavors working here, but I think they come off well together.
The mildly flavored, delicately fleshed haddock practically floats in this aromatic celery broth.
The minuscule Olympia oysters, merely warmed by the broth, disappear in your mouth
and melt like butter. The crab cake adds richness and a necessary heartiness, and the noodles
provide a sensual chewiness. Seaweed strands and kelp juices further accentuate the sea,
but the coup de théâtre is the sublime, exotic perfume of the kaffir lime.
This dish satisfies on all levels, not the least of which is an intellectual gratification.

Serves 4

5 ounces peekytoe crabmeat, cleaned

2 tablespoons chopped fresh chives

¼ cup diced red bell pepper

1 tablespoon freshly squeezed lime juice

2 tablespoons mayonnaise

1 teaspoon togarashi

½ cup bread crumbs

Salt and pepper

2 teaspoons butter

4 cups celery juice

32 Olympia oysters, shucked and juices reserved

10 kaffir lime leaves

8 1½-ounce pieces haddock, with skin and scored with a razor blade

4 ounces uncooked fresh thick Thai rice noodles

2 tablespoons julienned daikon

¾ cup sliced fresh bamboo shoots

2 teaspoons julienned wasabi

½ cup Japanese cucumbers, cut into small wedges

1½ cups fresh soybeans, blanched

¾ cup celery, julienned

¼ cup dried kelp, soaked in water and julienned

¼ cup celery leaves

4 teaspoons fine chiffonade of opal basil

4 teaspoons Basil Oil (see Appendices)

METHOD Place the crabmeat, chopped chives, red bell pepper, lime juice, mayonnaise, togarashi, and ¼ cup of the bread crumbs in a medium bowl. Toss together and season to taste with salt and pepper.

Fill four 1½-inch bottomless ring molds with the crab mixture and pack tightly. Dust the top and bottom of the molds with the remaining ¼ cup bread crumbs.

Just prior to use, sauté the crab in the molds in a very hot pan with the butter for 1 to 2 minutes on each side, or until each side is golden brown. Blot on a paper towel and carefully remove from the molds.

Simmer the celery juice in a medium saucepan for 5 to 6 minutes, or until the impurities rise to the surface. Strain through a fine-mesh sieve and return to the saucepan. Add the oyster juices and kaffir lime leaves. Simmer for 5 minutes or until the lime leaves turn dark green. Strain through a fine-mesh sieve and season to taste with salt and pepper.

Season the haddock with salt and pepper and steam, covered, for 2 to 3 minutes, or until just cooked.

Place the Thai rice noodles in boiling salted water and boil for 1 to 2 minutes, or until firm. Drain and use immediately.

ASSEMBLY Place a crab cake in the center of each bowl and arrange some of the Thai rice noodles around the crab cake. Place some of the daikon, bamboo shoots, wasabi, cucumbers, soybeans, celery, kelp, and oysters in each bowl. Place 2 pieces of the haddock next to the crab cake. Ladle in the hot broth and sprinkle the celery leaves and opal basil around the bowl. Top with a drizzle of the Basil Oil.

Recommended Substitutions

Cod, any type of crab, flounder, any type of oysters, scallop, whitefish

Wine Notes

This busy plate needs an aromatic and diverse wine companion. Probably the most spicy and perfumed Oregon Pinot Gris is the wonderful wine from Eyrie Vineyards, in the Willamette Valley. David Lett is the dean of Oregon winemaking and his wines are remarkably individual expressions of their varieties. The Pinot Gris is a stunning, fully fragrant wine, great for the sweet cakes and a successful companion to the Asian heat and vegetable elements here.

Tasmanian Salmon with Japanese Eggplant, Spring Peas, and Pea Sauce

Tasmanian salmon is luscious with fat and rich with sweet flavors. Japanese eggplant makes a sensual bed for the fish. Perfect, first-of-the-season peas add further sweetness, which helps to cut into the rich fish. Opal basil adds a subtle perfume that is echoed with a few drops of basil oil. This simple dish is profound with flavor and texture and would easily star as the focal point of a special spring meal.

Serves 4

4 tiny Japanese eggplant, cut in half

4 teaspoons olive oil

Salt and pepper

16 tiny Thai eggplant, steamed whole

2 tablespoons butter

1 cup water

2 tablespoons Basil Oil (see Appendices)

1 cup shucked sugar snap peas

4 4-ounce (1-inch-thick) pieces salmon, with skin

1 1/2 tablespoons grapeseed oil

Pea Sauce (recipe follows)

4 teaspoons small fresh opal basil leaves

METHOD Score the open halves of the Japanese eggplant with a knife, rub with the olive oil, and season with salt and pepper. Roast at 350 degrees for 15 to 20 minutes, or until done.

Carefully remove the skin from the Thai eggplant. Discard the seeds and skin and reserve the eggplant flesh. Season to taste with salt and pepper.

Just prior to use, place the butter, water, and Basil Oil in a small saucepan and bring to a simmer. Add the cleaned sugar snap peas and simmer for 30 to 45 seconds, or until the peas snap in your mouth. Drain the peas and season to taste with salt and pepper.

Season both sides of the salmon with salt and pepper. Score the skin with a razor blade and quickly sauté, skin side down first, in a very hot pan with the grapeseed oil. Sauté for 1 to 2 minutes on each side, or until just underdone.

ASSEMBLY Arrange some of the Thai eggplant pieces in the center of each plate and top with a piece of the salmon. Place 2 halves of the Japanese eggplant next to the salmon and spoon the cooked peas around the plate. Spoon some of the warm Pea Sauce around the peas and sprinkle the top with some of the opal basil leaves.

Pea Sauce

Yield: about 1/2 cup

1/2 cup shucked sugar snap peas (1 cup of reserved shells)

Salt

1/4 cup water

1 teaspoon freshly squeezed lemon juice

1/4 cup Basil Oil (see Appendices)

METHOD Quickly blanch the peas and shells in boiling salted water for 30 to 45 seconds. Immediately shock in ice water and drain. Purée the peas and shells with the water, lemon juice, and Basil Oil until smooth.

Recommended Substitutions

Catfish, halibut, salmon, scallops, red snapper, whitefish

Wine Notes

Salmon preparations are often well-suited to a fuller style of Oregon Pinot Gris. The King Estate Pinot Gris is full (14 percent alcohol) yet dry, structured more like white Burgundy than like Alsatian Pinot Gris or Italian Pinot Grigio. The variety has a nice effect with sweet peas and textural richness for the fish.

I hate people who are not serious about their food. – OSCAR WILDE

Gougeonettes of Walleye Pike with Sunflower Sprouts, Cilantro Vinaigrette, and Yellow Tomato Coulis

These little morsels of fried walleye pike are incredibly succulent inside and ever so delicately crispy on the outside. The crunchy sunflower sprouts provide a cleansing effect that further highlights the intense moistness of the fish. A complexly flavored cilantro vinaigrette incorporates an Asian influence that helps to guide the whole dish into a coherent blend.

Serves 4

16 purple pearl onions

1 teaspoon butter

1 cup fresh cilantro

1 teaspoon grapeseed oil plus extra for deep-frying

1 teaspoon ginger

2 teaspoons sesame oil

1 1/2 teaspoons tamari

1 1/2 tablespoons freshly squeezed orange juice

1 tablespoon rice wine vinegar

Salt and pepper

24 tiny yellow currant tomatoes, peeled

1/2 cup chopped yellow tomato, 1 teaspoon seeds reserved

1 egg yolk

2 tablespoons water

1 tablespoon togarashi

1/2 cup flour

8 1/2- by 4-inch strips walleye pike (about 1 1/2 ounces each), skin removed

2 cups sunflower sprouts

3/4 cup daikon sprouts

METHOD Blanch the purple pearl onions in boiling salted water for 3 minutes. Drain and shock in ice water. Remove the skins and warm in a small saucepan with the butter just prior to use.

Quickly sauté the cilantro in a very hot sauté pan with the grapeseed oil for 30 seconds. Immediately remove from the pan and cool in the refrigerator.

Place the cooled cilantro in a blender with the ginger, 1 teaspoon of the sesame oil, the tamari, orange juice, and vinegar. Purée until smooth, pass through a fine-mesh sieve, and season to taste with salt and pepper.

Gently warm the yellow currant tomatoes in a small saucepan and season to taste with salt and pepper. Place the chopped yellow tomato in the blender and purée until smooth. Pass through a sieve, allowing some of the pulp through. Whisk in 1 teaspoon of sesame oil and the reserved tomato seeds. Season to taste with salt and pepper and warm in a small saucepan.

Whisk the egg yolk and water together in a small bowl. Place the togarashi and flour in a small bowl, mix together, and season with salt. Lightly dust the walleye pike strips with some of the flour, dip in the egg yolk mixture, and dust once more with the flour mixture. Fry in the hot grapeseed oil until golden, remove from the oil, and blot on paper towels.

ASSEMBLY Arrange some of the sunflower sprouts, daikon sprouts, purple pearl onions, and yellow currant tomatoes in the center of each plate. Place 2 pieces of walleye pike on top of the sprouts. Spoon the cilantro vinaigrette and yellow tomato sauce around the plate.

Recommended Substitutions

Catfish, flounder, salmon, swordfish, tuna

Wine Notes

Cilantro adds a lively, peppy element to the vinaigrette here, and the melt-in-your-mouth pike needs an Italian-style light Pinot Grigio. Giovanni Puiatti's EnoFriulia makes a lively, fresh Friulian version of Pinot Grigio, clean and fresh. Ponzi Vineyards makes the best Oregon choice, a crisp, appley Pinot Gris that sets off these lively flavors very well. Moderate alcohol and low oak are keys here.

Shad Roe with Pea Shoots, Bacon Fat, Preserved Turmeric, and Spicy Pea Shoot Juice

Shad roe is a special treat that is only available for a short time in the spring. Bacon fat seems to nicely accentuate the shad roe's richness, while the pea shoots provide a refined, cleansing counterpoint. The preserved turmeric adds an exotic spiciness, and the Spicy Pea Shoot Juice delivers a playful but necessary heat. The roe can certainly be cooked all the way through, but it tends to dry out a little. I prefer it medium-rare, which superbly shows off all of its unique flavors, but more importantly, it allows you to revel in its sublime texture.

Serves 4

3 cups pea shoots

2 teaspoons butter

Salt and pepper

2 pairs shad roe, cleaned and separated into 4 whole pieces

2 tablespoons grapeseed oil

4 teaspoons freshly squeezed lemon juice

2 tablespoons Preserved Turmeric, syrup reserved (recipe follows)

½ cup julienned cooked bacon, warm rendered fat reserved

Spicy Pea Shoot Juice (recipe follows)

METHOD Quickly wilt the pea shoots in the butter for 1 minute over medium heat. Season to taste with salt and pepper.

Season both sides of the shad roe with salt and pepper. Place in a very hot nonstick pan with the grapeseed oil. Sauté for 1 to 2 minutes on each side, or until golden brown and just underdone. (Be careful not to break open the skin when flipping the shad roe.) Remove the ends of each shad roe and slice into 3 pieces. Spoon the lemon juice over the shad roe and season with salt and pepper.

Place the Preserved Turmeric and reserved syrup in a small saucepan and warm over medium heat.

ASSEMBLY Arrange some of the pea shoots and Preserved Turmeric in the center of each plate. Place 3 pieces of shad roe on top of the pea shoots. Arrange some of the bacon pieces around the plate. Spoon the rendered bacon fat, Spicy Pea Shoot Juice, and reserved Preserved Turmeric syrup around the plate. Top with freshly ground black pepper.

Preserved Turmeric

Yield: about 2½ tablespoons

3 tablespoons julienned fresh turmeric

1 cup sugar

METHOD Place the turmeric in a small saucepan with ½ cup of the sugar, cover with water, and bring to a simmer for 10 minutes. Drain, and repeat with fresh water and the remaining ½ cup sugar. Simmer for about 15 minutes, or until tender. Strain the turmeric and set aside. Return the cooking liquid to the heat and simmer for about 15 minutes, or until it coats the back of a spoon.

Spicy Pea Shoot Juice

Yield: about ½ cup

2 cups pea shoots

2 tablespoons grapeseed oil

3 tablespoons Spicy Vinegar (see Appendices)

Salt and pepper

3 tablespoons butter

METHOD Sauté the pea shoots in a large pan with 1 tablespoon of the grapeseed oil for 1 minute. Immediately remove from the pan and cool in the refrigerator. Once cool, coarsely chop and place in the blender with the Spicy Vinegar and the remaining 1 tablespoon of grapeseed oil. Purée until smooth, and pass through a fine-mesh sieve. Season to taste with salt and pepper. Place in a small saucepan and gently warm while whisking in the butter. Keep warm and use immediately. (Do not simmer or cook for more than 2 minutes or the sauce will break down and discolor.)

Recommended Substitutions

Lobster, monkfish liver, scallops, tuna

Wine Notes

Shad roe can have an intensity that is reminiscent of variety meat, and needs a bold wine. Pinot Gris delivers in yet another style, one that is densely concentrated yet only slightly sweet. The Zind-Humbrecht "Vieilles Vignes" leans ever so slightly to the sweet side, yet maintains balance while exerting power and spice. Even more bold and exciting is "Rangen de Thann" Grand Cru, also by Zind-Humbrecht, a wine of remarkable intensity and length on the palate.

John Dory, Foie Gras, and Hedgehog Mushrooms Wrapped in Napa Cabbage with Smoked Salmon Broth

This preparation is extravagant and light at the same time. The foie gras pushes it over the edge in terms of richness, but the John Dory is the real star of the show with its refined flavor and meltaway texture. The Smoked Salmon Broth provides an extraordinarily complex backdrop that shows off the other ingredients, yet it has its own identity. Finally, the napa cabbage and the mushrooms add a rusticity that helps steady these heavenly flavors.

Serves 4

1 cup roasted hedgehog mushrooms (see Appendices)

2 tablespoons chopped fresh chives

Salt and pepper

8 ounces foie gras, deveined and cut into 2 slices approximately 2 inches wide by 5 inches long

4 large leaves napa cabbage

2 4-ounce pieces John Dory, approximately 1 1/2 inches wide by 4 to 5 inches long

2 cups enoki mushrooms

1 teaspoon butter

2 tablespoons flat-leaf parsley chiffonade

Smoked Salmon Broth (recipe follows)

METHOD Chop the hedgehog mushrooms into a duxelle. Place in a small bowl, fold in the chives, and season to taste with salt and pepper.

Season the foie gras with salt and pepper and quickly sauté in a very hot pan for 1 to 2 minutes on each side until caramelized. Remove from the pan and blot on paper towels. Trim the foie gras pieces so they are the width and length of the John Dory.

Quickly blanch the napa cabbage leaves in boiling salted water. Shock in ice water and drain.

Season the John Dory with salt and pepper and place some of the hedgehog mushroom mixture on top of the fish. Lay the foie gras pieces on top of the hedgehog mushrooms. Wrap each piece of fish with 2 leaves of napa cabbage and place in a fish steamer for 4 to 5 minutes, or until the fish is cooked. Slice each piece of wrapped fish into 4 slices.

Quickly sauté the enoki mushrooms in a hot sauté pan with 1 teaspoon of butter and season to taste with salt and pepper.

ASSEMBLY Place 2 slices of the napa cabbage–wrapped fish in the center of each bowl. Arrange the enoki mushrooms and parsley around the bowl. Ladle the warmed Smoked Salmon Broth in the bowl and top with freshly ground black pepper.

Smoked Salmon Broth

Yield: about 3 cups

Skin of one side of smoked salmon

1 cup chopped Spanish onions

1 1/2 quarts Fish Stock (see Appendices)

1/2 cup chopped leek greens

1 teaspoon whole white peppercorns

METHOD Place all of the ingredients in a medium saucepan. Simmer over medium heat for 1 hour and strain through a fine-mesh sieve. Season to taste with salt and pepper.

Recommended Substitutions

Halibut, lobster, salmon, tuna

Wine Notes

Here, a dry style of Pinot Gris is well-suited to the lightly earthy and sweet mushrooms and broth. In Alsace, one of the most consistent is F. E. Trimbach's "Réserve Personnelle," a clean but full Pinot Gris that doesn't go overboard with spicy richness or overt sweetness. The rich-clean balance of the dish has a parallel with the wine, which cleanses and keeps the palate fresh.

Pinot Noir, of all the varieties, is, at times, the most frustrating wine for seafood because it is ephemeral and so delicate. But it can also surprise and delight in its many facets. More than other grapes, Pinot Noir has soul—an undefinable, intellect-feeding elusiveness. ❧ Adding meat to a seafood dish often brings it into the red wine realm. Sometimes the use of red wine or meat jus in a sauce can nudge the wine choice to red as well. But very few fish can handle tannin, so Pinot Noir seems to have the best chance with many seafood preparations because the tannins

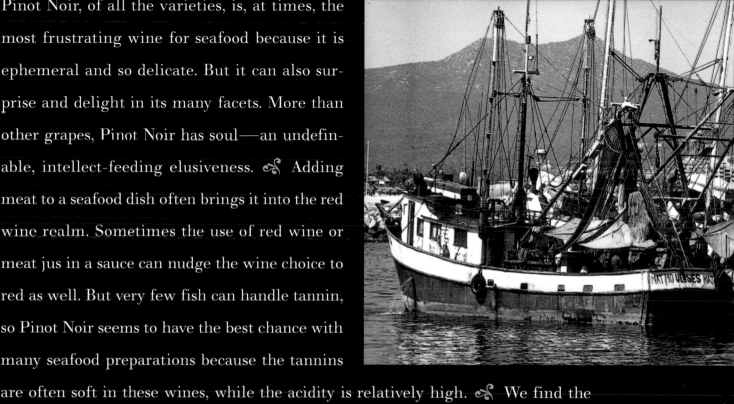

are often soft in these wines, while the acidity is relatively high. ❧ We find the greatest Pinots in Burgundy, although the freshness of fruit in many wines from Oregon and California often has more appeal. The transparency of Pinot to display *terroir* is one of its great virtues, but may not be the best attribute for seafood cookery. That lies in Pinot's ability to make sense with a wide range of flavors and cooking regimens. And in an age where red wine is on the table with diverse food-

Ragout of Small Thai Lobster, Pigeon Breast, and Black Trumpet Mushrooms with Pigeon Jus and Chervil

These small Thai lobsters are incredibly succulent and work perfectly with the richly flavored but lean pigeon. The ultra-earthy mushrooms add a restrained heartiness that helps to make this combination almost soulful comfort food. A drizzle of pigeon jus adds further richness, and chopped chervil and droplets of Chervil Oil provide a light, fragrant freshness.

Serves 4

4 live tiny Thai lobsters or very large crayfish

Salt and pepper

3 teaspoons butter, softened

8 baby zucchini

3 pigeon breasts

2 teaspoons grapeseed oil

1/2 cup Pigeon Reduction (recipe follows)

2 cups roasted black trumpet mushrooms, halved (see Appendices)

4 teaspoons chopped fresh chervil

4 teaspoons Chervil Oil (recipe follows)

METHOD Cook the tiny Thai lobsters in boiling salted water for 4 minutes and immediately shock in ice water. Carefully break open the shells and remove the claw and tail meat in whole pieces. Just prior to use, slice the lobster meat into thin medallions, season with salt and pepper, and lay the medallions and claws on a small sheet pan. Brush with 2 teaspoons of soft butter and bake at 350 degrees for 2 to 3 minutes, or until warm.

Blanch the baby zucchini in boiling salted water for 2 to 3 minutes, cut into quarters, toss with 1 teaspoon of the butter and season to taste with salt and pepper.

Season both sides of the pigeon with salt and pepper and place, skin side down first, in a very hot sauté pan with the grapeseed oil. Cook for 2 to 3 minutes, or until the skin is golden brown and crispy, turn over, and continue cooking for another 1 1/2 to 2 minutes. Remove from the pan and let rest for 2 minutes. Thinly slice, and season each slice with salt and pepper.

Place the Pigeon Reduction in a small saucepan and warm over medium heat.

ASSEMBLY Arrange some of the lobster meat, baby zucchini, pigeon slices, and roasted black trumpet mushrooms in the center of each plate. Sprinkle with chopped chervil and top with freshly ground black pepper. Spoon the warmed Pigeon Reduction and droplets of Chervil Oil around the ragout.

Pigeon Reduction

Yield: 1/2 cup

5 pounds squab bones

1 Spanish onion, chopped

1 carrot, chopped

2 stalks celery, chopped

1 head of garlic, cut in half

1 celery root, peeled and chopped

1/2 cup white wine

1/2 cup chopped tomato

Fresh thyme or tarragon (optional)

METHOD Roast the squab bones in the oven at 375 degrees for 40 to 60 minutes, or until browned.

Place the bones, vegetables, white wine, and tomato in a large pot and cover with about 3 quarts cold water. Bring to a boil. Lower the heat and simmer for 4 hours, skimming away any impurities that rise to the top. Strain and reduce to 1/2 cup. If desired, steep a few sprigs of thyme or tarragon in the reduction for 45 seconds, then remove.

Chervil Oil

Yield: about 1/2 cup

1 cup fresh chervil leaves

1/2 cup grapeseed oil

1/4 cup olive oil

METHOD Blanch the chervil in boiling salted water for 15 seconds. Immediately shock in ice water and drain. Squeeze out any excess liquid and coarsely chop. Purée in a blender with the oils for 3 to 4 minutes, or until bright green. Pour into a container, cover, and refrigerate for 1 day. Strain through cheesecloth, refrigerate for 1 more day, and then decant.

Recommended Substitutions

Crayfish, lobster, shrimp

Wine Notes

The marginalized status of Rosé in the hierarchy of fine wine is puzzling. Pinot Noir produces dazzling Rosé in some areas of the Burgundy region that are useful, young, varietally true refreshers. We find the Marsannay Rosé of Bruno Clair an exciting match for the delicate chervil-laced jus here. Pinot is a perfect fit for the squab, yet by absenting the deeper color (and tannin) one expects in Burgundy, the wine adds vitality and crispness for these sweet, tiny lobsters.

Arctic Char with White Bean Purée, Clam Mushrooms, Roasted Pearl Onions, and Red Wine Reduction

Arctic char is vaguely reminiscent of salmon in both texture and flavor, but it is slightly milder.
Here, the char, with its beautiful crispy skin, sits on a satiny purée of white beans.
The subtle strawlike clam mushrooms and the hearty Veal Stock Reduction are warm and
full-flavored, and the Red Wine Reduction grounds all of the extraordinary elements.
The char, because of its fat content, holds its own next to, and even supports, these robust ingredients.

Serves 4

12 pearl onions, blanched, peeled, and cut in half

2 teaspoons butter

2 cups cooked white beans, puréed

Salt and pepper

8 1½-ounce pieces arctic char, with skin

3 teaspoons grapeseed oil

3 cups roasted clam mushrooms, juices reserved (see Appendices)

¼ cup Veal Stock Reduction (recipe follows)

¼ cup Red Wine Reduction (see Appendices)

4 teaspoons chopped fresh herbs (such as fresh parsley and chives)

METHOD Caramelize the pearl onions in a hot sauté pan with the butter, keeping them intact.

Place the white bean purée in a small saucepan, warm over medium heat, and season to taste with salt and pepper.

Season both sides of the arctic char with salt and pepper and score the skin with a knife or razor blade. Place skin side down in a hot pan with the grapeseed oil and sauté on both sides for 1 to 2 minutes.

Warm the mushrooms in a sauté pan with the juices they were roasted in and season to taste with salt and pepper.

Place the Veal Stock Reduction and Red Wine Reduction in separate small saucepans and warm over medium heat.

ASSEMBLY Spoon some of the hot white bean purée in the center of each plate. Place 2 pieces of the arctic char on top and arrange some of the pearl onions and clam mushrooms around the plate. Spoon the Veal Stock Reduction and Red Wine Reduction on the plate and top with the chopped herbs.

Veal Stock Reduction

Yield: 1¼ cups

10 pounds veal bones
2 carrots, coarsely chopped
2 stalks celery, coarsely chopped
1 yellow onion, coarsely chopped
1 leek, cleaned and coarsely chopped
1 bulb garlic, cut in half
2 tablespoons grapeseed oil
½ cup tomato concassée
4 cups dry red wine (such as Burgundy)

METHOD Place the bones in a roasting pan and roast in the oven at 450 degrees for 2 hours, or until golden brown. When bones are browned, caramelize the carrots, celery, onion, leek, and garlic in the grapeseed oil in a large stockpot. Add the tomato concassée and cook for 5 minutes. Deglaze with the red wine and reduce until most of the wine has been cooked out. Add the browned bones and cover with cold water. Bring to a boil, then reduce heat and let simmer over medium heat for 8 hours. Strain through a fine-mesh sieve and simmer over medium heat for 45 minutes, or until it coats the back of a spoon. Extra reduction can be stored in the freezer for several months.

Recommended Substitutions

Halibut, flounder, salmon, red snapper, trout

Wine Notes

Earthier styles of Pinot Noir, some without high tannins, come from good Burgundy growers in the Côte de Nuits. One favorite for this range of earthy flavors is the Morey St. Denis *Vieilles Vignes* by Hubert Lignier. A more delicate vintage, such as 1991 or 1994, will provide the meaty fish with a structured wine and allow the bean, onion, and mushroom flavors to shine through as well. A classic Burgundy is ideal with this richer, fattier fish.

Barracuda and Veal Sweetbreads with Verjus Sauce and Wilted Mâche

*I gain immeasurable pleasure consuming an unabashedly aggressive creature.
The meat of this fish is fairly firm, and rather mild-tasting. Because of its fairly nondescript flavor
and texture characteristics, barracuda works well with vivid, robust flavors like the verjus sauce,
and easily shares the spotlight, as it does here with the veal sweetbreads. The wilted mâche provides
the perfect cutting element for the sweetbreads and barracuda, and in fact, almost melds them
together. Barracuda by itself also works quite nicely atop a mound of sautéed wild mushrooms.*

Serves 4

4 cups mâche

1 cup verjus

5 tablespoons grapeseed oil

2 tablespoons water

*2 tablespoons Red Wine Reduction
(see Appendices)*

6 tablespoons butter

Salt and pepper

4 3-ounce pieces barracuda, skin removed

Braised Sweetbreads (recipe follows)

METHOD In a medium sauté pan, wilt 2 cups of the mâche in 2 tablespoons of the verjus for 2 to 3 minutes. Immediately remove from the pan and refrigerate until chilled.

Place the cooled mâche in a blender with 3 tablespoons of the grapeseed oil and the water. Purée until smooth and strain through a fine-mesh sieve.

Place the remaining verjus in a small saucepan and simmer over medium-high heat until reduced to ¹/₂ cup. Add the Red Wine Reduction and whisk in 4 tablespoons of the butter.

In a small sauté pan, wilt the remaining mâche with 1 tablespoon of the butter for 2 minutes over medium-high heat. Season to taste with salt and pepper.

Season both sides of the barracuda with salt and pepper and place in a very hot sauté pan with the remaining grapeseed oil. Sauté for 2 to 2¹/₂ minutes on each side, or until golden brown (the fish should be cooked all the way through).

Just prior to use, place the mâche in a small saucepan and warm gently over medium heat. Whisk in 1 tablespoon of the butter and season to taste with salt and pepper.

ASSEMBLY Place some of the Braised Sweetbreads in the center of each plate. Arrange the wilted mâche on top of the sweetbreads and top with a piece of the barracuda. Spoon the red wine verjus sauce around the plate into a circle and spoon the warmed mâche sauce around the edges of the red wine verjus sauce.

Braised Sweetbreads

4 2- to 3-ounce sweetbread noisettes

1 cup chopped Spanish onions

1 cup chopped carrots

1 cup chopped celery

¹/₂ cup chopped leeks

3 tablespoons grapeseed oil

3 sprigs thyme

3 cups Chicken Stock (see Appendices)

Salt and pepper

1 teaspoon butter

METHOD Rinse the sweetbreads in cold running water for 30 to 45 minutes. In a medium saucepan, caramelize the onions, carrots, celery, and leeks with 2 tablespoons of the grapeseed oil. Add the sweetbreads and thyme and cover with the Chicken Stock. Simmer the liquid, gently poaching the sweetbreads for 7 to 8 minutes, or until tender. Remove from the liquid, clean off any membranes or veins, and lightly season with salt and pepper.

In a heavy-bottomed pan, sauté the sweetbreads in the remaining grapeseed oil and the butter over medium-high heat for 4 to 5 minutes, turning them from time to time until golden brown and crispy. Season to taste with salt and pepper.

Recommended Substitutions

Catfish, halibut, salmon, swordfish, tuna

Wine Notes

Burgundy from the southern end of the district, like the robust Givry by Domaine Joblot, gives more power and oak to the Pinot Noir but perhaps a touch less finesse. The meaty barracuda needs a more muscular Pinot, and the sweet oak of this wine matches up nicely to the sweetbreads and the tart verjus of the sauce.

Chilean Sea Bass with Pinot Noir—Stewed Shallots and Veal Stock Reduction

The high fat content of this fish results in a meltingly rich flavor. The Pinot Noir—stewed shallots provide just the right amount of acid for this full-flavored fish, and the Veal Stock Reduction lends a divine heartiness to this preparation. Earthy roasted vegetables—white carrots and matsutake mushrooms—round this preparation into a perfect fusion of land and sea.

Serves 4

6 shallots, thinly sliced
3 cups Pinot Noir
16 baby white carrots
2 tablespoons olive oil
4 medium matsutake mushrooms
2 cloves garlic
5 sprigs thyme
1 cup Mushroom Stock (see Appendices)
Salt and pepper
1 cup Veal Stock Reduction (recipe follows)
1 tablespoon hoisin sauce
3 teaspoons tamari
2 teaspoons rice wine vinegar
4 3-ounce pieces sea bass, skin removed
2 teaspoons grapeseed oil

METHOD Place the shallots in a small saucepan with the Pinot Noir. Simmer over medium heat for 20 to 30 minutes, or until all of the Pinot Noir has been absorbed into the shallots.

Place the carrots in an ovenproof pan with 1 tablespoon of the olive oil. Roast at 350 degrees, turning occasionally, for 15 to 20 minutes, or until tender.

Trim the stems of the mushrooms and rinse them clean. Place in an ovenproof pan with the garlic, thyme, Mushroom Stock, and remaining 1 tablespoon of olive oil. Season to taste with salt and pepper and cover with aluminum foil. Roast at 350 degrees for 45 minutes, or until the mushrooms are just cooked.

Place the Veal Stock Reduction, hoisin, tamari, and rice wine vinegar in a medium saucepan and bring to a simmer.

Season both sides of the bass with salt and pepper and quickly sauté in a very hot pan with the grapeseed oil for 1 to 2 minutes on each side.

ASSEMBLY Place some of the Pinot Noir shallots in the center of each plate and top with a piece of the bass. Arrange the roasted carrots and matsutake mushrooms behind the bass and spoon the Veal Stock Reduction around the plate.

Veal Stock Reduction

Yield: 1¼ cups

10 pounds veal bones
2 carrots, coarsely chopped
2 stalks celery, coarsely chopped
1 yellow onion, coarsely chopped
1 leek, cleaned and coarsely chopped
1 bulb garlic, cut in half
2 tablespoons grapeseed oil
½ cup tomato concassée
4 cups dry red wine (such as Burgundy)

METHOD Place the bones in a roasting pan and roast in the oven at 450 degrees for 2 hours, or until golden brown. When bones are browned, caramelize the carrots, celery, onion, leek, and garlic in the grapeseed oil in a large stockpot. Add the tomato concassée and cook for 5 minutes. Deglaze with the red wine and reduce until most of the wine has been cooked out. Add the browned bones and cover with cold water. Bring to a boil, then reduce heat and let simmer over medium heat for 8 hours. Strain through a fine-mesh sieve and simmer over medium heat for 45 minutes, or until it coats the back of a spoon. Extra reduction can be stored in the freezer for several months.

Recommended Substitutions

Catfish, halibut, snapper, swordfish, whitefish

Wine Notes

Pinot Noir from Oregon can have the juiciness of North American fruit with the structure of Burgundy. Yet some vineyards provide ample fruit without producing a coarse wine. An example is the Adelsheim "Ridgecrest Vineyard" Pinot Noir, a single-vineyard wine distinctive enough from the numerous lots used in Adelsheim Vineyard's Oregon Pinot Noir to establish itself separately. This wine explodes with rich cherry fruit yet not with tannin, and makes a fine companion to this delicate fish and its flavorful accompaniments.

Golden Trout with Black-Eyed Peas, Yellowfoot Chanterelles, Turnips, and Pinot Noir Reduction

The flavor of these little golden trout steaks vaguely resembles salmon, although it is a little more delicate. The skin is not only wonderfully crispy, but it's so full of flavor that it may be the star of the dish. The rustic quality of the black-eyed peas, chanterelles, and turnips implies that this preparation might be somewhat robust, when in fact it is really quite delicate. The Pinot Noir sauce coalesces the components into a coherent combination while providing just the right acid to tame the medium-rich fish.

Serves 4

2 cups roasted yellowfoot chanterelle mushrooms (see Appendices)

4 teaspoons butter

1 tablespoon chopped shallots

Salt and pepper

1 1/2 cups cooked black-eyed peas

1 cup diced turnips, blanched

8 1 1/2-ounce steaks of golden trout, skin on

4 teaspoons grapeseed oil

1/2 cup Pinot Noir Reduction (recipe follows)

4 teaspoons Basil Oil (see Appendices)

4 teaspoons fresh oregano leaves

METHOD Quickly sauté the mushrooms in a medium sauté pan with 2 teaspoons of the butter and the chopped shallots. Season to taste with salt and pepper.

Place the black-eyed peas in a small saucepan and warm over medium heat. Season to taste with salt and pepper. Place the diced turnips in a small saucepan with the remaining 2 teaspoons of butter and warm over medium heat. Season to taste with salt and pepper.

Season both sides of the trout with salt and pepper. Quickly sauté in a hot pan with the grapeseed oil for 1 to 2 minutes on each side.

Place the Pinot Noir Reduction in a small saucepan and gently warm over medium heat.

ASSEMBLY Arrange some of the mushrooms, black-eyed peas, and turnips in the center of each plate. Spoon some of the Pinot Noir Reduction over the vegetables and drizzle some of the Basil Oil around the plate. Place 2 pieces of the trout on top of the beans and top with freshly ground black pepper. Arrange some of the fresh oregano leaves around the plate.

Pinot Noir Reduction

Yield: 1/2 cup

1 Spanish onion, coarsely chopped

1 carrot, coarsely chopped

1 stalk celery, coarsely chopped

2 Granny Smith apples, coarsely chopped

1 orange, peeled and chopped

2 cloves garlic

2 tablespoons grapeseed oil

1 750-mL bottle Pinot Noir

1/2 cup Chicken Stock (see Appendices)

METHOD In a large saucepan, caramelize the onion, carrot, celery, apples, orange, and garlic in the grapeseed oil. Add the wine and reduce over medium heat for 2 hours. Strain and place in a small saucepan with the Chicken Stock. Continue to reduce over medium heat for 1 hour, or until you have 1/2 cup.

Recommended Substitutions

Salmon, snapper, trout, tuna, whitefish

Wine Notes

Etude Pinot Noir is a lively Carneros wine whose exuberant fruit is not surrendered to huge structure. The root vegetables and Pinot Noir Reduction used in this rich trout preparation merge beautifully with this plump style of Pinot. One might also consider the refreshing Etude Pinot Noir Rosé for a change of pace or with a lighter sauce for the same great fruitiness—without the oaky spine of the red.

Hebi with Quinoa and Roasted Hon-shimeji Mushrooms and Their Purée

While vacationing in Hawaii I went on a fishing outing with the incredible Sweeney family, owners of Vine Cliff Winery in Napa. About two hours out from Maui, I caught a 37-pound hebi, or shortbilled spearfish. That night, my Chef de Cuisine Guillermo Tellez and I cooked the fish over a grill and served it with a simple vinaigrette. It was truly one of the moistest and most flavorful pieces of fish I have ever eaten. Since then, I have served hebi at the restaurant on a regular basis. It works very well with strong heady flavors like wild mushrooms, Red Wine Reduction, and robust grains. This dish shows off the spearfish in a delicately hearty yet easy-to-make preparation.

Serves 4

1 cup (4 ounces) lentil stir-fry sprouts (such as adzuki bean, Alaskan pea, sunflower, mung bean)

2 tablespoons olive oil

Salt and pepper

2½ cups roasted hon-shimeji mushrooms, juices reserved (see Appendices)

¼ cup diced carrots

2 teaspoons butter

3 cups cooked quinoa

2 tablespoons Red Wine Reduction (see Appendices)

3 tablespoons white truffle oil

4 3-ounce pieces hebi (shortbill spearfish)

1 tablespoon grapeseed oil

4 teaspoons thyme leaves

4 teaspoons long-cut fresh chives

METHOD Toss the lentil stir-fry sprouts with the olive oil and season with salt and pepper. Spread out on a small sheet tray and bake at 375 degrees for 18 to 22 minutes, stirring occasionally, or until crispy and toasted.

Purée ½ cup of the roasted mushrooms with the reserved cooking juices until smooth. (Additional water may be needed to purée smoothly.) Season to taste with salt and pepper. Just prior to use, warm the purée in a small saucepan, reheat the remaining mushrooms if necessary and season to taste with salt and pepper.

In a small pan, sauté the diced carrots in the butter over medium-high heat. Fold the carrots and roasted lentil sprouts into the cooked quinoa and season to taste with salt and pepper.

In a small bowl, stir together the Red Wine Reduction and white truffle oil (it will appear broken).

Season both sides of the hebi with salt and pepper. Place in a hot pan with the grapeseed oil and sauté for 1 to 2 minutes on each side, until just underdone. Slice the fish in half and season the cut portion of the hebi with salt and pepper.

ASSEMBLY Place a large spoonful of the quinoa mixture in the center of each plate. Lay 2 halves of hebi on top of the quinoa. Arrange the mushrooms around the hebi and spoon the mushroom sauce and red wine–white truffle mixture around the plate. Sprinkle with fresh thyme and long-cut chives.

Recommended Substitutions

Lobster, scallops, red snapper, swordfish, tuna

Wine Notes

One Burgundy producer who turns out gorgeous wines in both lighter (1992) and richer (1990 or 1993) vintages is Mongeard-Mugneret. The Vosne-Romanée "Les Orveaux" 1992 shows amazing delicacy and transparency of *terroir* yet, though clearly oak-influenced, no harshness. In this preparation, the hebi basks in Burgundy-friendly flavors; the slight nuttiness and unique Burgundian perfume of the Vosne-Romanée is an ideal companion.

Strong flavors need strong wines, though neither Sangiovese nor Zinfandel packs the tannic punch of most Cabernet or Merlot. These grapes have guts! They both ripen in meridional climates but do not usually have the extract that would make them too hard. These wines can add rich dried berry flavors to many meat-enhanced dishes. ❧

Tuscany and, more recently, the Napa Valley are home to great Sangiovese. Zinfandel has long been a favorite wine-maker's variety throughout California, and almost nowhere else. Once thought to be an Italian variety closely related to Primitivo, current evidence points to Zinfandel's origins in Hungary or Croatia as the Plavác grape. It can be a lush, powerful wine (our favorite style) or an easy-drinking quaffer. Chianti, the best known Sangiovese-based wine, can take these directions too, especially when the traditional white wine grapes are omitted from the blend. These varieties may seem strange bedfellows, but they share many assets that match well with rich, hearty seafood dishes.

Monkfish Wrapped in Prosciutto and Mustard Greens with Shiitake Mushrooms and Red Wine Emulsion

Sturdy monkfish tail is roasted until caramelized and then basted with Dijon mustard, wrapped in mustard greens, wrapped again in prosciutto, and then finished in the oven. The meatlike preparation results in a robust and full-flavored yet refined preparation. An elegant red wine emulsion is spooned around the fish to add a delicate, woodsy touch and just the right amount of acid to help cut into the prosciutto and the meat of the fish. A side dish of wild mushroom risotto would be an ideal accompaniment to make this an entrée.

Serves 4

¹/₄ cup Red Wine Reduction (see Appendices)

6 large roasted shiitake mushrooms, cut into quarters, cooking juices reserved (see Appendices)

1 ¹/₂ cups Mushroom Stock (see Appendices)

¹/₂ cup butter

Salt and pepper

2 large monkfish tails (about 1 ¹/₂ pounds), cleaned and boned

3 tablespoons Dijon mustard

3 large mustard green leaves, blanched

6 large thin slices prosciutto

4 teaspoons olive oil

4 teaspoons Garlic Chive Oil (recipe follows)

4 tablespoons chopped fresh chervil

2 tablespoons long-cut fresh garlic chives

METHOD Place the Red Wine Reduction, reserved mushroom cooking juices, and Mushroom Stock in a small saucepan. Bring to a simmer over medium heat, whisk in 6 tablespoons of the butter, and season to taste with salt and pepper. Froth with a hand-held blender just prior to use.

Season the monkfish with salt and pepper, and quickly sauté in 2 tablespoons of the butter for 1 minute on each side. Remove from the pan and brush with Dijon mustard. Wrap each monkfish tail in 1¹/₂ of the mustard green leaves.

Lay 3 of the prosciutto slices flat, overlapping the edges. Carefully wrap the prosciutto around the mustard green—wrapped monkfish and brush with the olive oil. Repeat the process with the remaining monkfish and prosciutto. Place on a sheet pan and bake at 375 degrees for 4 to 5 minutes, or until the fish is just cooked. Slice each monkfish tail into 6 slices and season with salt and pepper.

ASSEMBLY Place some of the hot roasted shiitake mushrooms in the center of each bowl. Arrange 3 slices of the monkfish tail on top of the mushrooms. Spoon the red wine emulsion around the bowl and drizzle with the Garlic Chive Oil. Sprinkle with the chopped chervil and garlic chives.

Garlic Chive Oil

Yield: about ¹/₂ cup

³/₄ cup fresh garlic chives

³/₄ cup grapeseed oil

METHOD Blanch the garlic chives in boiling salted water and immediately shock in ice water. Drain and squeeze out the excess liquid. Chop and purée in the blender with the oil for 3 to 4 minutes, or until bright green. Refrigerate overnight and strain through a fine-mesh sieve. Refrigerate 1 more day and decant. Store in the refrigerator until needed.

Recommended Substitutions

Lobster, shrimp, red snapper, swordfish, tuna

Wine Notes

Delicious, forward Chianti Classico from a top producer puts to rest the impression of Chianti as a spaghetti or pizza wine. Producers like Castello di Ama and Isole e Olena care deeply about concentration and ripeness and the varietal identity of Sangiovese. The grape yields appropriate peppery and black cherry flavors for the juicy, prosciutto-wrapped monkfish, and punchy acidity for the mushroom and red wine emulsion flavors.

Oxtail-Stuffed Baby Squid with Cremini Mushrooms, Mustard Oil, and Oxtail Braising Juices

Tiny squid offer a perfect little pocket in which to tuck anything—fish, vegetables, or meat. Slowly braised oxtail seems the ideal companion for the barely firm, slightly chewy squid. Pieces of braised cremini mushrooms act as the perfect pedestal for the squid and the oxtail, while a few drops of mustard oil add a controlled zip. Finally, a loose salsify purée is drizzled around the plate for an element of lusciousness.

Serves 4

8 oxtail sections, approximately 2 inches long

2 tablespoons grapeseed oil

1/2 cup chopped carrots

1/2 cup chopped celery

1 cup chopped Spanish onions

3 tablespoons tomato paste

2 cups red wine

2 tablespoons chopped fresh cilantro

1 tablespoon minced jalapeño

1 teaspoon freshly squeezed lime juice

Salt and pepper

2 stalks (about 1 cup) salsify

2 cups milk

8 baby squids, cleaned, with tentacles separated

1 tablespoon butter

2 cups roasted cremini mushrooms (see Appendices)

8 teaspoons Mustard Oil (recipe follows)

METHOD Sear the oxtails in a large saucepan with the grapeseed oil. Remove the oxtails from the pan, add the carrots, celery, and onion, and cook until caramelized. Add the tomato paste and cook for 5 minutes. Deglaze with the red wine and return the oxtails to the pan. Add enough water to cover the oxtails and bring to a simmer. Cover and continue to simmer slowly for 2 to 3 hours, or until the meat easily falls off the bone. (Additional liquid may be needed during the cooking process.)

Remove the oxtails from the liquid and strain the braising liquid through a fine-mesh sieve. Return the braising liquid to the pan and simmer over medium heat for about 30 minutes, or until you have a sauce-like consistency.

Remove the oxtail meat from the bone and place in a small saucepan. Add the chopped cilantro, jalapeño, and lime juice, and warm over medium heat for 2 to 3 minutes. Season to taste with salt and pepper.

Peel the salsify, cut into 2-inch-long pieces, and immediately place in a medium saucepan with the milk. Simmer for 30 minutes, or until tender. Remove the salsify from the liquid and place in a blender with just enough of the cooking liquid to purée smoothly. Season to taste with salt and pepper.

Season the baby squids and tentacles with salt and pepper, and fill them with the oxtail mixture. In a medium sauté pan, sauté the stuffed squids with the butter for 2 to 3 minutes, turning occasionally. Add the tentacles and quickly sauté for 1 minute.

Slice the cremini mushrooms into thick slices and season to taste with salt and pepper. Warm in a small saucepan just prior to use.

ASSEMBLY Place a few slices of the cremini mushrooms in the center of each plate. Top mushrooms with 2 squids and a few of the tentacles. Spoon the salsify purée around the plate, along with some of the hot braising liquid, and mustard oil.

Mustard Oil

Yield: about 1/2 cup

1 1/2 teaspoons mustard seed

1/8 teaspoon turmeric

1/2 cup grapeseed oil

METHOD Roast the mustard seeds at 350 degrees for 5 minutes. Grind the mustard seeds and turmeric in a spice grinder. Put spices and oil in a blender and blend on high until spices are completely incorporated. Store, covered, for 1 day in the refrigerator. Strain through cheesecloth, refrigerate for 1 more day, and decant. Can be kept for up to 2 weeks in the refrigerator.

Recommended Substitutions

Lobster, salmon, scallops, swordfish, tuna

Wine Notes

Unique Sangiovese is produced in Carmignano, a small but historic DOCG district in Tuscany. These full-bodied wines give a distinct earthiness and backbone not always found in Chianti. Producers here traditionally use Cabernet Sauvignon to beef up the blend. Ambra is a fine example, from the Santa Cristina Vineyard, with a concentrated yet not overly powerful character for the oxtail-stuffed squid. The meat juices are also a perfect complement for the acidity of this wine.

Slow-Roasted Salmon with Red Wine Risotto, Wild Thyme, and Tiny White Asparagus

*In this dish, the salmon is covered with wild thyme and sits on a bed of braised celery
as it slowly roasts at 225 degrees. The result is a highly aromatic piece of fish that is so smooth
it literally has no texture as it melts in your mouth. Thus, the contrast of pairing it with
the pungent red wine risotto is all the more dramatic. This dish is extremely satisfying, true
good-for-the-soul food. The Veal Stock Reduction and tiny white asparagus
finish the dish with a touch of elegance that nicely elevates the overall preparation.*

Serves 4

1 clove garlic, minced

1/2 cup diced Spanish onions

2 tablespoons plus 1 teaspoon butter

1 cup uncooked Arborio rice

1 cup Red Wine Reduction (see Appendices)

*1 cup roasted woodear mushrooms, chopped
(see Appendices)*

Salt and pepper

4 3-ounce pieces salmon, skin removed

*4 stalks celery, peeled and cut
into long, thin strips*

1 1/2 cups fresh thyme

1 cup tiny white asparagus

1/2 cup Veal Stock Reduction (recipe follows)

METHOD Sweat the garlic and onion in a medium saucepan with 2 tablespoons of the butter. Add the Arborio rice, stir to coat with the onion and garlic, and cook for 3 minutes. Add 1/2 cup of the Red Wine Reduction and continue to cook over medium-low heat while gently stirring constantly. Once the rice has absorbed the Red Wine Reduction, add the remaining 1/2 cup, stirring constantly. After all of the Red Wine Reduction is absorbed, add 1/4 cup additions of water until the rice is just cooked. (It should be al dente, yet creamy.) Fold in the roasted woodear mushrooms and season to taste with salt and pepper.

Season both sides of the salmon with salt and pepper. Place the celery strips on a small sheet pan, creating a rack for the salmon. Place the salmon on top of the celery and cover with 1 1/4 cups of the fresh thyme. Roast at 225 degrees for 15 to 20 minutes, or until just done. Remove from oven, cut the celery into a small dice, and fold into the red wine risotto.

Quickly sauté the asparagus in a small pan with the remaining 1 teaspoon of butter. Season to taste with salt and pepper.

Warm the Veal Stock Reduction in a small saucepan.

ASSEMBLY Place a mound of the red wine risotto in the center of each plate and top with a piece of the salmon. Arrange some of the tiny white asparagus and remaining fresh thyme on top of the salmon. Spoon the Veal Stock Reduction around the risotto.

Veal Stock Reduction

Yield: 1 1/4 cups

10 pounds veal bones

2 carrots, coarsely chopped

2 stalks celery, coarsely chopped

1 yellow onion, coarsely chopped

1 leek, cleaned and coarsely chopped

1 bulb garlic, cut in half

2 tablespoons grapeseed oil

1/2 cup tomato concassée

4 cups dry red wine (such as Burgundy)

METHOD Place the bones in a roasting pan and roast in the oven at 450 degrees for 2 hours, or until golden brown. When bones are browned, caramelize the carrots, celery, onion, leek, and garlic in the grapeseed oil in a large stockpot. Add the tomato concassée and cook for 5 minutes. Deglaze with the red wine and reduce until most of the wine has been cooked out. Add the browned bones and cover with cold water. Bring to a boil, then reduce heat and let simmer over medium heat for 8 hours. Strain through a fine-mesh sieve and simmer over medium heat for 45 minutes, or until it coats the back of a spoon. Extra reduction can be stored in the freezer for several months.

Recommended Substitutions

Cod, lobster, scallops, red snapper, swordfish, tuna

Wine Notes

The development of Sangiovese in California vineyards has been rapid and exciting. The variety has a personality distinct from its forebears in Tuscany. The best producers are avoiding overoaking and overextracting, thus pushing forward the sour cherry and earthy tones that make Sangiovese as fine a variety for seafood as it is for meat. The supple fruit from the young Sangiovese vineyards at Swanson, Shafer's "Firebreak," or Staglin's "Stagliano" makes these wines good companions for this meltingly delicious approach to salmon. Thyme is a Sangiovese-friendly herb, and the risotto harks back to the grape's Italian origins.

Opah with Cipolline Onion Purée, Black Lentils, Lentil Juice, and Red Wine Reduction

Opah, or moonfish, is an open-ocean fish from the Hawaiian Islands.
Its flavor and texture are almost a cross between those of tuna and swordfish.
Here, I place the sliced fish on a bed of hot-and-sour cipolline onion slices
along with a satiny and sweet mound of cipolline onion purée. Sweet, terrestrial black lentils
give a meatlike quality to the plate. Red Wine Reduction provides a majestic and
complex fruity acid that helps to weave these extraordinary elements into a magnificent
combination of flavors and sensual textures. A simple mesclun salad, perhaps
with some goat cheese, would be a perfect accompaniment.

Serves 4

20 small cipolline onions, peeled

3 tablespoons butter

3 tablespoons Spicy Vinegar
(see Appendices)

Salt and pepper

2 cups cooked black lentils,
cooking juices reserved

1 12-ounce piece opah, 2½ inches wide
by 1¼ inches thick, skin removed

1 tablespoon grapeseed oil

4 teaspoons olive oil

¼ cup Red Wine Reduction
(see Appendices)

4 teaspoons chopped fresh chervil

METHOD Slice 12 of the cipolline onions into thirds horizontally, creating complete rings. Separate the rings and sauté in a large pan with 4 teaspoons of the butter for 3 to 4 minutes, or until translucent. Add the Spicy Vinegar and continue to sauté until all of the liquid is absorbed.

Chop the remaining cipolline onions and sauté in a medium pan with the remaining 5 teaspoons of butter until slightly caramelized. Purée the onions until smooth, pass through a fine-mesh sieve, and season to taste with salt and pepper. (The purée should be thick; if necessary, dry out the purée in a small pan over medium heat.)

Reheat the cooked lentils and reserved juices in a small saucepan. (If all of the liquid has been absorbed, add ¼ cup water and simmer the lentils for 5 minutes.) Season to taste with salt and pepper. Drain the cooking juices from the lentils and reserve.

Season the opah with salt and pepper. In a very hot sauté pan, sear the opah on each side with the grapeseed oil for 1 to 2 minutes, or until golden brown (the opah should be underdone). Remove the opah from the pan and slice into 20 thin slices.

ASSEMBLY Spoon some of the cipolline onion purée into a wide circle in the center of each plate. Top with some of the hot-and-sour cipolline onions and place 5 slices of the opah on top of the onions. Spoon the black lentils and the reserved lentil cooking liquid around the onion purée. Drizzle the olive oil and Red Wine Reduction around the lentils. Sprinkle with chopped chervil.

Recommended Substitutions

Lobster, red snapper, swordfish, tuna

Wine Notes

Softer Zinfandels such as Jed Steele's "Catfish Vineyard" rendition or Jerry Seps's Storybook Mountain "Eastern Exposures" version are not powerful but are still spicy enough for this meaty fish. The sweet onion purée and nutty lentil flavors are both cut nicely by this wine style's acidity and are well-seasoned by its peppery qualities. Lower alcohol also makes these wines less ponderous, and appropriate for the vegetable flavors.

Whole Roasted Moi with Porcini Mushrooms, Tripe, and Veal Stock Reduction

Moi is rich and luscious with its ultrasucculent flesh. When cooked whole, the delicate crispy skin highlights the moistness of the fish. Braised tripe and porcini mushrooms add a splendid rustic quality that contrasts beautifully against this Hawaiian reef fish. In all, this combination makes for a wonderful, sophisticated main course, ideal for a special party.

Serves 4

4 cups roasted porcini mushrooms (see Appendices)

2 tablespoons chopped shallots

2 tablespoons butter

Salt and pepper

4 small whole moi, gutted

4 tablespoons olive oil

2 tablespoons grapeseed oil

1/2 cup Veal Stock Reduction (recipe follows)

1/3 cup Red Wine Reduction (see Appendices)

Braised Tripe (recipe follows)

4 tablespoons chopped fresh chervil

METHOD Slice the roasted mushrooms and sauté in a medium pan with the shallots and butter for 3 to 4 minutes, or until slightly golden brown. Season to taste with salt and pepper.

Rub the moi with olive oil and season with salt and pepper. In a large, very hot pan, sauté the moi in the grapeseed oil for 4 to 6 minutes on each side. (The skin should be golden and crispy.)

Just prior to use, warm the Veal Stock Reduction and Red Wine Reduction in separate small saucepans over medium heat.

ASSEMBLY Arrange some of the Braised Tripe and roasted porcini mushrooms in the center of each plate. Top with a piece of moi and sprinkle with the chopped chervil. Spoon the Red Wine Reduction and Veal Stock Reduction around the plate.

Veal Stock Reduction

Yield: 1 1/4 cups

10 pounds veal bones

2 carrots, coarsely chopped

2 stalks celery, coarsely chopped

1 yellow onion, coarsely chopped

1 leek, cleaned and coarsely chopped

1 bulb garlic, cut in half

2 tablespoons grapeseed oil

1/2 cup tomato concassée

4 cups dry red wine (such as Burgundy)

METHOD Place the bones in a roasting pan and roast in the oven at 450 degrees for 2 hours, or until golden brown. When bones are browned, caramelize the carrots, celery, onion, leek, and garlic in the grapeseed oil in a large stockpot. Add the tomato concassée and cook for 5 minutes. Deglaze with the red wine and reduce until most of the wine has been cooked out. Add the browned bones and cover with cold water. Bring to a boil, then reduce heat and let simmer over medium heat for 8 hours. Strain through a fine-mesh sieve and simmer over medium heat for 45 minutes, or until it coats the back of a spoon. Extra reduction can be stored in the freezer for several months.

Braised Tripe

1 cup chopped carrots

1 cup chopped Spanish onions

1 cup chopped celery

1/2 cup chopped leeks

3 tablespoons grapeseed oil

1 tablespoon tomato paste

1/2 cup red wine (such as Zinfandel)

16 ounces tripe

3 sprigs thyme

1/2 cup butter

4 to 5 cups Chicken Stock (see Appendices)

METHOD In a medium saucepan, caramelize the chopped carrots, onions, celery, and leeks in the grapeseed oil. Add the tomato paste and continue cooking for 3 minutes. Deglaze with the red wine and then add the tripe, thyme, butter, and Chicken Stock. Simmer very slowly over medium-low heat for 4 to 5 hours, or until the tripe is very soft. Cool in the liquid and then cut the tripe into 1 1/2- by 1/2-inch strips. Reheat in the braising liquid just prior to use.

Recommended Substitutions

Flounder, halibut, trout, tuna, whitefish

Wine Notes

Zinfandel from old vines (some Californian vineyards are close to a century old, and still producing) can be far less aggressive and tannic than the wine of younger vines, which are more prolific but have less personality. A number of specialists in Zinfandel have sought out older vineyards to make ripe, plush red that is not shy in the alcohol department. This style delivers big flavors and intense fruit yet not the structure of more "classical" wines. Turley "Moore 'Earthquake' Vineyard" and Steele "Pacini Vineyard" are two Zinfandels that give rich, warm, spicy pleasure for the rich, textured mushrooms and tripe accompanying the delicate moi.

Haricot Vert-and-Anchovy—Larded Big-Eye Tuna with Roasted Garlic Purée and Black Olive—Meat Stock Reduction

Robust big-eye tuna is paired with the strong, salty flavors of anchovy, and heady, pungent roasted garlic. There is no more soul-satisfying plate of food in my entire repertoire. A full-flavored black olive sauce further envelops the tuna in wonderful, sweet earthiness. Even the most ardent meat lovers can find carnivorous satisfaction in this preparation.

Serves 4

1 12-ounce (5-inch-long) piece of big-eye tuna loin

8 salted anchovy fillets, rinsed

45 blanched thin haricots verts

Salt and pepper

4 tablespoons chopped fresh herbs (such as fresh chives and parsley)

2 tablespoons grapeseed oil

2 teaspoons butter

¼ cup finely chopped oil-cured French black olives

½ cup Beef Stock Reduction (see Appendices)

Roasted Garlic Purée (recipe follows)

Spicy Carrot Purée (recipe follows)

METHOD Using a small larding needle, lard the tuna loin with the anchovies and about 5 to 7 of the haricots verts. Season the loin with salt and pepper and roll in the chopped herbs. Sear all sides of the tuna loin in a very hot sauté pan in the grapeseed oil. Cut tuna into 8 slices and season to taste with salt and pepper.

Sauté the remaining haricots verts with the butter and season to taste with salt and pepper.

Place the olives in a small saucepan with the Beef Stock Reduction. Simmer over medium heat for 2 minutes.

Warm the Roasted Garlic Purée and Spicy Carrot Purée in separate saucepans just prior to serving.

ASSEMBLY Place a large spoonful of the Roasted Garlic Purée in the center of each plate. Arrange some of the haricots verts on the purée and top with 2 slices of the tuna. Spoon the Spicy Carrot Purée and Beef Stock Reduction around the plate.

Roasted Garlic Purée

Yield: about ¾ cup

4 bulbs garlic, tops removed

3 cups milk

½ cup olive oil

Salt and pepper

METHOD Place the garlic in a small saucepan, cover with the milk, and simmer for 10 minutes. Drain the milk, place the garlic bulbs bottom side down in an ovenproof pan, add the olive oil, and cover. Bake at 350 degrees for 1 to 1½ hours, or until the bulbs are soft. Once cool, squeeze the soft garlic out of the skins and place in a blender with the olive oil it baked in. Purée until smooth and season to taste with salt and pepper. If you prefer a thinner purée, you may adjust the consistency with Chicken Stock (see page 228) or water.

Spicy Carrot Purée

Yield: about ¾ cup

¾ cup chopped carrots

¼ cup Spicy Vinegar (see Appendices)

2 tablespoons butter

Salt and pepper

METHOD Place all of the ingredients in a small saucepan and cover with water. Simmer over medium heat for 30 minutes, or until the carrots are extremely tender. Purée until smooth and season to taste with salt and pepper.

Recommended Substitutions

Halibut, lobster, scallops, shrimp, red snapper

Wine Notes

Many bigger red wines can succeed here, but we find that the unique style of Tuscan Sangiovese known as Brunello di Montalcino can be exciting if the winemaker emphasizes fruit over tannins. Ciacci is a modern Brunello producer that makes a dark, almost brooding Brunello without sacrificing finesse. The meatlike tuna is buffeted by many intense flavors (olive, garlic, anchovy), suggesting a serious and even somewhat astringent wine of this magnitude.

This pair of varieties would almost never be seen together, but their peppery meatiness and earthy zestiness are useful characteristics with cured meats and amply seasoned vegetable flavors. Syrah is best in the Northern Rhône and increasingly in California and Washington State; Barbera's long undistinguished history in Piedmont and California has been transformed in recent vintages in both regions. These grapes have a "love it or hate it" character—assertive, boldly flavored, and sometimes oaky and/or tannic. ❧ We find both varieties thrilling for richer-textured fish, yet not all of the recipes in this chapter involve fleshy fish; it is the accompanying mushroom, meat, and stock flavors that balance these wines of structure and spice. Both grapes provide an aromatic enticement and smoky accents to these preparations.

Diver Scallops with Wild Mushroom Ragout in Swiss Chard, Butternut Squash Sauce, and Red Wine–Beef Stock Reduction

Scallops and mushrooms are an almost perfect combination. The sweet smoothness of the scallop almost begs to be paired with something intense and ultra-earthy like wild mushrooms. Here, a silky butternut squash sauce is also added to lend a sensual, textured note. An intense Red Wine–Beef Stock Reduction thoroughly grounds all of the flavors and adds an exquisite richness. Strands of sage and snow pea sprouts provide a refreshing whimsy. This preparation works well as either an appetizer or an entrée.

Serves 4

2 tablespoons chopped shallots

1 tablespoon butter

2 cups roasted cremini mushrooms, coarsely chopped (see Appendices)

2 tablespoons chopped fresh chives

Salt and pepper

4 large Swiss chard leaves

4 teaspoons Sage Oil (recipe follows)

1/2 cup cooked butternut squash

1/2 cup water

1/4 cup Red Wine Reduction (see Appendices)

3/4 cup Beef Stock Reduction (see Appendices)

4 large diver scallops

1 tablespoon grapeseed oil

4 teaspoons sage chiffonade

1 cup long-cut snow pea sprouts

METHOD In a medium sauté pan, sweat the chopped shallots in the butter until translucent. Add the cremini mushrooms to the pan and cook for 2 to 3 minutes. Add the chives and season to taste with salt and pepper.

Blanch the Swiss chard leaves in boiling salted water for 30 seconds and shock in ice water. Drain the water and carefully lay each leaf flat. Remove the thick inner stem from the leaf and blot dry with paper towels. Fill each of the Swiss chard leaves with some of the cremini mushroom mixture and carefully roll up into a tight cigar, folding in the ends as you roll. Lightly rub the outside of the Swiss chard roll with some of the Sage Oil, place on a small sheet pan, and heat in the oven at 400 degrees for 5 minutes. Remove from the pan and slice in half.

Purée the cooked butternut squash with the water, pass through a fine-mesh sieve, and season to taste with salt and pepper. Warm the butternut squash sauce in a small saucepan over medium heat.

Place the Red Wine Reduction and the Beef Stock Reduction in a small saucepan and warm over medium heat.

Season both sides of the scallops with salt and pepper and place in a very hot sauté pan with the grapeseed oil. Cook on each side for 1 to 2 minutes, or until slightly golden brown (the scallops should be just underdone).

ASSEMBLY Place 2 of the Swiss chard halves side by side in the center of each plate. Spoon the butternut squash sauce on top of the Swiss chard rolls and lay a scallop on top of the squash. Spoon the Red Wine–Beef Stock Reduction and the Sage Oil around the plate. Sprinkle the fresh sage around the Swiss chard rolls and arrange the snow pea sprouts standing upright around the scallop.

Sage Oil

Yield: about 1/2 cup

1/2 cup fresh sage leaves
1/2 cup grapeseed oil

METHOD Blanch the sage leaves in boiling salted water for 30 seconds and shock in ice water. Drain and squeeze out all of the excess liquid. Purée the sage leaves with the grapeseed oil for 4 minutes, or until smooth. Refrigerate overnight in a closed container and strain through a fine-mesh sieve. Refrigerate for another day, decant, and store in the refrigerator until needed. (The oil will keep for up to 2 weeks in the refrigerator.)

Recommended Substitutions

Catfish, halibut, lobster, shrimp, tuna

Wine Notes

The meat-imbued sweet flavors of scallops, chard, and squash are appropriate for a ripe, round red in the Rhône "range." Australian Shirazes like Penfolds "Magill Estate Shiraz" or Pikes Shiraz from Clare Valley in South Australia can be more ripe and supple than most Rhône or American Syrahs. Or try Cinsaut, typically a blending grape in the southern Rhône, with its ripe, plush character. Cline of California's Contra Costa County makes a small quantity of this warm but not too tannic wine, with a perfect illusion of sweetness for this flavor grouping and the surprising ability to not upstage the scallop that stars in this dish.

Crayfish Lasagne with Duck Rillette, Pickled Okra, and Gumbo Sauce

This flavorful dish is fun to prepare for special dinner parties.
It is merely a variation on a New Orleans gumbo with the addition of a pasta element.
If the idea of layering the lasagne noodles with the duck and the crayfish
seems too daunting, using a fettucine or capellini and tossing the pasta with the other ingredients
may make this preparation more appealing. The pickled okra and the spicy gumbo
offer very complex flavors and textures to go with the rich crayfish, duck, and chewy, neutral pasta.
No wonder this combination has been such a sensation in the history of Louisiana cooking.

Serves 4

Duck Confit (see Appendices)
36 tiny leeks or ramps
3 tablespoons butter
Salt and pepper
1 cup Pickling Juice (see Appendices)
12 fresh okra
72 large fresh crayfish, cooked and cleaned
Herb Pasta (recipe follows)
Gumbo Sauce (recipe follows)

METHOD Remove the duck confit from the fat and shred into small pieces. Place in a small saucepan and warm over medium heat.

Place the tiny leeks or ramps in a large sauté pan with 1 tablespoon of the butter and a little water. Slowly cook over low heat for 15 to 20 minutes, or until tender. Remove from the cooking liquid and season to taste with salt and pepper.

Bring the Pickling Juice to a boil in a medium saucepan and add the okra. Reduce heat and simmer for 3 minutes, then remove from the heat and cool in the Pickling Juice. Store the okra in the Pickling Juice and cut into small pieces on the bias just before using.

In a large pan, quickly sauté the crayfish with 2 tablespoons of the butter and season to taste with salt and pepper.

ASSEMBLY Lay 1 piece of pasta in the center of each plate. Arrange 6 crayfish on the pasta and top with a layer of Duck Confit and a layer of tiny leeks. Spoon some of the Gumbo Sauce over the leeks and top with another piece of pasta. Continue until you have 3 layers of crayfish, ending with a final layer of pasta. Arrange some of the pickled okra around the plate and spoon the remaining Gumbo Sauce around the okra.

Herb Pasta

Yield: ³/₄ pound

2 cups extra-fine semolina flour
3 eggs
1 cup fresh chervil leaves
1 teaspoon butter
Salt and pepper

METHOD Place the semolina flour and eggs in a mixing bowl. Using the dough hook, blend on low for 3 minutes, or until it comes together. Form into a ball, cover with plastic wrap, and refrigerate for 30 to 60 minutes before using.

Roll out the pasta using a pasta machine or by hand on a floured surface. Sprinkle the chervil along half the length of the pasta and fold over the remaining pasta. Run the dough through the pasta machine once more, or roll it by hand until thin to seal the chervil in the pasta. Using a pizza cutter, cut the pasta into sixteen 2-inch squares.

Cook the pasta in boiling salted water for 3 minutes, or until al dente. Toss with the butter and season to taste with salt and pepper.

Gumbo Sauce

Yield: about 1¹/₂ cups

1 jalapeño, chopped
¹/₄ cup chopped yellow peppers
¹/₄ cup chopped carrots
¹/₄ cup chopped Spanish onions
¹/₂ cup diced celery
¹/₄ cup grapeseed oil
2 tablespoons flour
3 cups Chicken Stock (see Appendices)
Salt and pepper

METHOD In a medium saucepan, caramelize the vegetables in the grapeseed oil over medium-high heat. Add the flour and stir with a wooden spoon for 15 minutes, or until the roux is a deep golden brown. Slowly whisk in the Chicken Stock and continue to cook for 20 to 30 minutes, or until the sauce coats the back of a spoon. Strain through a fine-mesh sieve and season to taste with salt and pepper.

Recommended Substitutions

Lobster, salmon, shrimp, swordfish, tuna

Wine Notes

A zesty Barbera can give great fruit in its youth without the tannins of Nebbiolo-based Piedmont wines. Giacomo Conterno's Barbera d'Alba offers beautiful rose and black cherry notes and does not overwhelm with tannin, and its spicy flavors are appropriate for a New Orleans–inspired dish. Crayfish and duck have a similar sweetness that works with the fruity character of a young, fresh Barbera.

Golden Spot Tile Fish with Blood Sausage, Asparagus, Asparagus Sauce, and Red Wine Reduction

Tile fish has a medium-firm flesh and a full enough taste to hold up well against stronger flavors, like spices or meat juices. Here, it sits on a piece of luscious but intense blood sausage and crisp, clean asparagus spears. Further enhancing the asparagus flavor is a sauce made from the tips. Red Wine Reduction adds a refined acid to all of the flavors. For something more substantial this preparation can be fortified with a mound of noodles.

Serves 4

1 1/2 cups blanched asparagus tips

2 tablespoons ice water

1/4 cup olive oil

Salt and pepper

3 cups thin stalks asparagus

1 tablespoon plus 1 teaspoon butter

1 tablespoon chopped shallots

4 1/4-inch slices blood sausage

1/4 cup Red Wine Reduction
(see Appendices)

4 2 1/2-ounce pieces golden spot tile fish, skin removed

2 tablespoons grapeseed oil

METHOD Purée the asparagus tips in a blender with the ice water and olive oil. Pass through a fine-mesh sieve and season to taste with salt and pepper. Gently warm in a small saucepan just prior to use.

Cut the whole asparagus into 3-inch-long pieces, with tips. Blanch in boiling salted water and shock in ice water. Coarsely chop half of the blanched asparagus. Heat the asparagus pieces in a sauté pan with 1 tablespoon of the butter. Season to taste with salt and pepper and remove the asparagus from the pan. Add the 1 teaspoon butter to the pan and sweat the shallots. Add the chopped asparagus and cook for 2 to 3 minutes, or until hot. Season to taste with salt and pepper.

Place the blood sausage on a sheet pan and bake at 400 degrees for 3 to 5 minutes, or until hot.

Warm the Red Wine Reduction in a small saucepan.

Season both sides of the golden spot tile fish with salt and pepper and quickly sauté in a very hot pan with the grapeseed oil for 2 minutes on each side.

ASSEMBLY Place a piece of the blood sausage in the center of each plate and top with a piece of the fish. Spoon some of the chopped asparagus-shallot mixture on top of the fish. Spoon some of the Red Wine Reduction and the asparagus sauce around the plate and arrange the asparagus spears around the blood sausage.

Recommended Substitutions

Catfish, halibut, salmon, scallops, trout, whitefish

Wine Notes

Long a devotee of traditional Italian varieties, Sonoma's Sebastiani Vineyards has made delicious Barbera for generations. It has a less zesty style, perhaps, than a Piedmont Barbera, yet is flavorful and peppery. For this red wine–friendly tile fish preparation, the Barbera merges beautifully with sweet blood sausage and does not overwhelm the asparagus elements.

Opakapaka with Bleeding Heart Radish, Morel Mushrooms, Morel Juices, and Turnip Sauce

Opakapaka, or crimson snapper, is a bottom-feeding fish from the Hawaiian Islands. It has a medium-firm flesh and a flavor that, although mild, can stand up to these beautifully rustic morels and to the intricate turnip theme that is woven throughout the dish. Julienned bleeding heart radish makes an exquisitely astringent bed for the fish and further augments the turnip flavor. Tiny roasted turnips stuffed with a morel and black trumpet mushroom duxelle provide a playful sweetness. A delicate turnip purée lends a wonderful butteriness, while wisps of chive and a drizzle of herb oil round out the dish with just the right amount of bite.

Serves 4

1/4 cup chopped carrots

1/4 cup chopped celery

1/4 cup chopped Spanish onions

2 tablespoons grapeseed oil

1 small bleeding heart radish

Salt and pepper

6 cups morel mushrooms

3 sprigs thyme

2 cloves garlic

2 tablespoons olive oil

1 cup water

1 cup chopped turnips

1 tablespoon plus 2 teaspoons butter

8 baby turnips, peeled

1/4 cup minced peeled celery root

1/4 cup roasted black trumpet mushrooms, minced (see Appendices)

1 teaspoon chopped fresh parsley

4 3-ounce portions opakapaka

4 teaspoons Herb Oil (see Appendices)

4 teaspoons long-cut fresh chives

METHOD Caramelize the chopped carrots, celery, and onions in a small saucepan with 1 tablespoon of the grapeseed oil. Add the bleeding heart radish and cover with water. Cover and simmer for 45 minutes, or until tender. Remove the radish from the liquid, peel, julienne, and season to taste with salt and pepper.

Soak the morel mushrooms in cold water for 5 minutes to remove the grit. Gently rinse and place in an ovenproof pan with the thyme, garlic, olive oil, water, and salt and pepper. Cover and roast in the oven at 375 degrees for 45 minutes, or until cooked.

Remove the mushrooms from the pan and strain the cooking juices. Set the mushrooms and cooking juices aside separately. Purée 1/2 cup of the morel mushrooms with 1/3 cup of the reserved cooking juices and season to taste with salt and pepper. Place the remaining mushroom juice in a small saucepan and simmer for 15 minutes, or until reduced by half.

Place the chopped turnips in a small saucepan with the 1 tablespoon of butter, cover with water, and simmer for 4 to 6 minutes, or until tender. Drain most of the liquid. Purée the turnips with just enough of the cooking liquid to purée smoothly. Season to taste with salt and pepper.

Cook the baby turnips in boiling salted water for 4 to 5 minutes, or until tender. Carefully remove the turnip tops and hollow out the bottoms using a small melon baller. Quickly sauté the celery root and black trumpet mushrooms in a small pan with the 2 teaspoons butter. Season to taste with salt and pepper and fold in the chopped parsley. Fill each of the baby turnips with some of the celery root mixture and place the top back on. Heat the baby turnips in the oven at 350 degrees for 3 to 5 minutes, or until hot.

Season both sides of the opakapaka with salt and pepper. Quickly sauté in a very hot pan with the remaining 1 tablespoon of grapeseed oil for 1 to 2 minutes on each side.

ASSEMBLY Arrange some of the julienned bleeding heart radish in the center of each plate. Place a piece of the opakapaka on top of the radish. Place 2 stuffed baby turnips at separate ends of the fish. Arrange the whole morel mushrooms around the plate. Spoon the morel purée and turnip purée around the morels. Spoon some of the reduced mushroom juice on top of the fish and around the plate. Drizzle some of the Herb Oil around the plate and sprinkle with the chives.

Recommended Substitutions

Salmon, shrimp, red snapper, swordfish, tuna

Wine Notes

Mushroom-evoking Barbera in a traditional style works wonders with this hearty dish. We like the almost tarlike notes in Parusso and Prunotto wines for the morels and radishes, both earthy flavors that embellish the meaty opakapaka. These producers allow Barbera to be suave and not overbearing, and do not mask this frisky variety in new oak.

Each morning the cuisinier must start again at zero, with nothing

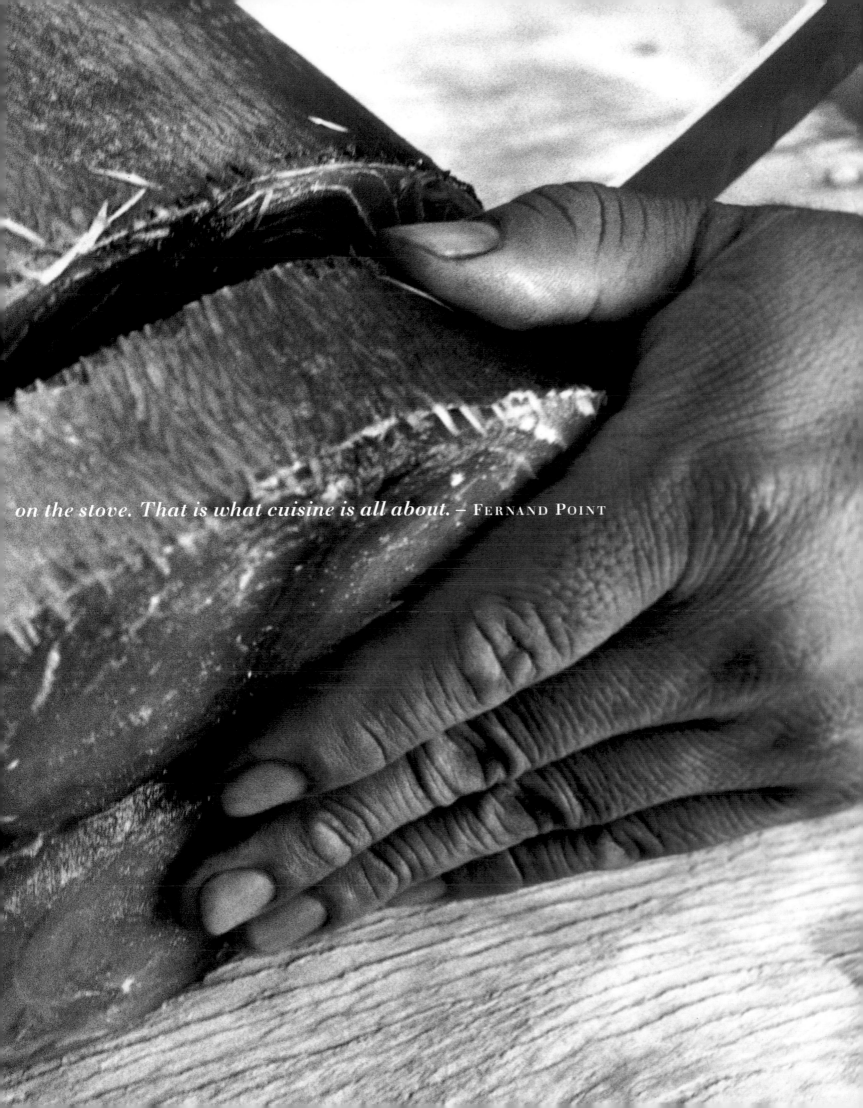

on the stove. That is what cuisine is all about. – FERNAND POINT

Ono with Eggplant Purée, Pancetta Bacon, Wilted Watercress, and Red Wine Emulsion

*Ono, also known as wahoo, is a sturdy, meaty fish that is best left medium-rare in the center.
Although it can stand up to strong flavors like pancetta and watercress, the flavors of the fish itself are
splendidly delicate. Here, it is served on a mound of sensuous eggplant purée that really helps
to show off the body of the fish, while a fruity and robust red wine emulsion adds an essential acidity.
By adding a grain or some potatoes, this dish moves from a simple appetizer to hearty entrée.*

Serves 4

1 large eggplant

Salt and pepper

Olive oil

¼ pound uncooked pancetta bacon, diced

*1 large bunch watercress, cleaned
and stems removed*

4 3-ounce pieces ono, skin removed

2 tablespoons grapeseed oil

*½ cup Red Wine Reduction
(see Appendices)*

3 tablespoons butter

METHOD Cut the eggplant in half and score with a knife. Season with salt and pepper and rub with olive oil. Place on a sheet pan, cut side up, with ¼ inch of water and bake at 375 degrees for 40 minutes, or until cooked. Remove the eggplant pulp from the skin and pass through a fine-mesh sieve (if it is not soft enough to pass through a sieve, purée in the blender with a touch of water and then sieve). Season to taste with salt and pepper.

Render the bacon in a hot sauté pan, remove, and blot on paper towels. Reserve 1 tablespoon of bacon fat. Just prior to serving, place the reserved bacon fat in a medium sauté pan, add the watercress, and quickly wilt it over medium heat for 1 to 2 minutes. Season to taste with salt and pepper.

Season both sides of the ono with salt and pepper and place in a very hot pan with the grapeseed oil. Sauté for 2 minutes on each side, or until golden brown.

Place the Red Wine Reduction in a medium saucepan and warm over medium heat. Whisk in the butter and season to taste with salt and pepper. Froth with a hand-held blender just prior to use.

ASSEMBLY Spoon some of the hot eggplant purée in the center of each plate. Place a piece of ono on top of the purée and arrange some of the wilted watercress and pancetta bacon on top of the ono. Arrange the remaining wilted watercress around the plate. Spoon the red wine emulsion around the ono.

Recommended Substitutions

Lobster, salmon, snapper, swordfish, tuna

Wine Notes

Good Syrah is grown throughout the Rhône Valley, but its purest varietal expression is restricted to the northern districts of Côte Rôtie, Hermitage, and Saint-Joseph. These first two are usually powerful, cellar-worthy reds—spicy, meaty, often tannic wines. Prettier and less concentrated Syrah in Saint-Joseph can still be smoky and wild violet–tinged, ideal aromatic accompaniments for the pancetta and eggplant flavors. The firm texture of ono works well with these additions and with the texture of the fine Saint-Joseph of Andre Perret, Raymond Trollat, or J. L. Chave.

Wild Loup de Mer with Collard Greens, Rice Beans, Lamb Tongue, Red Wine Reduction, and Mushroom Sauce

Wild loup de mer is a finely textured, delicately flavored fish. Here, it is paired with collard greens, which have just enough acid to cut into the fish without totally overpowering it. The lamb tongue and rice beans add a rich heartiness while the red wine essence and mushroom sauce bring forth a heady earthiness. I also like to fold finely diced aromatic vegetables into the beans at the last moment, a simple way to add a significant textural component. I love the way all of these flavors blend seamlessly in the mouth.

Serves 4

3 Pickled Lamb Tongues (see Appendices)

3 tablespoons grapeseed oil

1/2 cup chopped carrots

1/2 cup chopped celery

1 cup chopped Spanish onions

3/4 cup firmly packed brown sugar

1/4 cup chopped uncooked bacon

2 cups chopped collard greens

2 tablespoons rice wine vinegar

1 tablespoon granulated sugar

1/2 cup water

Salt and pepper

1 cup cooked rice beans

1/4 cup small-diced blanched carrots

1/4 cup small-diced blanched celery

2 tablespoons Basil Oil (see Appendices)

1 tablespoon chopped fresh herbs (such as fresh chives and parsley)

1/2 cup roasted shiitake mushrooms, juices reserved (see Appendices)

3 tablespoons Red Wine Reduction (see Appendices)

4 2 1/2-ounce pieces wild loup de mer, with skin

1/4 teaspoon sea salt

METHOD In a medium saucepan, sear the lamb tongues with 1 tablespoon of the grapeseed oil. Remove the tongues and caramelize the chopped carrots, celery, and onions in the same pan. Add the brown sugar and cook for 5 minutes. Return the lamb tongues to the pan and cover two-thirds of the way with water. Simmer, covered, for 2 to 3 hours, or until tender, adding additional water when necessary. Remove the lamb tongues and peel off the outer skin. Slice each tongue into 4 slices.

Render the bacon in a medium sauté pan. Add the collard greens to the bacon and the fat and continue to cook over medium heat for 3 minutes. Add the rice wine vinegar, sugar, and water and continue to cook for 15 minutes, or until tender. Season to taste with salt and pepper.

Place the cooked rice beans, diced carrots, diced celery, and Basil Oil in a small saucepan and warm over medium heat. Season to taste with salt and pepper and fold in the chopped herbs.

Purée the shiitake mushrooms and their juices until smooth (add some water if you don't have enough mushroom juices). Place in a small saucepan and warm over medium heat. Season to taste with salt and pepper.

Place the Red Wine Reduction in a small saucepan and warm over medium heat.

Season both sides of the fish with salt and pepper and score the skin side of the fish with a razor blade. Quickly sauté in a hot pan with the remaining 2 tablespoons of grapeseed oil for 1 to 2 minutes on each side.

ASSEMBLY Place some of the collard greens in the center of each plate and top with 3 slices of the lamb tongue. Place a piece of the fish on top of the tongue. Spoon some of the rice beans around the plate, along with some of the shiitake mushroom sauce and Red Wine Reduction. Sprinkle the sea salt on top of the fish.

Recommended Substitutions

Flounder, halibut, salmon, trout, whitefish

Wine Notes

One of the most impressive Syrah-based wines we know of is made by Bob Lindquist at Qupe in California's Santa Barbara County. Each vintage of this wine has improved upon its predecessor. The "Bien Nacido Reserve" Syrah 1994 has the classic smokiness and meatiness associated with Syrah, yet does not seem clumsy in its youth. Precise varietal expression makes it accommodating for this fish recipe, which features the sweet lamb tongue meat in a red wine format. Loup de mer is fleshy enough for this spicy but not too tannic Syrah.

APPENDICES

A GUIDE TO SEASONAL SEAFOOD

OILS

REDUCTIONS AND STOCKS

OTHER BASIC RECIPES

COOKING TERMS, EQUIPMENT, INGREDIENTS,
AND TECHNIQUES

WINE TERMS

SOURCES

PHOTO INDEX

A Guide to Seasonal Seafood

	Flavor	Texture	Cooking Methods	Seasons
Salmon and Trout				
White Salmon	D	Med.	Raw, Sear, Smoke, Broil, Steam, Sauté, Poach, Roast, Grill	Early Spring–late Summer, sporadic
Tasmanian Salmon	D	Med.	Raw, Sear, Smoke, Broil, Steam, Sauté, Poach, Roast, Grill	Late Summer–early Spring
Salmon	D	Med.	Raw, Sear, Smoke, Broil, Steam, Sauté, Poach, Roast, Grill	All year
Golden Trout	D	T	Broil, Sauté, Grill	All year
Rainbow Trout	D	T	Broil, Sauté, Grill	Spring and Summer
Whitefish	Mod.	T	Broil, Steam, Sauté, Grill	All year
Arctic Char	Mod.	T	Broil, Sauté, Grill	All year
Herring Family				
Shad Roe	R	F	Sauté	Spring–early Summer
Smelts	Mod.	Med.	Smoke, Broil, Sauté	Winter
Cod Family				
Cod	Mod.	F	Broil, Steam, Sauté, Poach, Grill	All year
Haddock	Mod.	Med.	Broil, Steam, Grill	All year
Perch-like Fish				
Amberjack	R	Med.	Broil, Sauté, Grill	All year, heavy in Summer
Daurade	Mod.	Med.	Steam, Sauté, Grill	All year
Wreck Bass	R	F	Sauté, Grill	All year, sporadic
Wild Stripe Bass	R	F	Broil, Steam, Sauté, Grill	Late Spring, Summer
Pink Porgy	R	Med.	Broil, Sauté	All year
Sea Bass	Mod.	Med.	Steam, Sauté, Grill	All year
Barracuda	R	F	Sauté, Grill	All year
Red Mullet	Mod.	T	Steam, Sauté, Roast	All year
Mahimahi	R	F	Broil, Sauté, Grill	Spring–early Fall
Wild Loup de Mer	Mod.	T	Broil, Sauté, Grill	All year, heavy during Fall
African Pompano	R	F	Broil, Sauté, Grill	Spring and Summer
Mackerel, Tuna, & Swordfish				
Tuna	Mod.	F	Raw, Sear, Broil, Sauté, Grill	All year
Albacore Tuna	Mod.	F	Raw, Sear, Broil, Sauté, Grill	All year
Mackerel	R	Med.	Sauté, Poach, Grill	Spring–early Fall
Swordfish	R	F	Sauté, Poach, Roast, Grill	All year
Hamachi	Mod.	T	Raw, Sear, Sauté, Grill	All year
Thin Bodied Fish				
Black Pomfret	R	F	Sear, Sauté, Grill	Winter, Spring, Fall
John Dory	R	F	Steam, Sauté, Grill	Winter, Spring, Fall
Flat Fish				
Dover Sole	Mod.	Med.	Steam, Sauté	Winter, Spring, late Fall
Turbot	Mod.	Med.	Raw, Broil, Sauté	All year
Flounder	Mod.	Med.	Broil, Sauté	All year
Fluke	Mod.	Med.	Raw, Steam, Sauté, Grill	Late Spring–early Fall
Halibut	Mod.	F	Raw, Smoke, Steam, Sauté, Poach, Grill	Winter, Spring, Fall
Fish without True Bones				
Skate Wing	R	Med.	Steam, Sauté	All year
Mako Shark	R	F	Broil, Sauté, Grill	Late Spring–early Fall
Sturgeon	R	F	Smoke, Sauté	Summer, Fall

Flavor: D = Delicate, Mod. = Moderate, R = Robust; Texture: F = Firm, Med. = Medium, T = Tender

	Flavor	Texture	Cooking Methods	Seasons
Crustaceans				
Peekytoe Crab	D	T	Poach	All year
Gooseneck Barnacles	R	F	Sauté, Poach	All year
Langoustine	D	Med.	Broil, Sauté, Poach	All year, except May and June
Spiny Lobster	Mod.	F	Raw, Broil, Sauté, Poach, Grill	All year, except May, June, and July
Thai Lobster	Mod.	F	Sauté, Poach	All year
Baby Maine Shrimp	D	T	Sauté, Poach, Grill	Fall—early Spring
Dungeness Crab	Mod.	Med.	Poach	Spring, Summer and early Fall
Soft Shell Crab	Mod.	Med.	Sauté	Late Spring, early Fall
Gulf Shrimp	D	Med.	Sauté, Poach, Grill	Late Spring, Fall
Crayfish	D	Med.	Sauté, Poach	All year
Lobster	D	Med.	Raw, Sauté, Poach, Grill	All year
Mollusks/Cephalopods				
Baby Octopus	Mod.	F	Sauté, Poach, Grill	All year
Baby Calamari	Mod.	F	Sauté, Grill	All year
Mollusks/Single Shells				
Periwinkles	Mod.	Med.	Steam, Sauté	All year
Baby Abalone	R	F	Sauté, Poach, Grill	All year
Conch	R	F	Sauté, Poach, Grill	All year
Mollusks/Bivalves				
Diver Scallops	D	Med.	Raw, Sear, Smoke, Broil, Sauté, Grill	Mid-October—mid-April
Cherrystone Clams	Mod.	Med.	Steam	All year
Countneck Clams	Mod.	Med.	Steam	All year
Geoduck Clams	Mod.	F	Poach	Sporadic all year
Pacific Coast Oysters	D	F	Raw, Smoke	Fall, Winter, mid-Spring
Razor Clams	R	F	Steam, Roast	Fall, Winter, sporadic Spring—Summer
Belon Oysters	Mod.	Med.	Raw, Smoke, Sauté	Fall, Winter, mid-Spring
Hawaiian Fish				
Hebi	Mod.	Med.	Raw, Sear, Sauté, Grill	Summer, mid-Fall
Gindai	D	T	Raw, Broil, Steam, Sauté, Grill	Late Fall, Winter, Spring
Nairagi	M	F	Raw, Sear, Broil, Sauté, Grill	Winter, Spring, late Fall
Hawaiian Blue Prawn	D	F	Sauté, Grill	All year sporadic
Opah	Mod.	Med.	Raw, Sear, Broil, Sauté, Grill	Mid-Spring, Summer, Fall
Opakapaka	D	Med.	Raw, Broil, Sauté, Grill	Fall, Winter
Ono	D	Med.	Raw, Broil, Sauté, Grill	Late Winter, Spring, Summer
Onaga	D	Med.	Raw, Broil, Sauté, Grill	Fall, Winter, Spring
Misc. Fish				
Monkfish	R	Med.	Sauté, Roast, Grill	Late Spring, Summer, mid-Fall
Frog Legs	R	F	Sauté	All year
Caviar	R	T	Raw	All year
Sea Urchin	R	T	Raw, Roast	Winter, Spring, early Summer, late Fall
Catfish	D	Med.	Smoke, Broil, Sauté, Grill	All year
Eel	R	F	Broil, Sauté, Grill	Late Summer, mid-Fall, and April
Moi	D	Med.	Broil, Sauté, Roast, Grill	All year
Escolar	R	F	Broil, Steam, Sauté, Grill	All year sporadic, heavy Summer—Fall
Walleye Pike	R	Med.	Steam, Sauté, Grill	Fall, early Winter
Golden Spot Tile Fish	R	F	Steam, Sauté, Grill	All year sporadic

Oils

Basil Oil

Yield: about 1/2 cup

1 1/2 cups fresh basil
1/2 cup grapeseed oil
1/4 cup olive oil

METHOD Blanch the basil in boiling salted water for 15 seconds. Immediately shock in ice water and drain. Coarsely chop the basil and squeeze out the excess water. Place in a blender with the oils and purée for 3 to 4 minutes, or until bright green. Pour into a container, cover, and refrigerate for 1 day. Strain through cheesecloth, refrigerate for 1 more day, and then decant.

Fennel Oil

Yield: about 1/2 cup

1 cup fennel fronds
3/4 cup grapeseed oil
1/2 cup olive oil

METHOD Blanch the fennel fronds in boiling salted water for 15 seconds. Immediately shock in ice water and drain. Coarsely chop the fennel and squeeze out the excess water. Place in a blender with the two oils, and purée for 3 or 4 minutes, or until bright green. Pour into a container, cover, and refrigerate for 1 day. Strain through cheesecloth, refrigerate for 1 more day, and decant.

Herb Oil

Yield: about 1/2 cup

1/4 cup fresh chives
1/4 cup flat-leaf parsley
1/4 cup fresh watercress
1/2 cup grapeseed oil
1/4 cup olive oil

METHOD Blanch the herbs in boiling salted water for 15 seconds. Immediately shock in ice water and drain. Coarsely chop the herbs and squeeze out the excess water. Place in a blender with the oils and purée for 3 to 4 minutes, or until bright green. Pour into a container, cover, and refrigerate for 1 day. Strain through cheesecloth, refrigerate for 1 more day, and decant.

Lemon Balm Oil

Yield: about 1/2 cup

1 cup fresh lemon balm leaves
1/2 cup grapeseed oil

METHOD Blanch the lemon balm in boiling salted water and shock in ice water. Drain and squeeze out the excess liquid. Coarsely chop the lemon balm and purée in a blender with the grapeseed oil for 3 to 5 minutes, or until bright green. Pour into a container, cover, and refrigerate for 1 day. Strain through a fine-mesh sieve, refrigerate for 1 more day, and decant. The oil will keep for up to 2 weeks in the refrigerator.

Rosemary Oil

Yield: about 1/2 cup

5 large sprigs rosemary,
leaves removed from the stem
1 cup flat-leaf parsley
1/2 cup olive oil

METHOD Blanch the rosemary leaves and parsley in boiling salted water, shock in ice water, drain, and squeeze out the excess liquid. Place in a blender with the olive oil and purée for 3 to 4 minutes. Pour into a container and refrigerate overnight. Strain through a fine-mesh sieve, refrigerate 1 more day, and decant.

Reductions and Stocks

Beef Stock

Yield: about 1 1/2 quarts

10 pounds beef bones
2 carrots, coarsely chopped
2 stalks celery, coarsely chopped
1 yellow onion, coarsely chopped
1 leek, cleaned and coarsely chopped
1 bulb garlic, cut in half
2 tablespoons grapeseed oil
1/2 cup tomato concassée
4 cups red wine

METHOD Place the bones in a roasting pan and roast at 450 degrees for 2 hours, or until golden brown. In a large stockpot, caramelize the carrots, celery, onion, leek, and garlic in the grapeseed oil. Add the tomato concassée and cook for 5 minutes. Deglaze with the red wine and reduce until most of the wine has been cooked out. Add the browned bones and cover with cold water. Bring to a boil, reduce the heat, and simmer over medium heat for 8 hours, skimming away the impurities that rise to the surface. Strain through a fine-mesh sieve.

Beef Stock Reduction

Yield: about 1 1/4 cups

1 cup chopped Spanish onion
1/2 cup chopped carrot
1/2 cup chopped celery
1/2 cup chopped leeks
1 tablespoon grapeseed oil
1/2 cup dry red wine (such as Burgundy)
2 quarts Beef Stock (see above)

METHOD Caramelize the vegetables in a medium saucepan with the grapeseed oil. Deglaze with the red wine and continue cooking for 2 minutes, or until most of the red wine has been absorbed. Add the Beef Stock and simmer over medium heat, skimming away the impurities that rise to the surface. Continue to simmer for 1 hour. Strain through a fine-mesh sieve. Return to the saucepan and simmer for 1 hour, or until you have about 1 1/4 cups of reduction.

Chicken Stock

Yield: about 6 cups

10 pounds chicken bones
2 Spanish onions, coarsely chopped
2 carrots, coarsely chopped
4 stalks celery, coarsely chopped
1 bulb garlic, cut in half
1 bulb celery root, peeled and chopped
1 tablespoon whole black peppercorns

METHOD Place all of the ingredients in a large stockpot. Cover with cold water (about 2 gallons). Bring to a boil, then reduce heat and simmer over medium heat for 4 hours, skimming away impurities that rise to the surface. Strain and reduce over medium heat for 45 minutes, or until reduced to about 6 cups.

Fish Stock

Yield: about 1½ quarts

3 pounds fish bones
1 cup chopped celery
1 cup chopped carrots
1 cup chopped Spanish onion
½ cup chopped leeks
½ cup dry white wine (such as Chardonnay)
1 teaspoon white peppercorns

METHOD Place all of the ingredients in a medium saucepan and cover with cold water. Bring to a boil and simmer for 40 minutes. Strain through a fine-mesh sieve and reduce to about 1½ quarts.

Mushroom Stock

Yield: 1½ cups

¼ cup chopped Spanish onions
2 cloves garlic
1½ pounds assorted wild mushrooms (such as shiitake, portobello, or cremini)
3 cups water

METHOD Place all of the ingredients in a medium saucepan. Simmer over medium heat for 40 minutes and strain through a fine-mesh sieve. Return the liquid to the saucepan and continue to simmer for 20 minutes, or until you have about 1½ cups of stock.

Red Wine Reduction

Yield: ½ cup

1 Spanish onion, coarsely chopped
1 carrot, coarsely chopped
1 stalk celery, coarsely chopped
1 Granny Smith apple, coarsely chopped
2 cloves garlic
2 tablespoons grapeseed oil
1 750-mL bottle Burgundy
2 cups Port
1 cup Chicken Stock (see page 228)

METHOD In a medium saucepan, caramelize the onion, carrot, celery, apple, and garlic in the grapeseed oil. Add the Burgundy and the Port and simmer over medium heat for 2 hours. Strain and place in a small saucepan with the Chicken Stock. Continue to simmer over medium heat for 1 hour, or until reduced to ½ cup.

Shellfish Stock

Yield: about 2 quarts

5 pounds fresh lobster shells
½ cup chopped carrots
½ cup chopped onions
½ cup chopped celery
½ cup chopped leeks
2 tablespoons grapeseed oil
3 tablespoons tomato paste
1 cup Burgundy

METHOD Roast the lobster shells at 400 degrees for 40 minutes. Caramelize all of the vegetables in the grapeseed oil over medium-high heat in a large, deep pan. Add the tomato paste and continue cooking for 2 to 3 minutes. Deglaze with the Burgundy and continue cooking for 3 minutes, or until most of the Burgundy has been absorbed. Add the lobster shells and cover with cold water. Simmer over medium heat for 3 hours. Strain through a fine-mesh sieve and return to the saucepan. Continue to reduce until the desired concentration of flavor is reached.

Other Basic Recipes

Brandade

Yield: about 1⅓ cups

⅔ cup salt cod
⅔ cup peeled and diced boiled potato
3 tablespoons Roasted Garlic Purée (see page 96)
2½ tablespoons olive oil
2½ tablespoons heavy cream
1 tablespoon chopped fresh parsley
Salt and pepper

METHOD Soak the salt cod in enough cold water to cover the fish and refrigerate. Repeat this process 3 or 4 times over a 48-hour period until the salty flavor is gone.

Place the salt cod in a saucepan and cover with water. Simmer for 10 to 20 minutes, or until the fish is tender. Do not let the fish boil or it will become tough. While it is still warm, place the cod in an electric mixer fitted with a paddle attachment and slowly beat it at medium speed to fluff. After about 1 minute, add the warm potato bit by

bit, until it is fully incorporated. Beat in the Roasted Garlic Purée. With the mixer still at medium speed, slowly drizzle in the olive oil and then the cream. Fold in the parsley and season to taste with salt and pepper.

Duck Confit

Yield: about 2 cups

6 duck thighs, barely trimmed, with bones
6 tablespoons kosher salt
1 tablespoon sugar
1 tablespoon coarsely ground black pepper
1 tablespoon sliced garlic
2 teaspoons chopped ginger
6 cups rendered duck fat

METHOD Rub the duck thighs with kosher salt, sugar, black pepper, garlic, and ginger. Pack tightly in a small container and cover with plastic wrap. Allow to marinate for 72 hours in the refrigerator, turning them over every 12 hours. When ready to cook, thoroughly rinse the marinade off the duck and place in a heavy-bottomed pot. Cover the thighs with duck fat and bake, covered with aluminum foil, at 180 degrees for about 4 hours, or until the meat is quite soft but still has some body left to it. Cool and store in the fat until ready to use.

Fennel Juice

Yield: about 2 cups

3 cups fresh fennel juice (about 4 to 5 bulbs of fennel)

METHOD Place the fennel juice in a small saucepan and simmer over medium heat for 15 to 20 minutes. Strain through a fine-mesh sieve and then through cheesecloth. Refrigerate until needed.

Olive Oil–Poached Tomatoes

Yield: about 2 cups

6 yellow or red plum tomatoes
2 cups olive oil
1 sprig rosemary

METHOD Remove the core from the tomatoes, leaving them whole. Place the tomatoes standing upright in an ovenproof dish just large enough to hold them. Add the olive oil and rosemary, and cover. Bake at

275 degrees for 3 to 4 hours, or until the skin easily comes off the tomatoes. Let the tomatoes cool, then remove the skin and seeds. Strain the olive oil and refrigerate until needed. (The oil will have a pleasant tomato aroma and can be used again.)

Pickled Lamb Tongues

Yield: about 1½ cups — *no*

3 lamb tongues
⅓ cup coarsely chopped celery
⅓ cup coarsely chopped Spanish onions
⅓ cup coarsely chopped carrots
2 cloves garlic
2 tablespoons reserved bacon fat
1 tablespoon grated ginger
12 pieces allspice, lightly pan-roasted
½ cup firmly packed brown sugar
1 cup rice wine vinegar
2 cups Chicken Stock (see page 228)
1 teaspoon salt

METHOD Soak the tongues in repeated changes of cold water for 1 day. In a medium sauté pan, sweat the celery, onion, carrots, and garlic in the bacon fat until softened. Add the tongues and brown lightly on all sides for about 15 minutes. Add the remaining ingredients, bring to a boil, and simmer for 2 to 3 hours, or until the meat is very tender. Cool in the liquid. Peel the sheath of skin away from the tongues. The tongues can be served immediately or refrigerated for up to 1 week.

Pickling Juice

Yield: 2 cups

1 cup water
½ cup rice vinegar
⅓ cup plus 2 tablespoons sugar
2 tablespoons kosher salt
1 whole clove
1 teaspoon mustard seed
1 teaspoon black peppercorns
1 teaspoon chopped ginger
½ jalapeño, seeded and chopped

METHOD Combine all of the ingredients in a small saucepan and bring to a simmer, allowing the salt and sugar to dissolve. Cool and use as needed.

Roasted Bell Peppers

Yield: about 1½ cups

4 red or yellow bell peppers
3 tablespoons olive oil

METHOD Coat the whole bell peppers with olive oil. Place on an open grill or flame and roast until black on one side, about 3 minutes. Turn, and repeat. Place the roasted peppers in a bowl, cover with plastic wrap, and let stand for 5 minutes. Peel off the skin. Seed the peppers, remove the stems, and cut the peppers to the desired size.

Roasted Mushrooms

Yield: about 2 cups

3 cups assorted wild mushrooms, cleaned (such as shiitake, cremini, black trumpet, hedgehog, portobello)
½ cup chopped Spanish onion
1 clove garlic
1 sprig thyme or rosemary
2 tablespoons olive oil
¾ cup Mushroom Stock (see page 229) or water
Salt and pepper

METHOD Place the mushrooms in an oven-proof pan and toss with the onion, garlic, thyme or rosemary, and olive oil. Add the stock or water and season to taste with salt and pepper. Cover and bake at 325 degrees for 30 to 40 minutes (some mushrooms may take more or less time), or until the mushrooms are tender. Remove from the oven and cool in the cooking juices.

Spicy Herb Sauce

Yield: about ¾ cup

1 bunch flat-leaf parsley
6 tablespoons grapeseed oil
2 tablespoons ice water
1 egg
2 teaspoons togarashi
1 tablespoon minced jalapeño
Salt and pepper

METHOD In a very hot pan, sauté the parsley for a few seconds in 1 tablespoon of the grapeseed oil. Immediately remove from

the pan and refrigerate. Coarsely chop the cooled parsley and place in a blender with the ice water and 3 tablespoons of the grapeseed oil. Blend thoroughly and strain through a fine-mesh sieve. Set aside. Place the egg in a small bowl with the togarashi and jalapeño and whisk together. Slowly whisk in the remaining grapeseed oil, creating a thick mayonnaise. Whisk in the parsley juice. Season to taste with salt and pepper and refrigerate until needed.

Spicy Peanut-Miso Sauce

Yield: about ¾ cup

1 tablespoon miso paste
2 tablespoons ground unsalted peanuts
½ cup Mushroom Stock (see page 229)
¼ cup roasted shiitake mushrooms (see this page)
1 tablespoon Spicy Vinegar (see this page)
Salt and pepper

METHOD Purée the miso, peanuts, Mushroom Stock, mushrooms, and Spicy Vinegar until smooth. Season to taste with salt and pepper. Place in a small saucepan and warm over medium heat just prior to serving.

Spicy Vinegar

Yield: about 3 cups

10 jalapeño peppers
10 red chile peppers
1 Spanish onion, julienned
2 cups sliced carrots
½ cup thyme sprigs
2 tablespoons black peppercorns
5 cloves
1 teaspoon allspice
Rice wine vinegar
½ cup olive oil

METHOD Place the jalapeño peppers, red chile peppers, onion, carrots, thyme, and spices in a jar just large enough to hold the ingredients. Cover with the rice wine vinegar and top off with the olive oil. Seal the jar and place in the refrigerator for 2 weeks before you break the seal. The vinegar can be kept for several months in the refrigerator. Use as needed.

Cooking Terms, Equipment, Ingredients, and Techniques

AMARANTH A high-protein, nutritious green leafy vegetable. The greens have a slightly sweet flavor. The seeds are used as cereal and can be ground into flour. The grains of amaranth have a highly complex flavor and texture.

BALSAMIC VINEGAR (aceto balsamico) A dark, sweet, mellow wine vinegar that is aged in a series of oak and hickory barrels. It is produced only in Modena, Italy, and is used primarily as a dressing. The older the vinegar, the sweeter and less acidic it is. Well-aged balsamic vinegars are available at gourmet food shops.

BATON (bâtonnet) A cut the size of a wooden matchstick (⅛ by ⅛ by 2 inches).

BLACK RADISH A large, round, turnip-sized radish with a thin black skin.

BLANCHING AND SHOCKING To plunge a food into boiling salted water briefly and then to immediately place into ice water to stop the cooking process. It is often used to firm the flesh or loosen the skins of fruits such as peaches or tomatoes. It is also used to heighten and set color and flavor of herbs and greens.

BRUNOISE A very fine dice, approximately ⅛ square inch.

CAUL FAT A thin, fatty membrane that lines the abdominal cavity, usually taken from pigs or sheep. Pork caul is considered superior. The caul resembles a lacy net and is used to encase various items.

CELLOPHANE NOODLES (bean threads, vermicelli) Clear noodles made from mung beans and sold in dry form. To cook, drop in boiling water for 1 minute. Available in Asian markets.

CHIFFONADE Fine strips, about 1/16 inch wide. Usually used in reference to leafy vegetables, which are rolled up and finely sliced.

CHINOIS A conical fine-mesh sieve used for straining. The mesh is so fine that a spoon or ladle must be used to press the food through it.

CRÈME FRAÎCHE A true crème fraîche is an unpasteurized 30-percent cream that has been allowed to ferment and thicken naturally. It has a nutty, faintly sour flavor. In the United States, crème fraîche is made with whipping cream and buttermilk. Do not substitute sour cream.

DAIKON A large, white Asian radish, relatively mild flavored. Excellent for adding texture and just the right amount of bite.

DEGLAZE When foods have been sautéed or roasted, the coagulated juices collect in the pan. Deglazing is the process of adding liquid to the pan and dissolving these flavorful deposits over heat.

DUXELLE A mixture of finely chopped mushrooms, shallots, and herbs.

ENNIS HAZELNUTS Organic hazelnuts from the Trufflebert Farm in Oregon.

FOIE GRAS Fatted goose or duck liver. All veins must be removed before using.

GELATIN Sheet gelatin is commonly used in Europe. In the United States you may find it at some specialty food shops. If unavailable, substitute 1 teaspoon of gelatin granules for each leaf of sheet gelatin.

HAWAIIAN GINGER (young ginger) A tamer, young, slightly more exotic-flavored ginger. It is not as harsh as regular ginger.

HOISIN A thick, sweet, brownish red sauce made with soybeans, vinegar, sesame seeds, chiles, and garlic. Used in Chinese cooking.

IRISH COBBLER POTATO A small creamy potato with a thin light brown skin and a soft, yellow interior.

ISRAELI COUSCOUS A larger grain of semolina, first manufactured in Israel and currently manufactured throughout the Middle East. It should be rinsed before and after cooking. It takes longer to cook than regular couscous.

JUICING Extracting the juice from fruits or vegetables. Electric kitchen juicers are most effective.

KELP (kombu, kónbu) A broad-leafed seaweed, commonly used in Japanese cooking for flavoring soups and sauces. Wonderful in broth-based dishes. Usually sold dried or frozen.

KIMCHI Spicy-hot, extraordinarily pungent fermented cabbage or turnips that have been pickled before being stored in tightly sealed pots or jars and buried in the ground. It is dug up and used as needed.

LARD To insert long, thin strips of fat or other ingredients into a fish or piece of meat. This is done with a larding needle.

LEMONGRASS A scented grass used as an herb in Southeast Asian cooking. Although the whole stalk may be used, usually the outer leaves are removed and only the bottom third of the stalk is used. Has a lemony, strawlike flavor.

LIPSTICK PEPPERS Small 2-inch-long red peppers, which are slightly pointy and have a thick flesh.

LOLLA ROSSA GREENS A frilly deep red lettuce that grows in small heads and has a sweet, delicate flavor.

LONGBEANS Green beans that are up to 2 feet long.

MIRLITON (chayote) This gourdlike fruit is the size and shape of a very large pear. Beneath the pale green skin is a white, rather crisp flesh surrounding one soft seed. It is grown in several states including California, Florida, and Louisiana.

MISO A fermented soy bean paste used in Japanese cooking for making soups, sauces, and dressings. Three types of miso are available at most supermarkets: red, yellow, and white. The three types are very distinct in flavor and should not be substituted for one another. We prefer miso that is made from a blend of fermented soy beans and white rice.

MITSUBA A small green herb or lettuce that resembles flat-leaf parsley. The leaves have a sharp pepper taste and the fragile stem has a somewhat stronger bite.

NAPE To just coat the back of a spoon.

NORI Paper-thin sheets of dried seaweed. The color can range from dark green to black. It is generally used for wrapping sushi. When finely cut it serves as a seasoning or garnish.

PARISIENNE BALL A small round ball about ¼ inch in diameter.

POACHING To cook food gently in liquid at or just below the boiling point.

QUENELLE An oval dumpling made with a forcemeat of fish, veal, or poultry. By extension, the term is also used to mean the typical oval shape. Quenelles can be easily formed with two spoons.

RAMP (wild leek) A wild onion that resembles a baby leek with broad leaves.

RENDER To slowly cook animal fat such as bacon until the fat separates from the meat.

RICE BEANS Small white beans that are slightly larger than a cooked piece of rice when dry. They have a delicate skin and sweet flavor.

SAFFRON The yellow-orange stigmas from a small purple crocus (Crocus sativus). It is the world's most expensive spice. Each flower provides only three stigmas, which must be carefully hand-packed and then dried, an extremely labor-intensive process.

SALSIFY A root vegetable imported from Belgium. It is available in specialty produce markets. When peeled, the flesh will discolor unless immediately placed in milk or acidulated water.

SAPOTE (white sapote) This fruit has a pale, creamy flesh that is usually soft and juicy. It has a very sweet, mild flavor that may hint of peaches, lemons, mango, and coconut.

SEAWEED SALAD A mixture of sea vegetables, seaweed, sesame oil, agar agar, chile peppers, sesame seeds, sugar, and vinegar. It can be purchased in most Asian markets.

SHISO (perilla, beefsteak plant) A member of the mint family. Somewhat tangy; tastes like a cross between lemon and mint. Often used as a garnish in Japanese cooking.

SQUID INK The ink extracted from the ink sacs in squid. It may used to color preparations such as pasta.

STEAMING A method of cooking whereby food is placed on a rack or in a special basket over boiling or simmering water in a covered pan. Steaming does a better job than boiling or poaching of retaining a food's flavor, shape, texture, and many of the vitamins and minerals.

STINGING NETTLES A wild green similar in flavor to the collard green. It is important to carefully remove the nettles with gloves because they can leave a slight stinging sensation if skin is pricked.

SUNCHOKE (Jerusalem artichoke) This vegetable is not truly an artichoke. It is a variety of sunflower with a lumpy, brown-skinned tuber that resembles ginger. The white flesh is nutty, sweet, and crisp.

SWEAT To cook slowly, uncovered, over medium or low heat with very little fat, until soft or translucent.

TAMARI A dark soy sauce, somewhat thicker and stronger than other soy sauces. It is cultured and fermented like miso. Used in Asian cooking. In Japanese cuisine it is used as a dipping or basting sauce.

TANGO GREENS A frilly bright green lettuce with a delicate flavor.

TATSOI A round small-leaf green with a mild flavor.

TERRINE A mold, usually rectangular in shape. Also, the food, which is usually layered, that has been prepared in the terrine. For recipes in this book, the terrine need not be ovenproof. If you have a terrine that is too large for a given recipe, you can reduce its capacity by filling the extra space with pieces of raw potato. Line the area to be used with plastic wrap or aluminum foil and proceed with the recipe.

TIMBALE A mold that is generally high-sided, drum-shaped, and slightly tapered at one end. It is often used to bake custard.

TOBIKO Flying fish roe. It comes in orange, red, or wasabi green.

TOGARASHI An Asian spice made of dried chiles, black sesame seeds, and dried herbs.

TOMATILLO A small, hard, round fruit that looks and tastes somewhat like a green tomato. Often sold with its peppery brown husk still on. Used extensively in Mexican and Southwestern cooking.

TOMATO CONCASSÉE Peeled, seeded, and diced tomato.

TRUFFLES A subterranean fungus that is highly prized for its pungent aroma and flavor; found only in certain regions of France and Italy. If fresh truffles are not available, substitute frozen truffles. Scrub thoroughly before using. White truffles are rarer and more expensive than black. Olive oils that have been infused with the highly pungent white truffle are available in gourmet shops.

TUILE A thin, crisp wafer that can be made out of potatoes or a sweet batter.

VERJUS A liquid made from green grapes that are harvested and crushed in mid-summer, when acid levels are high and sugar levels are low. The remaining (unfermented) liquid is delicately tart, and refreshing. It has many uses in cooking.

WASABI A pungent, green Japanese horse-radish. Available in paste or powder form. The powder is mixed with water to produce a smooth sauce.

WATER BATH A container filled with ice water that is used to quickly cool a food product (such as a stock or sauce). A second smaller container is placed in the water bath, allowing the food product to cool without directly touching the water bath.

WATER CHESTNUTS Fresh water chestnuts are so far superior to canned that you should accept no substitute. Boil for 10 minutes and peel before using. Available in most Asian markets.

WHITE ROSE POTATOES Sweet, creamy small potatoes with a thin, light brown skin and delicate flesh.

Wine Terms

CLASSIC A broad term used to suggest that a wine is consistent with the established characteristics of that particular wine's type and style.

COMPLEX A wine of multiple layers and nuances of aroma and flavor whose elements are perfectly balanced, completely harmonious, and eminently interesting.

EARTHY An aroma or flavor evocative of damp, rich soil, generally used in a positive sense, unless the characteristic is too pronounced.

FINESSE A descriptor for a wine that has distinction and grace, with perfect harmony among its components.

FRUITY A descriptor for a wine that has the flavor and smell of fresh fruit. Fruity characteristics can be reminiscent of everything from apples, pears, or berries to citrus and ripe tropical fruits.

MEATY A term describing wine (primarily red) that's so rich and full-bodied that it gives the sense of being chewable.

NOSE A general term referring to the aromas present in wine. Some common terms used to describe the nose of a wine are fruit, mineral, herbal, perfume, honey, and biscuity.

OAKY A term describing the flavor and fragrance in wines that have been aged in oak barrels. Some common terms used to describe the flavor oak adds to wine are smoky, toasty, vanilla, charred oak, grainy, buttery, round, and nutty.

PALATE The seat of the sense of taste. Some common wine descriptors derived from the palate are acid, rich, full-bodied, alcohol level, dense, creamy, firm, coarse, clean, crisp, balanced, bold, syrupy, and tannin.

STRUCTURE Refers to a wine's architecture, which includes the acid, alcohol, fruit, glycerol, and tannin.

TERROIR A French term that refers to geographic influences on wine grapes, including the type of soil, altitude, vine position relative to the sun, angle of incline, and water drainage.

Sources

Though it may take a little searching, you can probably find all of the ingredients you need right in your own area. For items that are not stocked by your supermarket, try local ethnic markets and specialty food stores. If that fails, you can contact the suppliers listed below.

Browne Trading Company
260 Commercial Street
Portland, Maine 04101
(207) 766-2402
Fresh fish and shellfish.

Charlie Trotter's
816 West Armitage
Chicago, Illinois 60614
(773) 248-6228
www.charlietrotters.com
The 8 by 1½- by 2¼-inch terrine mold, **Charlie Trotter's Smoked Salmon,** *fish spatula, and the ring cutters used in* Charlie Trotter's, Charlie Trotter's Vegetables, *and* Charlie Trotter's Seafood *may be purchased through the restaurant.*

Dean and Deluca
560 Broadway
New York, New York 10012
(800) 221-7714
White truffle oil, olive paste, balsamic vinegar, grains.

Garden & Valley Isle Seafood, Inc.
225 North Nimitz Highway, #3
Honolulu, Hawaii 96817
(808) 524-4847
Fresh seafood and shellfish.

Geo. Cornille & Sons Produce
60 South Water Market
Chicago, Illinois 60608
(312) 226-1015
Fresh and specialty produce.

Marinelli Shellfish
Pier 33, Space L-17
The Embarcadero
San Francisco, California 94111
(206) 870-0233
Fresh seafood and shellfish.

Star Market
3349 North Clark Street
Chicago, Illinois 60657
(773) 472-0599
Asian dry goods and produce.

Superior Ocean Produce
4106 North Avers Avenue
Chicago, Illinois 60618
(773) 463-2955
Fresh seafood and shellfish.

Wild Game, Inc.
2315 West Huron Street
Chicago, Illinois 60612
(773) 278-1661
Foie gras, squab, truffles.

Photo Index

End pages, Salmon Skin; 1 & 2 Clearwater Lake, Emo, Canada; 4 Uku; 6 Bar Harbor, ME; 8 Portland, ME; 11 NYC Chinatown, NY; 14 Oysters, Chemainus, Vancouver, B.C.; 15 Beluga Caviar Packing, Camden, ME; 22 & 23 Tuculet, Vancouver Island, B.C.; 30 Spot Prawns, Chinatown, Vancouver, B.C.; 31 Pike Place, Seattle, WA; 40 Dungeness Crab, Ufino, Vancouver Island, B.C.; 41 Sockeye Salmon, Seattle, WA; 48 & 49 Clearwater Lake, Emo, Canada; 58 *(Clockwise from top left)* Walleye Pike, Clearwater Lake, Canada; Salmon, Tucelet, Tofino, Vancouver; Halibut, Tucelet, Vancouver Island, B.C; Tuna, Baja, Mexico; 59 *(Clockwise from top left)* Swordfish, Baja; Mahimahi, Baja, Mexico; Salmon, Coast of Vancouver; Northern Pike, Clearwater Lake, Vancouver, B.C.; 68 Abalone, Portland, ME; 69 Tofino, Vancouver Island, B.C. ; 76 Wailea, Hawaii, 3 hours off Maui; 77 *(top)* Vancouver Island, B.C.; *(bottom)* Salmon, Tuculet, Vancouver Island, B.C.; 84 Red Mullet, ME; 85 Pibale Fishing, ME; 92 & 93 Dawn at the Fulton Market, NYC; 100 Thai Lobster; 101 Lobster Cage, ME; 106 & 107 Wild Stripe Bass, Portland, ME; 112 Halibut, Portland, ME; 113 Boathouse, Portland, ME; 120 Hawaii Tuna, Oahu Market; 121 *(Clockwise from top left)* Fulton Market, NYC (Swordfish); Guillermo Tellez, Oahu Market (Swordfish); Fulton Market, NYC (Tuna); Fulton Market (Swordfish); 126 Tuna, Baja, Mexico; 127 Maine/Canada, etc.; 136 *(Clockwise from top)* Salmon ladder, Ballard Locks, Seattle, WA; Portland, ME; Flounder, Portland, ME; 137 Fish Lumper, Portland, ME; 152 Italian Fish Market, Philadelphia, PA; 153 *(top)* NYC Chinatown; Italian Fish Market, Philadelphia; *(bottom)* Italian Fish Market, Philadelphia; 162 Brim Fish; 163 New Orleans, LA; 168 & 169 Randy Zweiban *(left)* holding Tuna, and Norman Van Aken *(right)* holding Black Grouper, in Coral Gables, Miami, FL; 176 Barracuda; 177 Fishing boat, Baja, Mexico; 184 *(Clockwise from top left)* Cod, Moi, Turbot, Loup De Mer; 185 *(Clockwise from top left)* Black Sea Bass, Onaga, Mahimahi, Salmon; 192 Opah (moonfish), Oahu Market, HI; 193 Charlie Trotter on the Sweeney boat, 3 hours off the coast of Maui, HI; 202 & 203 Belt Fish and Silver Fish; 208 Pink Singing Scallops, Vancouver, B.C.; 209 Diver 3 miles off coast of Maine; 218 & 219 Hebi; 224 Emeril Lagasse *(left)*, New Orleans; Back cover, Charlie Trotter, Maui, HI

Index

A

Abalone, Farmed Baby, with Bok Choy, Jicama, and Asian Vinaigrette, 82

African Pompano with Macadamia Nut Crust, Bok Choy, and Spicy Lemongrass-Coconut Emulsion, 70

Amaranth, Lobster-Strewn, Wreck Bass with Braised Scallions, Poached Quail Egg, Red Wine–Shellfish Sauce, and, 104

Amberjack with Periwinkle Vinaigrette, Wild Watercress, and Shallot Blossoms, 140

Apples
Smoked Catfish with Apple-Fennel Salad and Pickled Pearl Onions, 52

Steamed Lake Superior Whitefish with Fiddlehead Ferns and Potato-Apple-Celery Purée, 46

Turmeric Butter, 88

Arborio Rice–Crusted Belon Oysters with Baby Spinach and Sweet and Sour Beet Juice Emulsion, 18

Arctic Char with White Bean Purée, Clam Mushrooms, Roasted Pearl Onions, and Red Wine Reduction, 180

Arneis, 101

Artichokes
Baby Monkfish Tail Roasted on the Bone, with Hedgehog Mushrooms, Artichokes, Black Truffles, and Chicken Stock Reduction, 138

Escolar with Braised Endive, Fava Beans, and Veal Stock Reduction, 124

Langoustines with Braised Artichokes, Carrots, Onions, and Chervil-Infused Broth, 38

Olive Oil–Poached Swordfish with Oven-Dried Tomatoes, Roasted White Eggplant, and Black Olives, 122

Asparagus
Golden Spot Tile Fish with Blood Sausage, Asparagus, Asparagus Sauce, and Red Wine Reduction, 214

Lemon Balm–Infused Dungeness Crab Consommé with Crab-Stuffed Squash Blossoms, White Asparagus, and Ramps, 42

Slow-Roasted Salmon with Red Wine Risotto, Wild Thyme, and Tiny White Asparagus, 198

White Alaskan Salmon with Summer Truffles, White Trumpet Mushrooms, and Alaskan Peanut Potatoes, 158

Avocado
Fluke Sashimi with Baby Lettuces and Pickled Vegetable Maki Rolls with Spicy Peanut-Miso Sauce, 80

Hamachi Three Ways, 78

Tuna-Crab Roll and Tuna "Tartare" with Avocado, Crushed Black Sesame Seed Vinaigrette, and Coriander Juice, 128

B

Baby Eels with Seaweed Salad and Spicy Herb Sauce, 98

Baby Monkfish Tail Roasted on the Bone, with Hedgehog Mushrooms, Artichokes, Black Truffles, and Chicken Stock Reduction, 138

Bacon
Dairyless Three-Clam Chowder with Sweet Corn, Celery, and Bacon, 148

Ono with Eggplant Purée, Pancetta Bacon, Wilted Watercress, and Red Wine Emulsion, 220

Pink Porgy and Conch Fritter with Bacon Fat Vinaigrette, 102

Shad Roe with Pea Shoots, Bacon Fat, Preserved Turmeric, and Spicy Pea Shoot Juice, 172

Wild Loup de Mer with Collard Greens, Rice Beans, Lamb Tongue, Red Wine Reduction, and Mushroom Sauce, 222

Barbera, 209

Barracuda and Veal Sweetbreads with Verjus Sauce and Wilted Mâche, 182

Basil Oil, 228

Bass
Chilean Sea Bass with Pinot Noir–Stewed Shallots and Veal Stock Reduction, 186

Wild Striped Bass with Stinging Nettles, Wild Mushroom–Balsamic Emulsion, and Hot and Sour Golden Beet Sauce, 108

Wreck Bass with Lobster-Strewn Amaranth, Braised Scallions, Poached Quail Egg, and Red Wine–Shellfish Sauce, 104

Beans
Arctic Char with White Bean Purée, Clam Mushrooms, Roasted Pearl Onions, and Red Wine Reduction, 180

Baby Monkfish Tail Roasted on the Bone, with Hedgehog Mushrooms, Artichokes, Black Truffles, and Chicken Stock Reduction, 138

Black Pomfret with Garnet Yam, Yellow Wax Beans, Duck Gizzards, Veal Stock Reduction, and Olive Oil, 150

Escolar with Braised Endive, Fava Beans, and Veal Stock Reduction, 124

Golden Trout with Black-Eyed Peas, Yellowfoot Chanterelles, Turnips, and Pinot Noir Reduction, 188

Haricot Vert-and-Anchovy–Larded Big-Eye Tuna with Roasted Garlic Purée and Black Olive–Meat Stock Reduction, 206

Mahimahi with Wilted Greens, Chinese Long-beans, Fried Hawaiian Ginger, and Star Anise Vinaigrette, 74

Mako Shark with French Navy Beans, Bleeding Heart Radish, Crispy Pig's Feet, and Wild Mushroom–Foie Gras Sauce, 130

Rainbow Trout with Shellfish Eggdrop Soup, 118

Steamed Cod in Bok Choy with Preserved Ginger, Mung Bean Sprouts, and Flageolet Emulsion, 132

Wild Loup de Mer with Collard Greens, Rice Beans, Lamb Tongue, Red Wine Reduction, and Mushroom Sauce, 222

Beef Stock, 228

Beef Stock Reduction, 228

Beets
Beet Juice Reduction, 94

Whole Roasted Red Mullet with French Green Lentils, Roasted Yellow Beets, Baby Turnips, and Veal Stock Reduction, 90

Wild Striped Bass with Stinging Nettles, Wild Mushroom–Balsamic Emulsion, and Hot and Sour Golden Beet Sauce, 108

Bell peppers
Nairagi with Squid Ink Fettucine and Red Bell Pepper–Cardamom Emulsion, 64

Red Bell Pepper Juice, 110

Roasted Bell Peppers, 230

Yellow Bell Pepper Juice, 44

Black Pomfret with Garnet Yam, Yellow Wax Beans, Duck Gizzards, Veal Stock Reduction, and Olive Oil, 150

Bok choy
African Pompano with Macadamia Nut Crust, Bok Choy, and Spicy Lemongrass-Coconut Emulsion, 70

Farmed Baby Abalone with Bok Choy, Jicama, and Asian Vinaigrette, 82

Steamed Cod in Bok Choy with Preserved Ginger, Mung Bean Sprouts, and Flageolet Emulsion, 132

Braised Sweetbreads, 182

Braised Tripe, 204

Brandade, 229

Brandade and Mushroom Tart with Lobster Sauce and Braised Celery, 160

Broccoli Raab, Hokkaido Squash, and Red Wine–Beet Sauce, Scallop "Ravioli" with, 94

Broths. See Stocks and broths

C

Carrots
Langoustines with Braised Artichokes, Carrots, Onions, and Chervil-Infused Broth, 38

Spicy Carrot Purée, 206

Catfish, Smoked, with Apple-Fennel Salad and Pickled Pearl Onions, 52

Caviar
Rainbow Smelts with Caviar Rémoulade and Crispy Shallots, 16

Sea Urchin and Osetra Caviar with Vodka Crème Fraîche and Daikon, 26

Celery
Brandade and Mushroom Tart with Lobster Sauce and Braised Celery, 160

Dairyless Three-Clam Chowder with Sweet Corn, Celery, and Bacon, 148

Peekytoe Crab Cake, Haddock, and Olympia Oysters with Rice Noodles, Kelp, Wasabi Root, and Kaffir Lime–Celery Broth, 164

Steamed Lake Superior Whitefish with Fiddlehead Ferns and Potato-Apple-Celery Purée, 46

Champagne, 15

Chardonnay, 127

Chicken Stock, 228

Chilean Sea Bass with Pinot Noir–Stewed Shallots and Veal Stock Reduction, 186

Chiles
Cilantro-Chile Vinaigrette, 72

Red Chile Oil, 66

Spicy Vinegar, 230

Chowders. *See Soups*

Cilantro-Chile Vinaigrette, 72

Clams
Dairyless Three-Clam Chowder with Sweet Corn, Celery, and Bacon, 148
Turbot Ceviche Wrapped in Smoked Salmon with Razor Clam Vinaigrette, 34

Coconut Broth, 70

Cod
Brandade, 229
Steamed Cod in Bok Choy with Preserved Ginger, Mung Bean Sprouts, and Flageolet Emulsion, 132

Conch Fritters, 102

Coriander Juice, 128

Corn
Dairyless Three-Clam Chowder with Sweet Corn, Celery, and Bacon, 148
Rainbow Trout with Shellfish Eggdrop Soup, 118

Cortese, 101

Couscous, Israeli, and Cold Poached Halibut with Teardrop Tomato, Mint, and Red Jalapeño Vinaigrette, 116

Crab
Dungeness Crab Consommé, 42
Lemon Balm–Infused Dungeness Crab Consommé with Crab-Stuffed Squash Blossoms, White Asparagus, and Ramps, 42
Peekytoe Crab Cake, Haddock, and Olympia Oysters with Rice Noodles, Kelp, Wasabi Root, and Kaffir Lime–Celery Broth, 164
Soft-Shell Crab with Ennis Hazelnuts, Snow Pea Shoots, and Aromatic Vegetable Broth, 54
Tuna-Crab Roll and Tuna "Tartare" with Avocado, Crushed Black Sesame Seed Vinaigrette, and Coriander Juice, 128
Crayfish Lasagne with Duck Rillette, Pickled Okra, and Gumbo Sauce, 212

Crispy Pig's Feet, 130

Cucumber Sauce, 134

Cumin-Crusted Turbot with Yuca Purée, Wild Watercress, and Red Wine Vinaigrette, 86

Curry Butter, 154

D

Dairyless Three-Clam Chowder with Sweet Corn, Celery, and Bacon, 148

Daurade with Peruvian Potato Purée and Citrus-Tomato Vinaigrette, 32

Dill Oil, 34

Diver Scallop and Black Truffle Wrapped in Caul Fat with Saffron Fettucine Noodles, Portobello Mushrooms, and Rosemary, 146

Diver Scallop with Wild Mushroom Ragout in Swiss Chard, Butternut Squash Sauce, and Red Wine–Beef Stock Reduction, 210

Duck
Black Pomfret with Garnet Yam, Yellow Wax Beans, Duck Gizzards, Veal Stock Reduction, and Olive Oil, 150
Crayfish Lasagne with Duck Rillette, Pickled Okra, and Gumbo Sauce, 212
Duck Confit, 229

Dungeness Crab Consommé, 42

E

Eels
Baby Eels with Seaweed Salad and Spicy Herb Sauce, 98
Eel with Olive Oil–Poached Tomato, Cucumber Sauce, Petite Salad, and Horseradish Vinaigrette, 134

Eggplant
Frog Legs with Roasted Eggplant Purée and Saffron–Yellow Squash Coulis, 96
Olive Oil–Poached Swordfish with Oven-Dried Tomatoes, Roasted White Eggplant, and Black Olives, 122
Ono with Eggplant Purée, Pancetta Bacon, Wilted Watercress, and Red Wine Emulsion, 220
Tasmanian Salmon with Japanese Eggplant, Spring Peas, and Pea Sauce, 166

Escolar with Braised Endive, Fava Beans, and Veal Stock Reduction, 124

F

Farmed Baby Abalone with Bok Choy, Jicama, and Asian Vinaigrette, 82

Farmed Sturgeon with Banana Fingerling Potatoes, Veal Stock Reduction, and Truffle Oil, 114

Fennel
Fennel Juice, 229
Fennel Oil, 228
Fennel-Stuffed Dover Sole Wrapped in Black Radish with Fennel Broth, 144
Gulf Shrimp with Potato Purée and Turmeric-Fennel Emulsion, 88
Pacific Coast Oysters with Sweet and Sour Fennel, Tarragon Oil, and Peppercorns, 36
Smoked Catfish with Apple-Fennel Salad and Pickled Pearl Onions, 52

Fettucine, Squid Ink, 64

Fiddlehead Ferns and Potato-Apple-Celery Purée, Steamed Lake Superior Whitefish with, 46

Flounder with Pink Oyster Mushroom–Stuffed Mini Evergreen Tomato, Wilted Baby Beet Greens, and Beef Juices, 60

Fluke Sashimi with Baby Lettuces and Pickled Vegetable Maki Rolls with Spicy Peanut-Miso Sauce, 80

Foie gras
Foie Gras Butter, 130
John Dory, Foie Gras, and Hedgehog Mushrooms Wrapped in Napa Cabbage with Smoked Salmon Broth, 174

Mako Shark with French Navy Beans, Bleeding Heart Radish, Crispy Pig's Feet, and Wild Mushroom–Foie Gras Sauce, 130

Frog Legs with Roasted Eggplant Purée and Saffron–Yellow Squash Coulis, 96

Fruits. *See also individual fruits*
Hawaiian Blue Prawn with Tropical Fruit Salsa and Spicy Persimmon Sauce, 72
Pink Porgy and Conch Fritter with Bacon Fat Vinaigrette, 102

G

Garlic
Roasted Garlic Cloves, 156
Roasted Garlic Purée, 96
Garlic Chive Oil, 194

Gewürztraminer, 69

Gindai, Steamed, and Mussels with Lemongrass Broth, Braised Swiss Chard, and Soba Noodles, 62

Ginger
Ginger Oil, 66
Mahimahi with Wilted Greens, Chinese Long-beans, Fried Hawaiian Ginger, and Star Anise Vinaigrette, 74
Preserved Ginger, 18, 132

Golden Spot Tile Fish with Blood Sausage, Asparagus, Asparagus Sauce, and Red Wine Reduction, 214

Golden Trout with Black-Eyed Peas, Yellow-foot Chanterelles, Turnips, and Pinot Noir Reduction, 188

Gougeonettes of Walleye Pike with Sunflower Sprouts, Cilantro Vinaigrette, and Yellow Tomato Coulis, 170

Greens
Barracuda and Veal Sweetbreads with Verjus Sauce and Wilted Mâche, 182
Eel with Olive Oil–Poached Tomato, Cucumber Sauce, Petite Salad, and Horseradish Vinaigrette, 134
Flounder with Pink Oyster Mushroom–Stuffed Mini Evergreen Tomato, Wilted Baby Beet Greens, and Beef Juices, 60
Fluke Sashimi with Baby Lettuces and Pickled Vegetable Maki Rolls with Spicy Peanut-Miso Sauce, 80
Mahimahi with Wilted Greens, Chinese Long beans, Fried Hawaiian Ginger, and Star Anise Vinaigrette, 74
Seafood Sausage with Baby Greens, Pineapple Sage, and Peppered Pineapple Vinaigrette, 66
Wild Loup de Mer with Collard Greens, Rice Beans, Lamb Tongue, Red Wine Reduction, and Mushroom Sauce, 222

Gulf Shrimp with Potato Purée and Turmeric-Fennel Emulsion, 88

Gumbo Sauce, 212

H

Haddock, Peekytoe Crab Cake, and Olympia Oysters with Rice Noodles, Kelp, Wasabi Root, and Kaffir Lime–Celery Broth, 164

Halibut, Cold Poached, and Israeli Couscous with Teardrop Tomato, Mint, and Red Jalapeño Vinaigrette, 116

Hamachi Three Ways, 78

Haricot Vert-and-Anchovy–Larded Big-Eye Tuna with Roasted Garlic Purée and Black Olive–Meat Stock Reduction, 206

Hawaiian Blue Prawn with Tropical Fruit Salsa and Spicy Persimmon Sauce, 72

Hebi with Quinoa and Roasted Hon-shimeji Mushrooms and Their Purée, 190

Herb Oil, 228

Herb Pasta, 212

I

Israeli Couscous and Cold Poached Halibut with Teardrop Tomato, Mint, and Red Jalapeño Vinaigrette, 116

J

John Dory, Foie Gras, and Hedgehog Mushrooms Wrapped in Napa Cabbage with Smoked Salmon Broth, 174

K

Korean Hot Pot with Albacore Tuna and Somen Noodles, 24

L

Lamb tongue
Pickled Lamb Tongues, 230

Wild Loup de Mer with Collard Greens, Rice Beans, Lamb Tongue, Red Wine Reduction, and Mushroom Sauce, 222

Langoustines with Braised Artichokes, Carrots, Onions, and Chervil-Infused Broth, 38

Lemon Balm–Infused Dungeness Crab Consommé with Crab-Stuffed Squash Blossoms, White Asparagus, and Ramps, 42

Lemon Balm Oil, 228

Lemon Oil, 44

Lentils
Opah with Cipolline Onion Purée, Black Lentils, Lentil Juice, and Red Wine Reduction, 200

Whole Roasted Red Mullet with French Green Lentils, Roasted Yellow Beets, Baby Turnips, and Veal Stock Reduction, 90

Lobster

Brandade and Mushroom Tart with Lobster Sauce and Braised Celery, 160

Langoustines with Braised Artichokes, Carrots, Onions, and Chervil-Infused Broth, 38

Ragout of Small Thai Lobster, Pigeon Breast, and Black Trumpet Mushrooms with Pigeon Jus and Chervil, 178

Seafood Sausage with Baby Greens, Pineapple Sage, and Peppered Pineapple Vinaigrette, 66

Shellfish Stock, 229

Spiny Lobster with Potato Gnocchi, Wilted Spinach, and Saffron-Infused Mussel Emulsion, 110

Wreck Bass with Lobster-Strewn Amaranth, Braised Scallions, Poached Quail Egg, and Red Wine–Shellfish Sauce, 104

M

Mackerel, Pickled, with Caraway Vinaigrette and Warm Fingerling Potato Salad, 56

Mahimahi with Wilted Greens, Chinese Longbeans, Fried Hawaiian Ginger, and Star Anise Vinaigrette, 74

Maki Rolls, 80

Mako Shark with French Navy Beans, Bleeding Heart Radish, Crispy Pig's Feet, and Wild Mushroom–Foie Gras Sauce, 130

Marinated Onaga with Blood Orange Juice, Extra Virgin Olive Oil, and Lemon Thyme, 20

Marsanne, 113

Moi, Whole Roasted, with Porcini Mushrooms, Tripe, and Veal Stock Reduction, 204

Monkfish
Baby Monkfish Tail Roasted on the Bone, with Hedgehog Mushrooms, Artichokes, Black Truffles, and Chicken Stock Reduction, 138

Monkfish Wrapped in Prosciutto and Mustard Greens with Shiitake Mushrooms and Red Wine Emulsion, 194

Mullet, Whole Roasted Red, with French Green Lentils, Roasted Yellow Beets, Baby Turnips, and Veal Stock Reduction, 90

Muscat, 69

Mushrooms
Arctic Char with White Bean Purée, Clam Mushrooms, Roasted Pearl Onions, and Red Wine Reduction, 180

Baby Monkfish Tail Roasted on the Bone, with Hedgehog Mushrooms, Artichokes, Black Truffles, and Chicken Stock Reduction, 138

Brandade and Mushroom Tart with Lobster Sauce and Braised Celery, 160

Diver Scallop and Black Truffle Wrapped in Caul Fat with Saffron Fettucine Noodles, Portobello Mushrooms, and Rosemary, 146

Diver Scallop with Wild Mushroom Ragout in Swiss Chard, Butternut Squash Sauce, and Red Wine–Beef Stock Reduction, 210

Flounder with Pink Oyster Mushroom–Stuffed Mini Evergreen Tomato, Wilted Baby Beet Greens, and Beef Juices, 60

Golden Trout with Black-Eyed Peas, Yellowfoot Chanterelles, Turnips, and Pinot Noir Reduction, 188

Hebi with Quinoa and Roasted Hon-shimeji Mushrooms and Their Purée, 190

John Dory, Foie Gras, and Hedgehog Mushrooms Wrapped in Napa Cabbage with Smoked Salmon Broth, 174

Monkfish Wrapped in Prosciutto and Mustard Greens with Shiitake Mushrooms and Red Wine Emulsion, 194

Mushroom Stock, 229

Opakapaka with Bleeding Heart Radish, Morel Mushrooms, Morel Juices, and Turnip Sauce, 216

Oxtail-Stuffed Baby Squid with Cremini Mushrooms, Mustard Oil, and Oxtail Braising Juices, 196

Poached Octopus with Braised Leeks, Parsley Root, Tiny Zucchini, Barley, Marjoram, and Wild Mushroom Broth, 156

Ragout of Small Thai Lobster, Pigeon Breast, and Black Trumpet Mushrooms with Pigeon Jus and Chervil, 178

Roasted Mushrooms, 230

Skate Wing with Zucchini, Black Trumpet Mushrooms, Brussels Sprouts, Mushroom Sauce, and Curry, 154

Spicy Peanut-Miso Sauce, 230

White Alaskan Salmon with Summer Truffles, White Trumpet Mushrooms, and Alaskan Peanut Potatoes, 158

Whole Roasted Moi with Porcini Mushrooms, Tripe, and Veal Stock Reduction, 204

Wild Loup de Mer with Collard Greens, Rice Beans, Lamb Tongue, Red Wine Reduction, and Mushroom Sauce, 222

Wild Mushroom Broth, 156

Mussels
Spiny Lobster with Potato Gnocchi, Wilted Spinach, and Saffron-Infused Mussel Emulsion, 110

Steamed Gindai and Mussels with Lemongrass Broth, Braised Swiss Chard, and Soba Noodles, 62

Mustard Oil, 196

N

Nairagi with Squid Ink Fettucine and Red Bell Pepper–Cardamom Emulsion, 64

Noodles. *See* Pasta and noodles

O

Octopus, Poached, with Braised Leeks, Parsley Root, Tiny Zucchini, Barley, Marjoram, and Wild Mushroom Broth, 156

Oils
Basil Oil, 228

Dill Oil, 34

Fennel Oil, 228

Garlic Chive Oil, 194

Ginger Oil, 66

Herb Oil, 228

Lemon Balm Oil, 228

Lemon Oil, 44

Mustard Oil, 196

Red Chile Oil, 66

Rosemary Oil, 228

Saffron Oil, 142

Sage Oil, 210

Tarragon Oil, 36

Okra, Pickled, Crayfish Lasagne with Duck Rillette, Gumbo Sauce, and, 212

Olive Oil–Poached Swordfish with Oven-Dried Tomatoes, Roasted White Eggplant, and Black Olives, 122

Olive Oil–Poached Tomatoes, 229–30

Onaga, Marinated, with Blood Orange Juice, Extra Virgin Olive Oil, and Lemon Thyme, 20

Onions
Opah with Cipolline Onion Purée, Black Lentils, Lentil Juice, and Red Wine Reduction, 200

Smoked Catfish with Apple-Fennel Salad and Pickled Pearl Onions, 52

Ono with Eggplant Purée, Pancetta Bacon, Wilted Watercress, and Red Wine Emulsion, 220

Opah with Cipolline Onion Purée, Black Lentils, Lentil Juice, and Red Wine Reduction, 200

Opakapaka with Bleeding Heart Radish, Morel Mushrooms, Morel Juices, and Turnip Sauce, 216

Oven-Dried Tomatoes, 122

Oxtail-Stuffed Baby Squid with Cremini Mushrooms, Mustard Oil, and Oxtail Braising Juices, 196

Oysters
Arborio Rice–Crusted Belon Oysters with Baby Spinach and Sweet and Sour Beet Juice Emulsion, 18

Pacific Coast Oysters with Sweet and Sour Fennel, Tarragon Oil, and Peppercorns, 36

Peekytoe Crab Cake, Haddock, and Olympia Oysters with Rice Noodles, Kelp, Wasabi Root, and Kaffir Lime–Celery Broth, 164

P

Pacific Coast Oysters with Sweet and Sour Fennel, Tarragon Oil, and Peppercorns, 36

Papaya
Hamachi Three Ways, 78

Tuna-Crab Roll and Tuna "Tartare" with Avocado, Crushed Black Sesame Seed Vinaigrette, and Coriander Juice, 128

Parsley Juice, 26

Pasta and noodles
Crayfish Lasagne with Duck Rillette, Pickled Okra, and Gumbo Sauce, 212

Diver Scallop and Black Truffle Wrapped in Caul Fat with Saffron Fettucine Noodles, Portobello Mushrooms, and Rosemary, 146

Herb Pasta, 212

Korean Hot Pot with Albacore Tuna and Somen Noodles, 24

Nairagi with Squid Ink Fettucine and Red Bell Pepper–Cardamom Emulsion, 64

Peekytoe Crab Cake, Haddock, and Olympia Oysters with Rice Noodles, Kelp, Wasabi Root, and Kaffir Lime–Celery Broth, 164

Saffron Pasta, 146

Steamed Gindai and Mussels with Lemongrass Broth, Braised Swiss Chard, and Soba Noodles, 62

Peanut-Miso Sauce, Spicy, 230

Peas and pea shoots
Shad Roe with Pea Shoots, Bacon Fat, Preserved Turmeric, and Spicy Pea Shoot Juice, 172

Soft-Shell Crab with Ennis Hazelnuts, Snow Pea Shoots, and Aromatic Vegetable Broth, 54

Spicy Pea Shoot Juice, 172

Tasmanian Salmon with Japanese Eggplant, Spring Peas, and Pea Sauce, 166

Peekytoe Crab Cake, Haddock, and Olympia Oysters with Rice Noodles, Kelp, Wasabi Root, and Kaffir Lime–Celery Broth, 164

Peppers. See Bell peppers; Chiles

Percebes, Jasmine Rice, and Red Wine–Mushroom Juice–Saffron Oil Vinaigrette, 142

Periwinkle Vinaigrette, Wild Watercress, and Shallot Blossoms, Amberjack with, 140

Persimmon Sauce, Spicy, 72

Pickled Lamb Tongues, 230

Pickled Mackerel with Caraway Vinaigrette and Warm Fingerling Potato Salad, 56

Pickling Juice, 230

Pigeon
Pigeon Reduction, 178

Ragout of Small Thai Lobster, Pigeon Breast, and Black Trumpet Mushrooms with Pigeon Jus and Chervil, 178

Pig's Feet, Crispy, 130

Pike, Gougeonettes of Walleye, with Sunflower Sprouts, Cilantro Vinaigrette, and Yellow Tomato Coulis, 170

Pineapple
Seafood Sausage with Baby Greens, Pineapple Sage, and Peppered Pineapple Vinaigrette, 66

Pink Porgy and Conch Fritter with Bacon Fat Vinaigrette, 102

Pinot Gris, 163

Pinot Noir, 177

Pinot Noir Reduction, 188

Poached Octopus with Braised Leeks, Parsley Root, Tiny Zucchini, Barley, Marjoram, and Wild Mushroom Broth, 156

Poaching Liquid, 116

Pomfret, Black, with Garnet Yam, Yellow Wax Beans, Duck Gizzards, Veal Stock Reduction, and Olive Oil, 150

Pompano, African, with Macadamia Nut Crust, Bok Choy, and Spicy Lemongrass-Coconut Emulsion, 70

Potatoes
Brandade, 229

Brandade and Mushroom Tart with Lobster Sauce and Braised Celery, 160

Dairyless Three-Clam Chowder with Sweet Corn, Celery, and Bacon, 148

Daurade with Peruvian Potato Purée and Citrus-Tomato Vinaigrette, 32

Farmed Sturgeon with Banana Fingerling Potatoes, Veal Stock Reduction, and Truffle Oil, 114

Gulf Shrimp with Potato Purée and Turmeric-Fennel Emulsion, 88

Pickled Mackerel with Caraway Vinaigrette and Warm Fingerling Potato Salad, 56

Potato Tuiles, 88

Spiny Lobster with Potato Gnocchi, Wilted Spinach, and Saffron-Infused Mussel Emulsion, 110

Steamed Lake Superior Whitefish with Fiddlehead Ferns and Potato-Apple-Celery Purée, 46

White Alaskan Salmon with Summer Truffles, White Trumpet Mushrooms, and Alaskan Peanut Potatoes, 158

Prawn, Hawaiian Blue, with Tropical Fruit Salsa and Spicy Persimmon Sauce, 72

Preserved Ginger, 18, 132

Preserved Turmeric, 172

Prosciutto and Mustard Greens with Shiitake Mushrooms and Red Wine Emulsion, Monkfish Wrapped in, 194

Q

Quail eggs
Pickled Mackerel with Caraway Vinaigrette and Warm Fingerling Potato Salad, 56

Wreck Bass with Lobster-Strewn Amaranth, Braised Scallions, Poached Quail Egg, and Red Wine–Shellfish Sauce, 104

Quinoa and Roasted Hon-shimeji Mushrooms and Their Purée, Hebi with, 190

R

Radishes
Fennel-Stuffed Dover Sole Wrapped in Black Radish with Fennel Broth, 144

Mako Shark with French Navy Beans, Bleeding Heart Radish, Crispy Pig's Feet, and Wild Mushroom–Foie Gras Sauce, 130

Opakapaka with Bleeding Heart Radish, Morel Mushrooms, Morel Juices, and Turnip Sauce, 216

Ragout of Small Thai Lobster, Pigeon Breast, and Black Trumpet Mushrooms with Pigeon Jus and Chervil, 178

Rainbow Smelts with Caviar Rémoulade and Crispy Shallots, 16

Rainbow Trout with Shellfish Eggdrop Soup, 118

Red Bell Pepper Juice, 110

Red Chile Oil, 66

Reductions
Beef Stock Reduction, 228

Pigeon Reduction, 178

Pinot Noir Reduction, 188

Red Wine Reduction, 229

Veal Stock Reduction, 104, 114, 150, 180, 186, 198, 204

Rice
Arborio Rice–Crusted Belon Oysters with Baby Spinach and Sweet and Sour Beet Juice Emulsion, 18

Brandade and Mushroom Tart with Lobster Sauce and Braised Celery, 160

Percebes, Jasmine Rice, and Red Wine–Mushroom Juice–Saffron Oil Vinaigrette, 142

Slow-Roasted Salmon with Red Wine Risotto, Wild Thyme, and Tiny White Asparagus, 198

Riesling, 41

Roasted Bell Peppers, 230

Roasted Garlic Cloves, 156

Roasted Garlic Purée, 96

Roasted Mushrooms, 230

Rosemary Oil, 228

Roussanne, 113

S

Saffron Oil, 142

Saffron Pasta, 146

Sage Oil, 210

Salmon
John Dory, Foie Gras, and Hedgehog Mushrooms Wrapped in Napa Cabbage with Smoked Salmon Broth, 174

Seafood Sausage with Baby Greens, Pineapple Sage, and Peppered Pineapple Vinaigrette, 66

Slow-Roasted Salmon with Red Wine Risotto, Wild Thyme, and Tiny White Asparagus, 198

Tasmanian Salmon with Japanese Eggplant, Spring Peas, and Pea Sauce, 166

Turbot Ceviche Wrapped in Smoked Salmon with Razor Clam Vinaigrette, 34

White Alaskan Salmon with Summer Truffles, White Trumpet Mushrooms, and Alaskan Peanut Potatoes, 158

Sangiovese, 193

Sashimi, Fluke, with Baby Lettuces and Pickled Vegetable Maki Rolls with Spicy Peanut-Miso Sauce, 80

Sausage
Golden Spot Tile Fish with Blood Sausage, Asparagus, Asparagus Sauce, and Red Wine Reduction, 214

Seafood Sausage with Baby Greens, Pineapple Sage, and Peppered Pineapple Vinaigrette, 66

Sauvignon Blanc, 31

Scallops
Diver Scallop and Black Truffle Wrapped in Caul Fat with Saffron Fettucine Noodles, Portobello Mushrooms, and Rosemary, 146

Diver Scallop with Wild Mushroom Ragout in Swiss Chard, Butternut Squash Sauce, and Red Wine–Beef Stock Reduction, 210

Scallop "Ravioli" with Hokkaido Squash, Broccoli Raab, and Red Wine–Beet Sauce, 94

Seafood Sausage with Baby Greens, Pineapple Sage, and Peppered Pineapple Vinaigrette, 66

Sea Urchin and Osetra Caviar with Vodka Crème Fraîche and Daikon, 26

Seaweed Salad and Spicy Herb Sauce, Baby Eels with, 98

Shad Roe with Pea Shoots, Bacon Fat, Preserved Turmeric, and Spicy Pea Shoot Juice, 172

Shellfish Stock, 229

Shrimp
Gulf Shrimp with Potato Purée and Turmeric-Fennel Emulsion, 88

Sweet Baby Maine Shrimp with Arugula, Heart of Palm, Tomato Coulis, and Spicy Herb Sauce, 50

Skate Wing with Zucchini, Black Trumpet Mushrooms, Brussels Sprouts, Mushroom Sauce, and Curry, 154

Slow-Roasted Salmon with Red Wine Risotto, Wild Thyme, and Tiny White Asparagus, 198

Smelts, Rainbow, with Caviar Rémoulade and Crispy Shallots, 16

Smoked Catfish with Apple-Fennel Salad and Pickled Pearl Onions, 52

Smoked Salmon Broth, 174

Smoked Sturgeon Terrine with Petite Herb and Radish Salad and Yellow Bell Pepper Juice Vinaigrette, 44

Soft-Shell Crab with Ennis Hazelnuts, Snow Pea Shoots, and Aromatic Vegetable Broth, 54

Sole, Fennel-Stuffed Dover, Wrapped in Black Radish with Fennel Broth, 144

Soups
Dairyless Three-Clam Chowder with Sweet Corn, Celery, and Bacon, 148

Lemon Balm–Infused Dungeness Crab Consommé with Crab-Stuffed Squash Blossoms, White Asparagus, and Ramps, 42

Rainbow Trout with Shellfish Eggdrop Soup, 118

Sparkling wines, 15

Spicy Carrot Purée, 206

Spicy Herb Sauce, 230

Spicy Pea Shoot Juice, 172

Spicy Persimmon Sauce, 72

Spicy Vinegar, 230

Spinach
Arborio Rice–Crusted Belon Oysters with Baby Spinach and Sweet and Sour Beet Juice Emulsion, 18

Spiny Lobster with Potato Gnocchi, Wilted Spinach, and Saffron-Infused Mussel Emulsion, 110

Spiny Lobster with Potato Gnocchi, Wilted Spinach, and Saffron-Infused Mussel Emulsion, 110

Sprouts
Diver Scallop with Wild Mushroom Ragout in Swiss Chard, Butternut Squash Sauce, and Red Wine–Beef Stock Reduction, 210

Gougeonettes of Walleye Pike with Sunflower Sprouts, Cilantro Vinaigrette, and Yellow Tomato Coulis, 170

Hebi with Quinoa and Roasted Hon-shimeji Mushrooms and Their Purée, 190

Steamed Cod in Bok Choy with Preserved Ginger, Mung Bean Sprouts, and Flageolet Emulsion, 132

Squash and squash blossoms. *See also* **Zucchini**
Diver Scallop with Wild Mushroom Ragout in Swiss Chard, Butternut Squash Sauce, and Red Wine–Beef Stock Reduction, 210

Frog Legs with Roasted Eggplant Purée and Saffron–Yellow Squash Coulis, 96

Israeli Couscous and Cold Poached Halibut with Teardrop Tomato, Mint, and Red Jalapeño Vinaigrette, 116

Lemon Balm–Infused Dungeness Crab Consommé with Crab-Stuffed Squash Blossoms, White Asparagus, and Ramps, 42

Mahimahi with Wilted Greens, Chinese Longbeans, Fried Hawaiian Ginger, and Star Anise Vinaigrette, 74

Rainbow Trout with Shellfish Eggdrop Soup, 118

Scallop "Ravioli" with Hokkaido Squash, Broccoli Raab, and Red Wine–Beet Sauce, 94

Spiny Lobster with Potato Gnocchi, Wilted Spinach, and Saffron-Infused Mussel Emulsion, 110

Squid
Oxtail-Stuffed Baby Squid with Cremini Mushrooms, Mustard Oil, and Oxtail Braising Juices, 196

Squid Ink Fettucine, 64

Steamed Cod in Bok Choy with Preserved Ginger, Mung Bean Sprouts, and Flageolet Emulsion, 132

Steamed Gindai and Mussels with Lemongrass Broth, Braised Swiss Chard, and Soba Noodles, 62

Steamed Lake Superior Whitefish with Fiddlehead Ferns and Potato-Apple-Celery Purée, 46

Stinging Nettles, Wild Mushroom–Balsamic Emulsion, and Hot and Sour Golden Beet Sauce, Wild Striped Bass with, 108

Stocks and broths. *See also* Reductions
Beef Stock, 228

Chicken Stock, 228

Coconut Broth, 70

Fish Stock, 229

Mushroom Stock, 229

Shellfish Stock, 229

Smoked Salmon Broth, 174

Vegetable Stock, 132

Wild Mushroom Broth, 156

Sturgeon
Farmed Sturgeon with Banana Fingerling Potatoes, Veal Stock Reduction, and Truffle Oil, 114

Smoked Sturgeon Terrine with Petite Herb and Radish Salad and Yellow Bell Pepper Juice Vinaigrette, 44

Sushi, 28

Sweet Baby Maine Shrimp with Arugula, Heart of Palm, Tomato Coulis, and Spicy Herb Sauce, 50

Sweetbreads
Barracuda and Veal Sweetbreads with Verjus Sauce and Wilted Mâche, 182

Braised Sweetbreads, 182

Swiss chard
Diver Scallop with Wild Mushroom Ragout in Swiss Chard, Butternut Squash Sauce, and Red Wine–Beef Stock Reduction, 210

Farmed Sturgeon with Banana Fingerling Potatoes, Veal Stock Reduction, and Truffle Oil, 114

Steamed Gindai and Mussels with Lemongrass Broth, Braised Swiss Chard, and Soba Noodles, 62

Swordfish, Olive Oil–Poached, with Oven-Dried Tomatoes, Roasted White Eggplant, and Black Olives, 122

Syrah, 209

T

Tarragon Oil, 36

Tart Dough, 160

Tasmanian Salmon with Japanese Eggplant, Spring Peas, and Pea Sauce, 166

Tile Fish, Golden Spot, with Blood Sausage, Asparagus, Asparagus Sauce, and Red Wine Reduction, 214

Tomatoes
Eel with Olive Oil–Poached Tomato, Cucumber Sauce, Petite Salad, and Horseradish Vinaigrette, 134

Flounder with Pink Oyster Mushroom–Stuffed Mini Evergreen Tomato, Wilted Baby Beet Greens, and Beef Juices, 60

Gougeonettes of Walleye Pike with Sunflower Sprouts, Cilantro Vinaigrette, and Yellow Tomato Coulis, 170

Israeli Couscous and Cold Poached Halibut with Teardrop Tomato, Mint, and Red Jalapeño Vinaigrette, 116

Olive Oil–Poached Swordfish with Oven-Dried Tomatoes, Roasted White Eggplant, and Black Olives, 122

Olive Oil–Poached Tomatoes, 229–30

Sweet Baby Maine Shrimp with Arugula, Heart of Palm, Tomato Coulis, and Spicy Herb Sauce, 50

Tripe
Braised Tripe, 204

Whole Roasted Moi with Porcini Mushrooms, Tripe, and Veal Stock Reduction, 204

Trout
Golden Trout with Black-Eyed Peas, Yellowfoot Chanterelles, Turnips, and Pinot Noir Reduction, 188

Rainbow Trout with Shellfish Eggdrop Soup, 118

Truffles and truffle oil
Baby Monkfish Tail Roasted on the Bone, with Hedgehog Mushrooms, Artichokes, Black Truffles, and Chicken Stock Reduction, 138

Diver Scallop and Black Truffle Wrapped in Caul Fat with Saffron Fettucine Noodles, Portobello Mushrooms, and Rosemary, 146

Farmed Sturgeon with Banana Fingerling Potatoes, Veal Stock Reduction, and Truffle Oil, 114

Fennel-Stuffed Dover Sole Wrapped in Black Radish with Fennel Broth, 144

Hebi with Quinoa and Roasted Hon-shimeji Mushrooms and Their Purée, 190

Percebes, Jasmine Rice, and Red Wine–Mushroom Juice–Saffron Oil Vinaigrette, 142

White Alaskan Salmon with Summer Truffles, White Trumpet Mushrooms, and Alaskan Peanut Potatoes, 158

Tuna
Haricot Vert-and-Anchovy–Larded Big-Eye Tuna with Roasted Garlic Purée and Black Olive–Meat Stock Reduction, 206

Korean Hot Pot with Albacore Tuna and Somen Noodles, 24

Tuna-Crab Roll and Tuna "Tartare" with Avocado, Crushed Black Sesame Seed Vinaigrette, and Coriander Juice, 128

Turbot
Cumin-Crusted Turbot with Yuca Purée, Wild Watercress, and Red Wine Vinaigrette, 86

Turbot Ceviche Wrapped in Smoked Salmon with Razor Clam Vinaigrette, 34

Turmeric
Preserved Turmeric, 172

Turmeric Butter, 88

Turnips
Golden Trout with Black-Eyed Peas, Yellowfoot Chanterelles, Turnips, and Pinot Noir Reduction, 188

Opakapaka with Bleeding Heart Radish, Morel Mushrooms, Morel Juices, and Turnip Sauce, 216

Whole Roasted Red Mullet with French Green Lentils, Roasted Yellow Beets, Baby Turnips, and Veal Stock Reduction, 90

Wreck Bass with Lobster-Strewn Amaranth, Braised Scallions, Poached Quail Egg, and Red Wine–Shellfish Sauce, 104

V

Veal
Barracuda and Veal Sweetbreads with Verjus Sauce and Wilted Mâche, 182

Veal Stock Reduction, 104, 114, 150, 180, 186, 198, 204

Vegetables
Dairyless Three-Clam Chowder with Sweet Corn, Celery, and Bacon, 148

Escolar with Braised Endive, Fava Beans, and Veal Stock Reduction, 124

Fluke Sashimi with Baby Lettuces and Pickled Vegetable Maki Rolls with Spicy Peanut-Miso Sauce, 80

Langoustines with Braised Artichokes, Carrots, Onions, and Chervil-Infused Broth, 38

Vegetable Stock, 132

Vinegar, Spicy, 230

Viognier, 85

W

Watercress
Amberjack with Periwinkle Vinaigrette, Wild Watercress, and Shallot Blossoms, 140

Cumin-Crusted Turbot with Yuca Purée, Wild Watercress, and Red Wine Vinaigrette, 86

Ono with Eggplant Purée, Pancetta Bacon, Wilted Watercress, and Red Wine Emulsion, 220

White Alaskan Salmon with Summer Truffles, White Trumpet Mushrooms, and Alaskan Peanut Potatoes, 158

Whitefish, Steamed Lake Superior, with Fiddlehead Ferns and Potato-Apple-Celery Purée, 46

Whole Roasted Moi with Porcini Mushrooms, Tripe, and Veal Stock Reduction, 204

Whole Roasted Red Mullet with French Green Lentils, Roasted Yellow Beets, Baby Turnips, and Veal Stock Reduction, 90

Wild Loup de Mer with Collard Greens, Rice Beans, Lamb Tongue, Red Wine Reduction, and Mushroom Sauce, 222

Wild Mushroom Broth, 156

Wild Striped Bass with Stinging Nettles, Wild Mushroom–Balsamic Emulsion, and Hot and Sour Golden Beet Sauce, 108

Wines
Arneis, 101

Barbera, 209

Champagne, 15

Chardonnay, 127

Cortese, 101

Gewürztraminer, 69

Marsanne, 113

Muscat, 69

Pinot Gris, 163

Pinot Noir, 177

Riesling, 41

Roussanne, 113

Sangiovese, 193

Sauvignon Blanc, 31

sparkling, 15

Syrah, 209

Viognier, 85

Zinfandel, 193

Wreck Bass with Lobster-Strewn Amaranth, Braised Scallions, Poached Quail Egg, and Red Wine–Shellfish Sauce, 104

Y

Yam, Yellow Wax Beans, Duck Gizzards, Veal Stock Reduction, and Olive Oil, Black Pomfret with, 150

Yellow Bell Pepper Juice, 44

Yuca Purée, Wild Watercress, and Red Wine Vinaigrette, Cumin-Crusted Turbot with, 86

Z

Zucchini
Poached Octopus with Braised Leeks, Parsley Root, Tiny Zucchini, Barley, Marjoram, and Wild Mushroom Broth, 156

Skate Wing with Zucchini, Black Trumpet Mushrooms, Brussels Sprouts, Mushroom Sauce, and Curry, 154

Zucchini Sauce, 154